Modelling Systems: Practical Tools and Techniques in Software Development

John Fitzgerald

and

Peter Gorm Larsen

CAMBRIDGE
UNIVERSITY PRESS

PUBLISHED BY THE PRESS SYNDICATE OF THE UNIVERSITY OF CAMBRIDGE
The Pitt Building, Trumpington Street, Cambridge CB2 1RP, United Kingdom

CAMBRIDGE UNIVERSITY PRESS
The Edinburgh Building, Cambridge CB2 2RU, United Kingdom
40 West 20th Street, New York, NY 10011-4211, USA
10 Stamford Road, Oakleigh, Melbourne 3166, Australia

First published 1998

Printed in Great Britain at the University Press, Cambridge

Typeset in 11/14pt Computer Modern

A catalogue record of this book is available from the British Library

ISBN 0 521 626056 hardback (with CD-ROM)
ISBN 0 521 623480 paperback (with CD-ROM)

Modelling Systems: Practical Tools and Techniques in Software Development

Software is pervasive, error-prone, expensive to develop and, as an engineering medium, extraordinarily seductive. Some of the major challenges in software development lie not so much in the details of design but in gaining confidence that the software under development will actually meet its requirements.

This book provides an insight into established techniques which help developers to overcome the complexity of software development by constructing models of software systems in early design stages. The analysis and testing of models allows feedback before an expensive commitment is made to detailed design and coding. Aimed at software developers in industry and university students on software engineering courses, the text provides a remarkable new introduction to modelling using a leading technology: ISO Standard VDM-SL. The text breaks new ground by combining training in modelling techniques with commercial-strength tool support on a PC Windows platform.

Teaching is done by example with modelling techniques being introduced through a series of studies derived from industrial applications. At each stage the main components of the modelling technology are introduced as they are needed. The tool included with the book allows readers to check their understanding by developing their own models, validating them by syntax- and type-checking, execution and testing.

The authors, who are leading authorities on the use of modelling techniques in software development, have based the book on successful material from industrial and university training courses given in North America, Europe and Asia.

John Fitzgerald is a lecturer in computer science at the University of Newcastle upon Tyne, UK, and works there in the Centre for Software Reliability.

Peter Gorm Larsen is currently Research & Development Manager at the Institute for Applied Computer Science (IFAD) in Odense, Denmark.

CONTENTS

Foreword		ix
Preface		xi
1	**Introduction**	**1**
	1.1 Software	1
	1.2 Modelling and analysis	2
	1.3 This book	3
	1.4 VDM-SL	4
	1.5 The structure of a VDM-SL model	5
	1.6 Analysing a model	10
2	**Constructing a Model**	**13**
	2.1 Introduction	13
	2.2 Requirements for an alarm system	13
	2.3 Constructing a model from scratch	14
	2.4 Reading the requirements	15
	2.5 Sketching type representations	16
	2.6 Defining the functions	22
	2.7 Completing the type definitions	23
	2.8 Completing the function definitions	25
	2.9 Reviewing requirements	29
3	**Toolbox Lite**	**36**
	3.1 Introduction	36
	3.2 Installing Toolbox Lite	37
	3.3 Configuring the alarm example	37
	3.4 Syntax and type checking models	38
	3.5 Interpreting and debugging models	43
	3.6 Setting options	46

4 Describing System Properties Using Logical Expressions 50

4.1 Introduction   50

4.2 The temperature monitor   50

4.3 Logical expressions   52

4.4 Presenting and evaluating predicates   60

4.5 Using quantifiers   61

4.6 Coping with undefinedness   66

5 The Elements of a Formal Model   72

5.1 Introduction   72

5.2 A traffic light control kernel   73

5.3 Union and basic types   76

5.4 Basic type constructors   78

5.5 Record types   79

5.6 Invariants   80

5.7 Explicit function definitions   82

5.8 Functions for changing signals   83

5.9 Reviewing the safety requirements   90

5.10 Optional types: modelling failure behaviour   91

6 Sets   93

6.1 Introduction   93

6.2 The set type constructor   95

6.3 Defining sets   95

6.4 Modelling with sets   97

6.5 Distributed set operators   110

6.6 Summary   113

7 Sequences   116

7.1 Introduction   116

7.2 The sequence type constructor   117

7.3 Defining sequences   117

7.4 Modelling with sequences   121

7.5 Further operators on sequences   128

7.6 Level of abstraction   131

7.7 Recursive data structures   132

8 Mappings **137**
   8.1 Introduction 137
   8.2 The mapping type constructor 139
   8.3 Defining mappings 139
   8.4 Modelling with mappings 140
   8.5 Summary 155

9 Validating Models **157**
   9.1 Introduction 157
   9.2 Internal consistency: proof obligations 159
   9.3 Visualisation of a model 167
   9.4 Systematic testing 170
   9.5 Using proofs 172
   9.6 Choosing a validation technique 174

10 State-Based Modelling **176**
   10.1 Introduction 176
   10.2 State-based modelling 177
   10.3 A state-based model of the explosives store controller 178
   10.4 A state-based model of the trusted gateway 183
   10.5 Validation of state-based models 187

11 Large-Scale Modelling **190**
   11.1 Introduction 190
   11.2 A structure for the tracker model 191
   11.3 Information hiding 199
   11.4 Supporting reuse through parameterisation 202
   11.5 Object-orientated structuring 207

12 Using VDM in Practice **209**
   12.1 Introduction 209
   12.2 The traditional life-cycle model 210
   12.3 Common development problems 213
   12.4 Advantages of VDM technology 215
   12.5 Getting started 218

A Language Guide **224**
   A.1 Identifiers 224
   A.2 Type definitions 225
   A.3 Basic data types and type constructors 225

A.4   Data type operator overview   226
A.5   Expressions   235
A.6   Patterns   237
A.7   Bindings   238
A.8   Explicit function definition   239
A.9   Implicit functions   239
A.10 Operations   240
A.11 The state definition   240
A.12 Syntax overview   241

B Solutions to Exercises   **251**

Bibliography   **262**

Subject Index   264
Definitions Index   268

FOREWORD

Software engineers produce many descriptions: those of the environment or domain in which a desired computing system software is to exist; descriptions of the requirements put on the software; and descriptions of the software design that implements the requirements. Thus the descriptions span the spectrum from application domain, via requirements and software architecture, program organisation and lower level designs, to executable code. While its concerns may be general, software engineering is unique among engineering disciplines in that its primary products are descriptions that must eventually satisfy the laws of mathematical logic and metamathematics.

Other engineering disciplines have to handle a quantum leap into physical reality – the stuff of natural science. In software engineering there is a different quantum leap: that from description to execution. Software engineering is thus about structuring and relating descriptions.

Abstraction and modelling taken together are the keys to mastering the complexity of environments and systems. Formal specification is employed to express abstractions and to ensure affinity to real domains. Such specifications open up ways to establish the proper relation between domain and requirements models as well as potentially verifying the links between software architecture, requirements models, and the stages of design. This increases the chance of achieving a proper fit to the environment, to user expectations and of the correctness of implementation.

VDM was first conceived at the IBM Vienna Laboratory during the summer of 1973. The quarter of a century which separates that date from the publication of this book has shown that VDM is characterised by having remarkably robust, yet simple and elegant, means of abstraction and modelling. Careful attention was paid during the 1980s to ensuring a consistent and comprehensive final version of the VDM Specification Language (VDM-SL). This was supported by a method for specification refinement (reification) including a Logic for Partial Functions Proof System. VDM is today as powerful a tool and technique for software development as any available.

Software development is pursued in a world where the engineer is not always allowed to pursue the ideas of formal development as epitomised by VDM-SL. But anyone who is aware of the fundamental idea of building abstract models can benefit from its immense power to aid understanding and communication.

In this delightful book former students of ours bring you realistic and effective techniques for abstraction and modelling. The practical, tool based, approach is one which should give their readers and students (present and future software engineers) the ability to employ these techniques in their everyday work.

Dines Bjørner
Cliff Jones

Hiroshima, November 1997

PREFACE

For developers of computer-based systems, capturing and understanding the complex functional requirements and behaviour of software components has come to represent a considerable challenge. This book aims to equip readers with skills and techniques which will help them to address this challenge. It does so by stressing the value of abstract system models which can be analysed and tested before an expensive commitment is made to a particular design strategy. The book enables the reader to understand the role and nature of abstract models as well as gaining practical experience in their creation.

In order to permit machine-supported analysis, system models must be formulated in a well-defined notation. In this text, we use a formally defined language called VDM-SL (the Vienna Development Method Specification Language). The Vienna Development Method is a collection of techniques for developing computing systems from models expressed in the language. Since its origin in an industrial environment, VDM has become one of the most widely used of a class of techniques known as *model-oriented formal methods*. The language VDM-SL was recently standardised by the International Organization for Standardization (ISO). Although VDM-SL is used as a teaching medium in this text, the principles taught apply equally well to other model-based formal methods such as B, RAISE and Z.

In this book we take a pragmatic approach to the use of formal methods. We aim to illustrate the concepts and techniques used in VDM without overwhelming the reader with mathematics. Unlike most teaching texts on formal methods, this book does not treat formal refinement or formal proof. Instead it focusses on the construction of abstract and formal models for a range of computer systems. Mastering the construction and validation of abstract models is in our view a prerequisite for entering the world of verification.

This book is unusual in two other respects as well. First, the majority of the examples presented are inspired by models developed in industrial projects over recent years. We believe that examples grounded in industrial practice provide motivating illustrations of the fact that this technology can be used for development of real systems and not simply for stacks and vending machines. Second, the skills to develop abstract models can only be acquired through practice. Throughout the text, the use of an industrial quality tool is encouraged, in order to develop the reader's intuitive grasp of the reality of modelling.

Hands-on experience is stressed in the exercises throughout this book. The authors recommend the use of either the Toolbox Lite tool designed to accompany the text, or the IFAD VDM-SL Toolbox[1]. It is possible to carry out the exercises without tool support, but this will not give the reader an appreciation of what can be expected from such tools. The CD-ROM accompanying this text provides all the example models presented in the book, additional models used for exercises and an HTML version of the BNF grammar for the VDM-SL subset supported by Toolbox Lite. This book uses the (ASCII) interchange syntax of VDM-SL rather than the mathematical syntax which is used in most existing texts. It is our experience that this notation presents less of a barrier to the novice who does not have experience in mathematical logic.

The subset of VDM-SL used in this book includes facilities for state-based specification. However, readers already familiar with VDM will notice that the tutorial content is biased towards a functional modelling style. The functional style provides an environment in which type constructors and operators can be covered without the distraction of operation syntax, side-effects and access restrictions to external variables. Once the elements of data and functional modelling have been covered, the "state and operations" paradigm is introduced. The text omits a discussion of explicit operations, because it is our experience that those who learn abstraction skills within the language subset we have chosen, can learn to use explicit operations very easily based on experience from programming languages.

---

[1] Toolbox Lite is supplied on the CD-ROM which accompanies this book. Readers who do not have the CD-ROM are referred to the IFAD World Wide Web site for further information on this and the full IFAD VDM-SL Toolbox. The URL is http://www.ifad.dk/.

Using this book

This tutorial text is aimed at software engineers who wish to investigate how the use of models can improve the software development process, and at university students studying software engineering or computing science. The material in the book has been used successfully on industrial training courses and at second-year undergraduate level. No formal mathematical background is assumed, but the authors find that students gain most benefit when they have some familiarity with the structure and difficulties of software development on a realistic scale. In the university context, students' experience of constructing a large piece of software in a group project, and suffering serious setbacks during integration, has been found to provide a valuable motivating lesson.

The objective of this book is to bring readers to a point where they are able to read and write formal models of computer systems using VDM-SL and have a better understanding of the kind of problems to which these techniques can be applied cost-effectively using industrial strength tool support.

The book contains twelve chapters and divides into four main parts. Chapters 1 to 3 form the introductory material. The first two chapters motivate and introduce the notion of modelling using a formal language and indicate a systematic approach for using this kind of technology. On reaching the end of Chapter 2, the reader will have seen most of the elements of VDM-SL covered in the book. Chapter 3 introduces Toolbox Lite, the tool support provided for the tutorial material. Chapters 4 to 8 form the core of the book, covering the use of logic, basic data types, type constructors and functions in constructing models. Each of these chapters contains a description of the requirements for an application for which a model is developed, introducing each modelling construct in VDM-SL as it is needed. Chapters 9 to 11 are concerned with the use of models in practice, in particular validation techniques, the representation of persistent state and dealing with large-scale system models. The final part of the book examines the introduction and use of formal modelling in the commercial context. Chapter 12 discusses the introduction of modelling technology in the industrial environment. The appendices include a language guide for the subset of VDM-SL used in the text and supported by Toolbox Lite along with solutions to exercises.

Students using the book as an introduction to formal modelling can follow the text in the order in which it is presented. Practising software engineers may prefer to read Chapter 12 after Chapter 1 for a consideration of the costs and benefits of applying the techniques covered in depth in the remainder of the book.

Although the book is intended to embody a single course in use of formal modelling techniques, Chapters 1 to 8 would be suitable for a course covering modelling only. Chapters 9 to 12 could be used in a second and more advanced course including a significant assignment in which students can explore the construction and analysis of a model.

Exercises are included in the flow of the text and should be attempted as they are encountered by the reader. In addition, a small number of more substantial exercises are normally included at the end of each of the central chapters. Those exercises marked with a star ($\star$) are slightly more demanding than the average. It is our experience presenting this material that instructors are asked for large numbers of small exercises which increase familiarity with the language. Often, lecturers also require more demanding exercises for the most enthusiastic and capable students. Teaching material including samples of lecture notes, slides and exercises of both these kinds will become available from the World Wide Web Page at URL:

`http://www.csr.ncl.ac.uk/modelling-book/index.html`

> The production of a formal model is much less straightforward than a textbook might lead one to suppose. By presenting particular models as solutions to problems, we do not intend to imply that they are the only, or even the best, solutions. In addition, the developer of a model runs into many dead ends before reaching a good solution. We are unable to present this process in all its detail in this volume, but we do record some aspects of our practical experience which we feel would be most helpful. This is done in distinguished boxes of text such as this.

Acknowledgements

First and foremost we would like to thank our former professors Cliff Jones and Dines Bjørner for introducing us to the subject of formal methods and to VDM in particular. Our thanks also go to our supportive and patient editor David Tranah from Cambridge University Press; to

Benny Graff Mortensen from IFAD for enabling us to include an educational version of the IFAD VDM-SL Toolbox with this book.

Many colleagues have provided valuable comments on drafts of the book: Sten Agerholm, Bernhard Aichernig, Mo Ajmal, Paul Ammann, Peer Bonnerup, Carsten Breum, Hanne Carlsen, Tim Clement, Ian Cottam, Lionel Devauchelle, Albert Esterline, Kelsey Francis, Brigitte Fröhlich, Anne Haxthausen, Niels Kirkegaard, Ole Bjerg Larsen, Janusz Laski, Yves Ledru, David Morgan, Paul Mukherjee, Anne Berit Nielsen, Erik Toubro Nielsen, Takahiko Ogino, José Olivera, Lars Toftegaard Olsen, Jan Storbank Pedersen, Marie-Laure Potet, Abd-El-Kader Sahraoui, Paul Smith, Vincent Stephan, Elliot Sullivan, Marcel Verhoef, Henrik Voss, Mark Wigmans and the students who have participated in the Newcastle University and IFAD courses during which we have presented this material. Finally, we would like to thank our closest friends and family for being so patient with us while we have been writing this book.

John Fitzgerald
Peter Gorm Larsen
Odense

1
Introduction

Aims

The aim of this chapter is to provide a motivation for studying the modelling of computing systems by discussing the challenges of developing correct software. On completion of this chapter, the reader should be aware of the main concepts to be presented in the book and know where to find the relevant material in the text.

1.1   Software

Software is pervasive, error-prone, expensive to develop and, as an engineering medium, extraordinarily seductive. Its seemingly infinite flexibility, increasing power and the absence of physical characteristics, such as weight, make it an ideal medium in which to express complex models which might not exist at all were it not for software. As a result, software is often developed for applications which are critical either to an enterprise's mission or the quality of life of those with whom the system interacts.

Challenged by the variety and scale of software applications, the participants in the 1968 NATO Conference on Software Engineering foresaw a discipline of software development with a sound scientific basis [Naur&69]. Over the last 30 years, there is little doubt that enormous advances have been made in our ability to control software development. However, software projects continue to suffer from serious difficulties which can lead to the delivery of faulty goods that are over budget and behind schedule.

The rapid increase in processor power has naturally led to increasing demands being made on software and its developers. Software is almost always developed as part of a larger system involving computing hardware, special systems such as sensors and actuators, human-computer interfaces and human beings. However, the long lead-times associated with the production of special items of hardware mean that additional functionality caused by changes in customers' requirements are often realised in software because that medium is seen as more flexible.

A comparison between software engineering and the engineering in other media, whether mechanical, fluid, chemical or electronic, is difficult because of the different characteristics of those media. However, there is little doubt that software engineers can still learn from other more mature engineering disciplines.

1.2   Modelling and analysis

One of the major differences between software engineering and other forms of engineering is that the other disciplines have a longer tradition of constructing abstract models of the product in the early stages of development. Such models serve as a proving ground for design ideas and as a communication medium between engineers and customers. As a result of modelling, engineers can avoid errors which might otherwise only become obvious in the very late stages of development, when expensive commitments have been made to materials and designs. There are two aspects of these models which are crucial to their successful use: abstraction and rigour.

Engineering models are abstract in the sense that aspects of the product not relevant to the analysis in hand are not included. For example, an aeronautical engineer investigating the aerodynamics of an aircraft design may model the air flow over the surfaces (mathematically or in a wind tunnel) because air flow is a dominant design parameter. The model is unlikely to include the user interface of the cockpit instruments. Similarly, human factors engineers who design cockpit instruments model the cockpit, not the aerodynamics of the wing surfaces. The choice of which aspects of a system should be included in the model (its level of abstraction), is a matter of engineering skill.

Perhaps the most significant property of a system model is its suitability for analysis. The purpose of such an analysis is to provide an objective assessment of a model's properties. For example, a model of a new design of bridge might be used to assess the design's ability to withstand physical stresses with acceptable risk of collapse. This contrasts with the more subjective analysis of a review or inspection in which the outcome may depend on the consultants carrying out the job. It is also important to be able to repeat the assessment on alternative models and to be able to perform as much as possible of the analysis mechanically, in order to minimise the risk of subjectivity and error as well as the required human effort. To obtain this level of objectivity, mechanisation and repeatability, mathematics is often used in the analysis. Indeed, many system models exist only as mathematical constructions and not as physical entities at all.

How do these concepts of system modelling transfer to the development of computing systems, and in particular to software? A wide range of modelling techniques have been developed for computing systems, including pseudo-code, natural language, graphical and mathematical notations. Data flow modelling, often applied in the analysis of information systems, is one particularly widely-used technique. Ultimately, a computer program could be seen as a model of the system which is to be provided: an executable model which meets all the relevant user requirements, or at least a large enough subset of them to make the product acceptable. Although a wide variety of modelling techniques are available, comparatively few provide the combination of abstraction and rigour which could bring the benefits of early detection of errors and increased confidence in designs.

This book describes well-established modelling techniques which combine abstraction with rigour. We will introduce the elements of a modelling language that can be combined effectively with existing software engineering techniques, opening up the possibility of improved analysis in early development stages.

Models expressed very abstractly in the early stages of system development would normally be treated as *specifications* of a system. If the models instead are described at a lower level of abstraction later in the process, they will normally be called *designs*. The borderlines between specification, design and implementation are not clearly defined and the modelling and analysis techniques discussed in this book are not confined to any particular stage of software development. We will therefore tend to avoid loaded terms such as "specification" and use the general term "model" to refer to the system descriptions we develop. Nevertheless, we focus on requirements analysis and early design stages because these are the phases in which the application of modelling is most beneficial.

1.3 This book

This book is concerned with the construction of abstract models for computing systems. The notation used to describe such models is

a subset of the ISO standardised language VDM-SL [ISOVDM96]. The
VDM-SL notation supports abstraction in a variety of ways which will
be introduced in the text. The rigour of the language lies mainly in its
definition in the ISO standard, which is extremely thorough and detailed.
Indeed, the language is referred to as a *formal* modelling language because its syntax and the meaning of models expressed in the language are
so thoroughly defined. This formality allows analyses to be carried out
consistently because the formal definition of the meaning of the language
constructs leaves little or no room for interpretations to differ between
support tools or practitioners.

This book is about the practical exploitation of modelling techniques.
Our pragmatic approach is realised in three ways. First, the book is
accompanied by Toolbox Lite, a limited training version of the commercial IFAD VDM-SL Toolbox, available on a Windows®95 platform on a
CD-ROM. Most exercises in this book are designed to provide training
in both modelling concepts and tool support. Second, we take a practical approach by using concrete examples to motivate the introduction
of language features. The majority of these examples are derived from
commercial models either directly developed by industrial engineers or in
close collaboration with industry. Third, the validation approach we use
in this book exploits testing rather than refinement and proof, which we
see as more advanced techniques to be used when occasion demands, but
which do not form a part of the initial training offered here.

1.4   VDM-SL

The *Vienna Development Method* (VDM) is a collection of techniques for modelling, analysing and developing sequential software systems. VDM's modelling language, which we use as the main vehicle in
this book, is commonly known as *VDM-SL* (the VDM Specification Language). It is one of the most widely used modelling languages, having
been applied to the construction of a variety of software systems. Its
name refers to its origin in IBM's Vienna Development Laboratory.

The VDM-SL notation is fixed in an ISO standard [ISOVDM96]. It
permits both abstraction from the data structures to be used in the final
implementation of the system, and also algorithm abstraction where one
can state *what* a function shall do without having to provide detail on
how it shall do it.

The analysis techniques for models in VDM-SL covered in this text include static checking of syntax and type-correctness of models, and animation of models by execution. Mathematical proof can be used to show internal consistency of models and to show that less abstract models are faithful to more abstract models of the same system. However, this book does not seek to cover the proof techniques, instead focussing on the construction of models and analysis by the other means mentioned above.

1.5   The structure of a VDM-SL model

This section provides a very brief introduction to the structure of a VDM-SL model through the example of a simple air traffic control system which monitors the movements of aircraft in the airspace around an airport. In what follows, we are not concerned with notational detail, but only with the general form and content of the model. As each main feature of the model emerges, a reference is given to the relevant part of the book. The process of deriving a VDM-SL model from a collection of customer requirements is discussed in Chapter 2.

A VDM-SL model, like many programs, is structured around descriptions of data and functionality. Data are described through a collection of type and value (constant) definitions; functionality is described through function definitions. Each kind of definition is considered in turn below.

1.5.1   *Modelling data in VDM-SL*

Data are mainly modelled by means of *type definitions*. A type is a collection of values which might arise in the model of a system. In our air traffic control model, for example, we could have types to represent the positions of aircraft, their latitude, longitude and altitude. A type definition gives a representation to a type. For example, the author of the air traffic control model could choose a representation for latitudes. In VDM-SL, the modeller would write the following[1]:

```
Latitude = ???
```

How could a latitude be represented? A latitude is usually a number between 0 and 360, assuming a representation in degrees. The modelling language VDM-SL provides the modeller with a collection of basic types from which to build representations of new types such as `Latitude`. The

---

[1] In this book, VDM-SL models will be presented in a `typewriter` typeface.

basic types include collections of values such as the natural numbers, integers, real numbers, Boolean values and characters. The basic types from which models can be constructed are introduced in Chapter 5. In this example, the representation of a latitude could be as a real number. This would be written as follows:

```
Latitude = real
```

However, it is still necessary to record the restriction that the latitude must be between 0 and 360. Such additional restrictions on the values included in a type are recorded by means of *invariants*. An invariant is a property which must always be true of values in a certain type. If a type has an invariant associated with it, the invariant is stated as a Boolean expression on a typical element of the type. Thus, the following type definition defines a type called `Latitude` which contains all real numbers from 0 up to, but not including, 360. It does this by describing the property that a typical latitude `lat` is greater than or equal to 0 and strictly less than 360. Thus:

```
Latitude = real
inv lat == lat >= 0 and lat < 360
```

The Boolean expression defining the invariant on the type `Latitude` is written and interpreted using the logic of VDM-SL. This logic, which incorporates operators like **and**, **or** and **not**, is introduced in Chapter 4.

In VDM-SL there is no limit to the precision or size of the numbers in the basic type **real**. This is an example of abstraction from computer systems where a limit will exist. When the precision or maximum size of a number is a significant factor in the model, this is expressed by defining a new type (e.g. one called `LongReal`) which respects the relevant restrictions.

Types such as `Latitude` can be used in the representations of other, more complex, types. For example, aircraft positions can be modelled by a type `AircraftPosition` defined as follows:

```
AircraftPosition :: lat  : Latitude
                    long : Longitude
                    alt  : Altitude
```

Here `AircraftPosition` is represented as a *record type*. A record type is similar to a record or struct type in other programming languages such as Ada or C++. Its elements are values which are each made up of several components. This definition says that an aircraft position will consist of three things: a latitude, which is a value from the type `Latitude`; a longitude, which is a value drawn from the type `Longitude` and an altitude modelled by a value drawn from the type `Altitude`. Records, and other ways to construct more complex types from simple types are introduced in Chapter 5.

Often it is necessary to model more elaborate data than just single numbers, characters or records. Frequently we will need to model collections such as sets of values, sequences of values, or mappings from values of one collection to values of another. These three kinds of data type (sets, sequences and mappings) are central to the construction of models in VDM-SL – so much so that they each warrant an entire chapter later in the book (Chapters 6 to 8). As an example of their use, we could here define a model of the flight information on a radar screen as a mapping from aircraft identifiers to aircraft positions. The mapping can be thought of as a table associating aircraft identifiers with positions. In VDM-SL, we would make the following type definition:

```
RadarInfo = map AircraftId to AircraftPosition
```

The type `AircraftId` would be defined elsewhere in the model. In a programming language there are many different ways of implementing this data structure (e.g. pointer-based tree structures, arrays, hash tables) but, early in the development process, we may not be interested in precisely which structure should be chosen. If the model has been constructed in order to analyse, for example, the possibility of a "near miss" between aircraft being alerted, the space efficiency of the data structure used to model the mapping is not a dominant consideration, and so does not form part of the abstract model. At a later development stage, this issue may become significant and so could form part of a model used for space efficiency analysis. The use of an abstract modelling language like VDM-SL in the early stages of design naturally encourages one to think in this way, in terms of *what* concepts are needed in the model and not *how* they are to be implemented.

1.5.2 *Modelling functionality in VDM-SL*

Given a collection of type definitions modelling system data, the system's behaviour is modelled by means of functions and operations defined on the data model. For example, two functions of interest in the air traffic control system might be functions to add a new aircraft, with its position, to the radar information and a function to choose an aircraft to which landing permission is to be granted.

The first function, to add a new aircraft which has just been detected by the system, could be modelled as follows. Suppose the function is to be named `NewAircraft`. When a function is defined, the types of its inputs and result are given. In this case, the inputs are some radar information, the identifier of the new aircraft and the position of the new aircraft. The result returned will be a radar information mapping, the same as the input mapping, but with the new aircraft and its position added. The types of the input and result are given and the action performed by the function is described on some input parameters. The function definition so far would be written as follows:

```
NewAircraft: RadarInfo * AircraftId * AircraftPosition ->
             RadarInfo
NewAircraft(radar,airid,airpos) == ???
```

The "???" contains the body of the definition: an expression showing the value of the result in terms of the input values supplied. In this case the result is just the input mapping `radar` with `airid` and `airpos` added to it so that `airid` maps to `airpos`. The details of the expression in the body of the function are not of concern here: they will be dealt with in full in later chapters. In VDM-SL this is written as follows:

```
NewAircraft: RadarInfo * AircraftId * AircraftPosition ->
             RadarInfo
NewAircraft(radar,airid,airpos) ==
   radar munion {airid |-> airpos}
```

The `NewAircraft` function should not be applied to add just any aircraft to the radar information. It should only be applied when the newly detected aircraft is indeed new, i.e. it does not already occur in the mapping. To record a restriction on the circumstances in which a function may be applied, a *pre-condition* is used. A pre-condition is a Boolean expression which is true only for those input values to which the function may be applied. In this example, the pre-condition must state that the input

airid is not already in the input mapping radar. Again, the details of
the expression are not important and will be discussed in later chapters.

```
NewAircraft: RadarInfo * AircraftId * AircraftPosition ->
              RadarInfo
NewAircraft(radar,airid,airpos) ==
  radar munion {airid |-> airpos}
pre airid not in set dom radar
```

The function definition given here is abstract. There is no information
about the details of how the new information is to be added to the mapping. It simply states that the new identifier and position are to be added.

In some cases, it is possible to have an even more abstract function
definition. An *implicit* function definition, rather than stating what the
result of the function should be, simply characterises the result by saying
what properties are required of it. This technique is often valuable where
we do not wish to have to give an algorithm for calculating a result. For
example, we may not be interested in modelling the algorithm which is
used to select an aircraft for landing, but we do need a function which
describes the selection of an aircraft, because we will wish to model its
removal from the radar information once the aircraft has landed. In this
case, we do not give a result expression, but instead give a *post-condition*.

A post-condition is a logical expression which states how the result is to
be related to the inputs. For this example, the function SelectForLanding
takes the radar information as input and returns an aircraft identifier as
the result. The post-condition states that the result is an identifier from
the mapping, but goes no further in suggesting how the result is chosen.
A pre-condition is recorded to assert that this function should only be
applied when the radar information is non-empty, i.e. there are some aircraft identifiers to choose from. Again, the details of the expressions used
will be dealt with in later chapters. The function definition is as follows:

```
SelectForLanding(radar:RadarInfo) aircraft:AircraftId
pre  dom radar <> {}
post aircraft in set dom radar
```

In a VDM-SL model, each function is self-contained in that the only
data which can be referred to in the function body are the input parameters. In particular, the function body has no access to any global
variables. However, in this example it is likely that many of the functions would need to access and possibly update the radar information.

There is a clear sense in which the radar information is persistent, and the functions merely make changes to part of that radar information. The functions in this case might be better expressed as procedures with side-effects on global variables. For such situations it is possible to describe the persistent data in a *state definition* and record the modifications to the state as operations. This state-based modelling style is the subject of Chapter 10.

The example used in this section does not reflect the size and complexity of a realistic computing problem. Indeed, any course on modelling must use examples which fit into the textbook space available. However, Chapter 11 deals with techniques for structuring large-scale models by splitting them into manageable, and sometimes re-usable, modules.

1.6   Analysing a model

Once a model has been developed, what can be done with it? If the model is to form the basis for the development of software, it is important to have confidence both in the model's internal consistency and in the accuracy with which it records the customer's original requirements. Checking internal consistency involves ensuring that the language syntax has been correctly followed and that the functions can indeed be calculated on the values provided as inputs (this is done say by ensuring that operators like numeric addition or union of mappings are applied to values of the correct types). A range of more subtle checks can also be performed: for example, making sure that a function definition does not allow the invariant on a data type to be violated. In addition, the model can be tested by supplying sample input values and calculating the results of applying the functions to these.

The process of increasing confidence in a model is called *validation* and is described in detail in Chapter 9. When inconsistencies are discovered, or the model does not correspond to expectations in some way, the model can be modified at this early stage in the development of the computing system, before going on to detailed design. Early identification and resolution of errors prevents their propagation into detailed design and code and subsequent, late and expensive, correction. The issues surrounding the use of modelling in the commercial development process are the subject of Chapter 12.

Summary

- Software developers have a difficult task, because of the complexity of the systems they build and the characteristics of the material out of which they are built. Nevertheless, some useful lessons can be learned from other engineering disciplines. One of these is the value of models of systems in the early stages of development.

- If used in the early stages of software development, models can ease communication between developers and between developers and clients. They can help identify deficiencies in understanding and in requirements and thus help to reduce rework costs in later development stages.

- To be useful, a model should be abstract (so that it is not too complex) and rigorously defined, so that objective and repeatable analyses can be performed.

- Formulating an abstract model using a notation with a fixed syntax and semantics enables machine support and provides a communication medium without ambiguity. Such a formal definition of a notation also provide a means of resolving disputes about the meaning of a model.

- VDM-SL is an ISO-standard modelling language which has a formal definition. It is part of a collection of techniques for analysing models and developing software from them. In this book we will concentrate only on the system modelling and analysis aspects.

- A model in VDM-SL contains definitions of the data and functionality of a system.

- The data is represented through types which are built from simple basic types such as characters and numbers. Values of these basic types can be grouped into elements of more elaborate types such as records, sets, sequences and mappings. Types may be restricted by invariants. Abstraction is obtained, where required, by allowing data values of arbitrary size and precision. A modelling language such as VDM-SL allows the modeller the freedom to choose a level of abstraction appropriate to the analysis in hand. In contrast, a model in a traditional programming language may have to contain machine-specific details not relevant to the model or analysis.

- Functionality in a VDM-SL model is defined through function definitions. For each function, the types of the inputs and result are given. The input values to which a function may be applied can be restricted by means of a pre-condition. Abstraction is obtained because the function definitions only state the result of application, without giving details of any particular algorithms to be used. An implicit function definition only characterises the result, without explicitly stating what result value is to be returned.

2

Constructing a Model

Aims

The aim of this chapter is to provide the reader with an understanding of the process of developing a model and the kind of components present in a model. This will be illustrated by developing a model from scratch for a small alarm system showing the main elements of data type and function definitions in VDM-SL.

2.1 Introduction

This chapter tells the story of how a simple formal model is developed from informally expressed requirements. The model under consideration, the call-out mechanism for a chemical plant alarm system, illustrates most of the features of models developed in this book. Although this is a great deal of material for a single chapter, there is no need to be able to understand all the details of the language as these will be covered at a slower pace later in the book. The intention is to provide an overview of the concepts which will be covered in depth later, and to provide some initial guidance on how one can start developing formal models using VDM-SL.

2.2 Requirements for an alarm system

This section contains the requirements for a simple alarm system for a chemical plant. The example was inspired by a subcomponent of a large alarm system developed by IFAD, a Danish high-technology company, for the local telephone company, Tele Danmark Process.

A chemical plant is equipped with a number of sensors which are able to raise alarms in response to conditions in the plant. When an alarm is raised, an expert must be called to the scene. Experts have different qualifications for coping with different kinds of alarm. The individual requirements are labelled R1-R8 for reference.

R1 A computer-based system is to be developed to manage the alarms of this plant.

R2 Four kinds of qualification are needed to cope with the alarms. These are electrical, mechanical, biological, and chemical.

R3 There must be experts on duty during all periods which have been allocated in the system.

R4 Each expert can have a list of qualifications.

R5 Each alarm reported to the system has a qualification associated with it along with a description of the alarm which can be understood by the expert.

R6 Whenever an alarm is received by the system an expert with the right qualification should be found so that he or she can be paged.

R7 The experts should be able to use the system database to check when they will be on duty.

R8 It must be possible to assess the number of experts on duty.

2.3   Constructing a model from scratch

There is no right or wrong way to compose a model from a requirements description. However, faced with a collection of requirements, it is useful to have a rough procedure to follow which at least helps in getting a first attempt down on paper. This section presents such a procedure. However, before beginning the process of developing a model, it is vital to consider the model's *purpose*. A model is normally developed so that some analysis can be performed on it. For example, in the development of a single system, a model might be constructed in order to help determine the resource requirements for the system; to clarify the rules under which the system must operate; or to assess security or safety. The purpose for which a model is constructed determines the model's abstraction: which details will be represented and which will be ignored because they are not relevant to the analysis. When we introduce the examples in each core chapter of this book, we will try to make the purpose of the model clear. In this chapter, the purpose of the model is to clarify the rules governing the duty roster and calling out of experts to deal with alarms.

After establishing the purpose of the model, the following list of steps can be a helpful guide to its construction:

1. Read the requirements.

2. Extract a list of possible data types (often from nouns) and functions (often from actions).
3. Sketch out representations for the types.
4. Sketch out signatures for the functions.
5. Complete the type definitions by determining any invariant properties from the requirements and formalise these.
6. Complete the function definitions, modifying the type definitions if necessary.
7. Review the requirements, noting how each clause has been treated in the model.

This procedure will be followed in our analysis of the chemical plant alarm system.

2.4   Reading the requirements

In constructing a model of a computing system it is necessary to find representations for the data and computations involved. While reading the requirements, it is worth noting the nouns and actions which typically may correspond to types and functions in the model.

Statements of requirements, like the example above, can contain undesirable features such as noise, silence, ambiguity, wishful thinking and misstated intention. Look out for these when developing the formal model: when imprecision is encountered, it is necessary to resolve the issue and record the resolution in order to keep track of all the decisions made during the analysis.

Examining each of the requirements listed above yields possible types and functions:

R1 This concerns the entire system and suggests that a type could be introduced to represent the various alarms which can arise. Call this type `Alarm`. The requirement also suggests that a type could be introduced to represent the overall condition of the plant. This type will be called `Plant`.

R2 This requirement mentions a collection of kinds of qualification, so a type `Qualification` is suggested. `Alarms` are also mentioned again.

R3 This requirement mentions experts and periods of duty, suggesting types `Period` and `Expert`.

R4 Here `Qualification` and `Expert` are mentioned again.

R5 Descriptions appear to be associated with alarms, so this suggests
a type called `Description`. The types `Alarm`, `Qualification` and
`Expert` are mentioned again.

R6 This requirement refers to the action of finding an expert with the
right qualification to handle an alarm. This suggests that a function is required to find an expert to page. Let this function be called
`ExpertToPage`. The types `Alarm`, `Expert` and `Qualification` are all
mentioned again.

R7 This requirement refers to the action of checking when experts are
on duty, suggesting that a function is needed to perform this check.
Call the function `ExpertIsOnDuty`. In addition, the type `Expert` is
mentioned again.

R8 A function to return the `NumberOfExperts` on duty is suggested, and
the type `Expert` is mentioned again.

This suggests the following list of possible types and functions:

Types	Functions
Plant	ExpertToPage
Qualification	ExpertIsOnDuty
Alarm	NumberOfExperts
Period	
Expert	
Description	

It would be reasonable to expect that functions would be needed to
add and remove alarms and experts from the system, but these are not
mentioned in the simplified requirements presented here. For the rest of
this chapter, the list of types and functions above will suffice.

2.5   Sketching type representations

How would one go about writing the type definitions for the types
identified above? Requirement *R2* states the four kinds of qualifications
needed in this system. This suggested a type `Qualification`. Its definition has the following form, where "???" stands for some representation
for the type:

```
Qualification = ???
```

The qualifications are all mentioned by name and it is simply necessary to be able to distinguish between them: the details of their representations (as strings of characters, numbers etc.) are not significant factors at this stage of development. It is therefore possible to abstract away from the particular representation of these four values (as strings, numbers etc.), but we would like to provide a name for each of them. In VDM-SL this is done by means of an enumerated type, similar to the enumerated types found in programming languages. In this case the type `Qualification` could be defined as follows:

```
Qualification = <Elec> | <Mech> | <Bio> | <Chem>
```

This type definition says that a qualification is either `<Elec>`, `<Mech>`, `<Bio>` or `<Chem>`. Thus this type has four members corresponding to the four kinds of qualification needed in this system. The "<" and ">" symbols simply indicate a special named value.

In Requirement *R2* `Alarm` was identified as a potential type. Requirement *R5* states that an alarm "has a qualification associated with it". In this case, we will assume that exactly one qualification is associated with each alarm and record this assumption in the model. However, the phrase could be understood to state that each alarm has *at least one* qualification associated with it. This is an example where the textual description might be interpreted in different ways by different readers. An advantage of building a model at this stage is that the assumption is explicitly recorded and, if necessary, can be corrected when the model is analysed and reviewed. In this case we will assume that an alarm has exactly one qualification and one description.

We have already modelled qualifications, but we need to decide what a description is like. Requirement *R5* emphasises that the description should be made so that it can be understood by the experts. This could indicate that the description is a piece of text (a sequence of characters) which is to be sent to the pager of the selected expert. Note that there is no guarantee that the sequence of characters present here actually can be understood by an expert. Thus, at a later stage of development it would be necessary to review the "alarm text" to check that they are actually clear. The notion of clarity is subjective and beyond the scope of a model in VDM-SL.

In VDM-SL, a *record type*, similar to the record or struct in a programming language, is used to model values made up of several components. The definition of an alarm is:

```
Alarm :: alarmtext : seq of char
         quali     : Qualification
```

This states that an alarm is composed of two fields called `alarmtext` and `quali`. The type `char` used in the definition is a basic type of characters in VDM-SL. The keywords `seq of` produce a sequence type so that the `alarmtext` is represented by a sequence of characters.

Suppose a value `a` belongs to the type `Alarm`. The components can be selected from `a` using a dot notation. For example, the description of an alarm `a` is written `a.alarmtext`. Thus if `a` is of type `Alarm` then `a.alarmtext` is a sequence of characters representing the text for the alarm.

Having modelled alarms, we now consider the experts. Requirement *R4* states that an expert can have *a list of* qualifications. Whenever we encounter a requirement stating that a list should be used, we must ask ourselves how the elements of the list should be ordered. In this example, the order cannot be deduced from the requirements, so we must note this as a point to be resolved and record in the model any assumption made. In this case we assume that the order is not significant and use an unordered collection of qualifications in form of a *set* here.

In order to distinguish two experts from each other, some kind of unique identification of experts is needed. Thus the type of an `Expert` can be modelled using another record type:

```
Expert :: expertid : ExpertId
          quali    : set of Qualification
```

The representation of `ExpertId` is important in the final implementation, but in this model none of the functions need to be concerned with its final representation. All that is required at this level of abstraction is for the identifiers to be values that can be compared for equality. In VDM-SL, the special type representation called `token` is used to indicate that we are not concerned with the detailed representation of values, and that we only require a type which consists of some collection of values. This is usually the case when the functions in the model do not need to read or modify the information stored in an element of the type. For example, if we were to include a function which modifies `ExpertIds`, then we would need to model the identifiers in detail in order to be able to describe the modification. No such function is required in this model, so the representation of expert identifiers is immaterial and the completed type definition in VDM-SL is:

```
ExpertId = token
```

Notice that no kind of unique identification of experts was mentioned explicitly in the requirements although requirement *R6* indicated the need for it. This is an example where an extra clause like: *All experts must be uniquely identified* could be added to the requirements.

Now let us turn to the modelling of `Period` mentioned in *R3*. It is not important whether the periods are represented as character strings or reference numbers with some fixed syntax, and we cannot deduce from the requirements whether a period is composed of entire working days, hours or some other time period. In the final implementation this needs to be clarified. However, none of the functions we develop in the model here require access to the representation of `Period`, so this is not a core part of the model. It is enough to know that a period has some identifier and that it is possible to compare periods to see if they are the same or not. Abstracting from this detail, the `token` type can be used once again:

```
Period = token
```

Requirement *R3* suggests that there must be a schedule relating periods to the experts who are on duty in each period. We therefore identify `Schedule` as a possible type. Note that we did not manage to identify `Schedule` as part of the initial "nouns and actions" analysis of the requirements. The "nouns and actions" approach is certainly not foolproof – it may fail to come up with types which are only implied by the text. Moreover, some types corresponding to nouns may not be needed.

For each allocated period, the schedule must record the collection of experts on duty during that period. The schedule can therefore be thought of as a *mapping* from periods to collections of experts. Given a period, we can look up the collection of experts in the mapping. Should the collections of experts be sets or sequences? We resolve this by assuming that experts are not recorded in any particular order, enabling us to use sets. If the requirements did suggest that there was a significant ordering among the experts, we could use sequences.

Figure 2.1 *A possible schedule.*

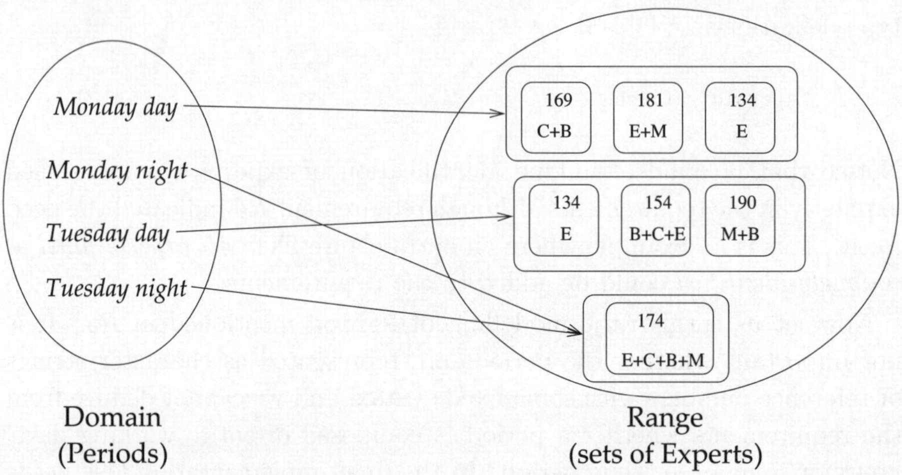

Domain
(Periods)

Range
(sets of Experts)

The schedule is therefore represented as a mapping from periods to sets of experts. An example of such a schedule is shown schematically in Figure 2.1. The corresponding type definition in VDM-SL is as follows:

```
Schedule = map Period to set of Expert
```

The `map _ to _` notation represents mappings from the first type (e.g. `Period`) to the second type (e.g. `set of Expert`). Consider a schedule `sch`. The collection of periods in `sch` is called the *domain* of `sch`: in Figure 2.1 the domain has four elements. The sets of experts in the mapping are collectively called the *range* of `sch`: the range of the schedule in Figure 2.1 has three elements. If a period is in the domain, then it is part of the "allocated" schedule and points across the mapping to a set of experts on duty in this period. If a period `per` is in the domain of `sch`, we write `sch(per)` to represent the range element (the set of experts) in `sch` to which `per` points. If a period `per` has not yet been planned and assigned a collection of experts, it is not in the domain of the mapping `sch` and so `sch(per)` is not defined.

Finally, consider Requirement *R1*. This combines the type definitions we have made into a top level type definition modelling the entire `Plant`. This must be a record with the schedule for experts that are on duty and a collection of alarms which can be activated. We use a record type definition again:

```
Plant :: schedule : Schedule
         alarms   : set of Alarm
```

The model so far

Representations have now been presented for the main types which arose from a reading of the requirements. A considerable part of the VDM-SL notation has been introduced, so it is worth taking stock. Each type has been given a *representation* in terms of other types. Some of the representations have been basic types which are already part of the VDM-SL language, e.g. `token` and `char`. Enumerated types allow collections of named values to be represented. More complex records can be built up from components, each of which has their own type. Collections of values can be built up as sets (where the ordering of the elements is insignificant), sequences (where the ordering is significant) and mappings (which represent relationships from values of one type to values of another).

The type definitions for the chemical plant alarm system developed so far are shown below. At this point it is worth making a remark about how models are presented.

Models written in a special notation such as VDM-SL should *never* be presented without comment to support the reader. Throughout this book, we intersperse the VDM-SL text with natural language explanations typeset separately. We expect this to be the normal mode of presentation of models. However, it may be necessary to have the text and VDM-SL in the same source file. In this case, the natural language text can be presented in comments using the syntax shown below. Note that definitions are separated by semicolons and that comments are put on lines beginning with "--" in common with many programming languages, for example Ada.

```
-- Expert call-out system.
-- VDM-SL model Version 1.01
-- Date: 21 August 1997
-- Engineer: JSF

-- Overall plant contains a schedule relating each period to
-- the set of experts on duty in the period; the alarms component
```

```
-- records the alarms which can possibly arise.

Plant :: schedule : Schedule
         alarms   : set of Alarm;

Schedule = map Period to set of Expert;

Period = token;

-- Experts represented by unique identifier and a
-- set of qualifications.

Expert :: expertid : ExpertId
          quali    : set of Qualification;

ExpertId = token;

Qualification = <Elec> | <Mech> | <Bio> | <Chem>;

Alarm :: alarmtext : seq of char
         quali     : Qualification
```

The data types are presented in a top-down order with the `Plant` type first. It is quite common to do this because data type definitions are often more readable this way. However, in VDM-SL, the names of types do not have to be defined in any particular order, as long as they are all defined somewhere in the model. The particular order of presentation is therefore left to the author of the model.

2.6   Defining the functions

Now it is possible to consider the functionality provided by the system, beginning with the function signatures. Recall the functions identified from the requirements (Section 2.4):

> ExpertToPage
> ExpertIsOnDuty
> NumberOfExperts

A function takes a number of input parameters and returns a result. The *signature* of a function gives the name of the function, the types of its input parameters, and the type of the result.

First consider the `ExpertToPage` function. From Requirement *R6*, it appears that this function must take an alarm as input. In order to find the appropriate expert it also needs an identification of the period and requires access to the overall plant structure in order to read the schedule. The *signature* of `ExpertToPage` lists the types of the inputs and result as follows:

> `ExpertToPage: Alarm * Period * Plant -> Expert`

where `*` is used to separate the types of inputs from one another and `->` is used to separate the types of the inputs from the type of the result.

Requirement *R7* suggests that the function `ExpertIsOnDuty` must take an expert and a plant as inputs. The function must check when the expert is on duty according to the schedule of the plant. The assumption is made here that the order in which the periods are presented is not relevant to the model's purpose, and so the result is a *set* of periods rather than a sequence. The signature of `ExpertIsOnDuty` is as follows:

> `ExpertIsOnDuty: Expert * Plant -> set of Period`

Finally, Requirement *R8* identifies a function `NumberOfExperts`. This function must certainly take the plant as input. However, the requirement is not very precise about whether this is for a specific period. We assume that this is the case but we would need to record this imprecision and our assumption that we are dealing with a specific period here. Thus, the signature is:

> `NumberOfExperts: Period * Plant -> nat`

The result type `nat` is a basic type in VDM-SL. It represents the natural numbers 0,1,2,3, ...

2.7   Completing the type definitions

At this stage, when all the type definitions and function signatures have been sketched out, it is worth considering whether there are any constraints that must hold in the model at all times. Such constraints are called *invariants*. Each invariant is recorded immediately after the definition of the type to which it refers. Indeed, the invariant forms part of the type's definition so, for a value to belong to the type, it must respect the invariant.

To state an invariant formally, we express the property which all values must satisfy as a Boolean expression on a typical element of the type. As an example, consider Requirement *R4*; arguably it should be strengthened. Experts with no qualifications are not of much use in this plant. If the expert is called `ex` this can be expressed by a Boolean expression as follows:

```
ex.quali <> {}
```

This expression can be used to introduce an invariant for the type `Expert` as follows:

```
Expert :: expertid : ExpertId
          quali    : set of Qualification
inv ex == ex.quali <> {}
```

Requirement *R3* indicates that there must be at least one expert on duty in all periods for which the system has assigned a group of experts. This is a constraint on schedules, so it should be defined as part of the `Schedule` type definition. Consider a typical schedule (called `sch`, say). Now, `sch` is a mapping from periods to sets of experts. The constraint is that all the sets of experts in the range of the mapping are non-empty. Put formally:

```
forall exs in set rng sch & exs <> {}
```

The Boolean expression used here is called a *quantified* expression. It states that, for all sets of experts in the range of the mapping, the set must be non-empty. Quantified expressions are often used to express properties which should hold for collections of values. This language of logical expressions will be introduced in Chapter 4.

However this constraint is not sufficient because we would also like to ensure that the expert identifiers are unique in each set of experts in order that one could not erroneously have two experts with different qualifications having the same expert identification. Put formally:

```
forall ex1, ex2 in set exs & ex1 <> ex2 =>
                        ex1.expertid <> ex2.expertid
```

Again a quantified expression is used, but this time two experts called `ex1` and `ex2` are selected from the set `exs`. In case they are different experts their identifications must also be different. The `=>` symbol is used for implication and this will also be introduced in Chapter 4.

Including both of these constraints into the invariant for `Schedule` gives us:

```
Schedule = map Period to set of Expert
inv sch ==
    forall exs in set rng sch &
            exs <> {} and
            forall ex1, ex2 in set exs &
                    ex1 <> ex2 => ex1.expertid <> ex2.expertid
```

The invariant is formulated as a logical expression that limits the elements belonging to the type being defined (in this case `Schedule`) to those satisfying both the type description and the invariant.

2.8   Completing the function definitions

It has already been seen that the data descriptions in a formal model need not contain all the intricate detail found in a program's data structures. We have simplified the model by abstracting away from a number of aspects which are not important for the functionality we want to describe. Indeed, a good general principle is that a model should contain no more detail than is relevant to its analysis. A similar principle applies to the definition of functions, so VDM-SL provides facilities to give a function definition *explicitly*, stating how a result can be calculated from the inputs. However, the language also provides for *implicit* function definition, where the result is characterised, but no specific "recipe" for calculating the result is used. This section illustrates first the explicit style and later the implicit.

Let us first consider the `NumberOfExperts` function. Requirement *R8* said: "*It must be possible to assess the number of experts that are on duty.*" In sketching the function signatures we decided that it would be natural to take a `Period` as an input to this function. The signature is therefore as follows:

```
NumberOfExperts: Period * Plant -> nat
```

The function is defined by giving its result in terms of its inputs. Thus, we need to look up the set of experts on duty for the given period in the schedule and return the size of the set. This can be defined as follows:

```
NumberOfExperts: Period * Plant -> nat
NumberOfExperts(per,plant) ==
    card plant.schedule(per)
```

The **card** notation indicates the *cardinality* (or size) of a set. It is applied
to the set of experts obtained by looking up the input period **per** in the
schedule component of the plant record (**plant.schedule**). The operators
and expressions used here will be introduced in greater depth in later
chapters.

The function **NumberOfExperts** may not be applied to just any inputs.
Calling the function only makes sense when the period **per** is actually
described in the plant's schedule. We record this restriction by means
of a *pre-condition*, a logical expression over the input parameters saying
that the function may be applied when it is true.

So the pre-condition can be formulated as:

```
NumberOfExperts: Period * Plant -> nat
NumberOfExperts(per,plant) ==
   card plant.schedule(per)
pre per in set dom plant.schedule
```

The pre-condition says that the input period **per** must be in the set of
periods which forms the domain of the schedule mapping. We do not
guarantee anything about what happens if a function is applied to inputs
which do not meet the pre-condition. In a model at a later stage of design,
we may wish to provide an error message in the situation where the pre-
condition is violated and this can be done quite easily. However, at this
early stage of analysis, we prefer to abstract away from this and record
the restriction that the function must not be applied in this way.

Now consider the **ExpertIsOnDuty** function required by *R7*. In the case
of **ExpertIsOnDuty**, the function returns a set of all the periods where
the expert is on duty. Thus, in this case we need to select all the periods
in the **schedule** which have the expert **ex** as one of the experts on duty in
that particular period. The full function definition for **ExpertIsOnDuty**
is as follows:

```
ExpertIsOnDuty: Expert * Plant -> set of Period
ExpertIsOnDuty(ex,plant) ==
   {per| per in set dom plant.schedule &
         ex in set plant.schedule(per)}
```

The body of this function is expressed using a *set comprehension* expression which collects all periods **per** (from the domain of the schedule) for

which the expert `ex` is registered. In Chapter 6 we will return to the notion of sets and explain how this can be understood.

Notice that the definition of the function `ExpertIsOnDuty` selects the `schedule` component from the `plant` value twice. It may be worth using a more general pattern in the parameter list to avoid this.

```
ExpertIsOnDuty: Expert * Plant -> set of Period
ExpertIsOnDuty(ex,mk_Plant(sch,-)) ==
   {per| per in set dom sch & ex in set sch(per)}
```

We will return to more explanation about patterns in Chapter 5. At the moment patterns should simply be viewed as a way to provide names to the components of the `Plant` rather than having to use the dot notation for selecting the `schedule` component all the time. The `alarms` component is not needed in the function definition, and so is represented by a "-" symbol.

From a system point of view, it should also be ensured that the experts have the computing or telephone equipment they need to allow them to check whether they are on duty. However, this model abstracts away from the communication mechanism and interface.

Finally, consider the `ExpertToPage` function. Requirement *R6*, which gives rise to the function, states: "Whenever an alarm is received by the system an expert with the right qualification should be found so that he or she can be paged." Note that the requirement does not mandate any method for determining *which* expert has to be found: any expert will do as long as he or she has the correct qualification. There is some *looseness* in the requirement: the designer of the system is free to choose a mechanism for deciding which expert to call. This sort of looseness suggests that an *implicit* definition may be appropriate. Recall that an implicit function definition characterises the result without giving a particular mechanism for calculating it.

It is possible to model a function by stating what properties are required of the result it returns, without indicating how the result is to be calculated. This is done by means of an *implicit* function definition. The main advantage of using implicit function definitions is the ability to state the required properties of a result without biasing a subsequent developer towards any particular way of producing the result from the input parameters. An implicit definition of `ExpertToPage` is as follows:

```
ExpertToPage(a:Alarm,per:Period,plant:Plant) r: Expert
pre per in set dom plant.schedule and
    a in set plant.alarms
post r in set plant.schedule(per) and
    a.quali in set r.quali
```

Notice that no separate signature is given, but that the types of the inputs and results are given together in a header. A pre-condition describes a condition under which the function can be applied and a post-condition describes the result without giving a particular algorithm for calculating it. The pre-condition is similar to that of the `ExpertIsOnDuty` function except that we also require the alarm `a` to be known for the plant. The post-condition states that the expert to be paged, `r`, must belong to the collection of experts on duty in this period, and one of his or her qualifications should be the one required to deal with the given alarm. If more than one such expert is available the post-condition above does not state who should be chosen. A definition that does not narrow the result down to a single possible outcome is said to be *loose*. We will return to the subject of looseness in Chapter 6.

By this stage one problem with the model may have become apparent. The requirements have been silent about the question: "How can we be sure that an expert with the required qualification exists in the required period?" The `ExpertToPage` function cannot yield a satisfactory result if no expert is available. How can the situation be resolved? Either the pre-condition can be made more restrictive (requiring that a suitable expert should be available before an attempt is made to find one), or an invariant can be imposed on the type `Plant` to require that, at all times, there is at least one expert for each kind of qualification. This choice, between representing constraints as pre-conditions and recording them as invariants, is commonly faced by modellers. As a general rule, it is best to model this kind of constraint as an invariant if the property should hold at all times. If the restriction is only required to hold when a function is applied, then a pre-condition is more appropriate. In this example, we will assume that for each qualification, at least one expert has to be available at any time. Thus, we should modify the invariant. The modified `Plant` type definition would be:

```
Plant :: schedule : Schedule
         alarms   : set of Alarm
inv mk_Plant(schedule,alarms) ==
    forall a in set alarms &
```

```
forall per in set dom schedule &
    QualificationOK(schedule(per),a.quali)
```

and the function `QualificationOK` is defined explicitly as:

```
QualificationOK: set of Expert * Qualification -> bool
QualificationOK(exs,reqquali) ==
  exists ex in set exs & reqquali in set ex.quali
```

The body of this function is a Boolean expression which is **true** if an expert with the required qualifications (`reqquali`) exists in the given set of experts `exs`. Note that the function `QualificationOK` has been written purely for notational convenience: it makes the invariant easier to read. Unlike the other functions defined so far, it is not required to be implemented in the system under development. Such functions, defined for convenience rather than implementation, are called *auxiliary functions*. The use of auxiliary functions is to be encouraged, as they improve the ease with which a model can be read and analysed.

There is an obligation (called a *proof obligation*) on the writer of function definitions to check that each function will be able to produce a result whenever its pre-condition is satisfied. Note that without the addition of the invariant to the `Plant` type we would not have been able to meet this obligation for the `ExpertToPage` function. The role of such obligations will be examined more closely when we look at validation and consistency checking in Chapter 9.

2.9   Reviewing requirements

Having completed the formal model we look through the requirements one last time to review how each clause has been considered:

R1 A computer-based system managing the alarms of this plant is to be developed. *Considered in the overall* `Plant` *type definition and the function definitions.*

R2 Four kinds of qualifications are needed to cope with the alarms. These are electrical, mechanical, biological, and chemical. *Considered in the* `Qualification` *type definition.*

R3 There must be experts on duty during all periods which have been allocated in the system. *Invariant on type* `Schedule`.

R4 Each expert can have a list of qualifications. *Assumption: non-empty set instead of list in* `Expert`.

R5 Each alarm reported to the system has a qualification associated with it and a description which can be understood by the expert. *Considered in the* `Alarm` *type definition assuming that it is precisely one qualification.*

R6 Whenever an alarm is received by the system an expert with the right qualification should be found so that he or she can be paged. *The* `ExpertToPage` *function with additional invariant on the* `Plant` *type definition.*

R7 The experts should be able to use the system to check when they will be on duty. *The* `ExpertIsOnDuty` *function.*

R8 It must be possible to assess the number of experts on duty. *The* `NumberOfExperts` *function with assumption for a given period.*

Weaknesses in the requirements document

The development of the formal model has helped to identify some weaknesses in the original requirements document. We made assumptions to resolve these, so it is important to record them. Below we list some of the deficiencies spotted:

- No explicit mention of unique identification of experts.
- Experts without qualifications are useless, and may not be considered 'experts' at all.
- How can we be sure that an expert with the required qualification is on duty in the required period?
- Should the number of experts must be relative to a period?
- "a qualification" means "exactly one" or "at least one"?

Summary

In this chapter we have used a systematic approach to analyse the requirements for an alarm system. In practice, there is no right or wrong way to compose a model from a requirements description, but the following list of steps can be a helpful guide for the novice:

1. Read the requirements.
2. Extract a list of possible data types (often from nouns) and functions (often from actions).
3. Sketch out representations for the types.
4. Sketch out signatures for the functions.

5. Complete the type definitions by determining any invariant properties from the requirements and formalise these.

6. Complete the function definitions, modifying the type definitions if necessary.

7. Review the requirements, noting how each clause has been considered.

The presentation given here is a simplification of what would happen in the development of an industrial system. Depending upon the context, involvement from customers and/or local domain experts could be necessary to resolve the unclear points discovered and the assumptions made during the construction of a formal model. It is important to note, however, that the construction of a model allows us to expose and record these assumptions at an early stage in system development.

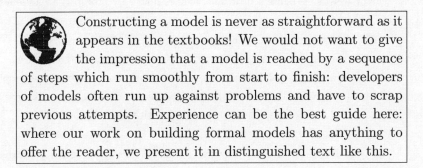 Constructing a model is never as straightforward as it appears in the textbooks! We would not want to give the impression that a model is reached by a sequence of steps which run smoothly from start to finish: developers of models often run up against problems and have to scrap previous attempts. Experience can be the best guide here: where our work on building formal models has anything to offer the reader, we present it in distinguished text like this.

The approach to developing a model which has been presented in this chapter underlies the models developed subsequently. However, when we are presenting an example for the purpose of introducing some types or operators, we will not explicitly describe the individual steps in the process.

We have gone through the process of constructing a formal model. The language, no doubt, still seems unfamiliar. However, most of the features of the modelling language have been introduced: the main part of this book aims to help the reader develop confidence using the logic employed for writing invariants, pre-conditions and post-conditions, and familiarity with the operators on the data types (sets, mappings, sequences and records, mostly). The subsequent chapters take a much more detailed look at these, with plenty of examples. Appendix A provides an overview of all the constructs in the subset of VDM-SL used in this book and serves as a quick reference on the usage of the language's constructs.

Exercise 2.1 This exercise is based on a (fictional) technical report written by an engineer working on another part of the chemical plant alarm system and describes a first attempt at a model for the system under development. Read the report and then consider the questions which follow it. The object of this exercise is simply to increase your familiarity with models expressed in VDM-SL. Reading and considering the report are more important than getting "correct" answers!

We have been asked to develop a detector for alerting the chemical plant's experts whenever there is a certain kind of failure in the sensors in any of the reactor vessels. When a sensor fails, it does not reply promptly to a request for data.

The detector will broadcast requests for data to all the sensors in the plant at certain times. A functioning sensor will reply to such a request within a time limit (called `maxtime`). A malfunctioning sensor will not reply within the time limit. If a malfunctioning sensor is discovered an alarm is to be raised. The qualification needed to deal with these alarms is always electrical knowledge.

It was decided to develop a system model in VDM-SL in order to clarify the rules for raising this alarm. Obviously, other kinds of failure are possible (sensors sticking on a value, for example) but we were asked only to analyse the rules for detecting this particular kind of failure, so the model abstracts away from other factors which are not material to this analysis.

The system consists of a collection of sensors, each with their own identifier. In addition, we keep a record of the times when requests are sent out and the collection of replies obtained to each request. The system is modelled as the type **System** shown below. The sensors are modelled as a set of sensor identifiers while the requests and answers from the sensors are recorded as a mapping from times (the times at which requests were issued) to sets of replies.

```
System :: sensors: set of SensorId
          answers: map Time to set of SensorReply
```

Recall that the purpose of the model is to allow analysis of the alarm-raising mechanism. The detailed representation of sensor identifiers is not a significant aspect of this, and so the `token` type representation is used.

```
SensorId = token
```

Also for the purposes of the model, time is represented by a natural number denoting the number of elapsed time units since the combined sensors and alarm system were started up.

```
Time = nat
```

The sensor replies contain information about the time of the request being responded to, the sensor replying and the data it is carrying (a real number representing reactor temperature):

```
SensorReply :: request: Time
               sid : SensorId
               data: Data
```

The data types for alarms and qualifications are taken from the current model of the expert call-out system:

```
Alarm :: alarmtext : seq of char
         quali     : Qualification;

Qualification = <Elec> | <Mech> | <Bio> | <Chem>
```

We begin defining the functionality with a simple function which clears the current record of requests and replies:

```
Clear: System -> System
Clear(sys) ==
  mk_System(sys.sensors,{|->})
```

The function `Request` models the issuing of a new request. This adds the request time to the domain of the `answers` mapping, pointing to an empty set of replies:

```
Request: System * Time -> System
Request(mk_System(sens,ans),t) ==
  mk_System(sens, ans munion {t |-> {}})
pre forall t1 in set dom ans & t1 < t
```

When sensor replies are received they must be registered in the system for the request made at the time given in the **request** field of the reply. Thus the **answers** mapping must be updated with this information:

```
Reply: System * SensorReply -> System
Reply(mk_System(sens,ans),sr) ==
  mk_System(sens,
                ans ++ {sr.request |-> ans(sr.request)
                                      union {sr}}
            )
      pre sr.request in set dom ans
```

An alarm is to be constructed if there is some request issued more than **maxtime** time units ago to which not all of the sensors have yet replied. The function **RaiseAlarm** is called with a system **sys** and the current time (**now**) as inputs. It constructs an alarm, but should be called only if there are still some outstanding responses to one of the requests. The precise definition of the alarm condition is in the function **CheckAlarm**.

```
RaiseAlarm: System * Time -> Alarm
RaiseAlarm(sys,now) ==
  mk_Alarm("Sensor Malfunction", <Elec>)
pre CheckAlarm(sys,now)
```

The function **CheckAlarm** returns a Boolean value which is **true** if there exists some request in the **answers** component of the system which is more than **maxtime** time units old and there is at least one sensor which has not returned a reply. Its definition will be given in the next draft of this report.

The report presented above was reviewed by several other engineers. They wrote the following comments and questions on the report. In each case, consider whether you agree with the comment or try to answer the question. Remember that it is more important to think about the model and its level of abstraction than to get a "correct" answer.

1. *Why do you represent the* **Data** *field in the* **SensorReply** *record? As far as I can see, it never gets used.*
2. *Presumably you need to make sure that, when you issue a new request, the time of the new request is later than all the other times in the system. How does the model ensure this?*
3. *What do you need the function* **Clear** *for?*
4. *I heard that the team working on the expert call-out software had changed their model of an alarm so that it includes a call-out time*

as well as a message and a qualification. What parts of your model would be affected by this?

The last comment raises a significant point. If several parts of a large system are being developed simultaneously, it is helpful to have a mechanism for defining the interfaces between those subsystems, so that it is possible to check that data types and functions provided by the model of one subsystem are used correctly in the models of other subsystems. The modular structuring mechanism in VDM-SL (introduced in Chapter 11) allows for this kind of checking. It is often the case in software developments that misunderstanding about the interfaces between subsystems are responsible for considerable reworking costs after deficiencies are discovered when modules are tested together. □

3
Toolbox Lite

Aims

The aim of this chapter is to introduce the functionality of Toolbox Lite. This is done by providing a "hands-on" tour of the tool's functionality using the alarm example introduced in the previous chapter. This chapter should enable the reader to use Toolbox Lite for exercises in the remaining part of this book.

3.1   Introduction

Much of the benefit of developing a formal model lies in the ability to analyse the model to check that it reflects intuition about the real system it describes. Such an analysis often reveals gaps in the understanding of the system, allowing these to be resolved before an expensive commitment is made to detailed code. Software tools play an important role in supporting this analysis. This book is accompanied by an educational version of the IFAD VDM-SL Toolbox, called *Toolbox Lite*. This provides much of the functionality of the commercial tool, but it is restricted to the subset of VDM-SL covered in the book. Unlike the full Toolbox, Toolbox Lite is not suited to systems development on the medium to large scale[1], but it is powerful enough to provide an insight into the value of tool support when developing formal models on a commercial scale.

This chapter introduces Toolbox Lite as a preparation for the examples and exercises of later chapters. The chapter takes the form of a tour through the facilities for performing syntax checking, type checking, testing and debugging of models in VDM-SL, using the alarm example which was presented in the previous chapter. The reader is encouraged to use the Toolbox Lite or the full version of the IFAD VDM-SL Toolbox for all the exercises in this and subsequent chapters.

[1] There is an upper limit on the size of models which can be handled by Toolbox Lite, but all the examples presented in this book can be analysed using this educational version of the full Toolbox.

36

Figure 3.1 *Startup window for Toolbox Lite*

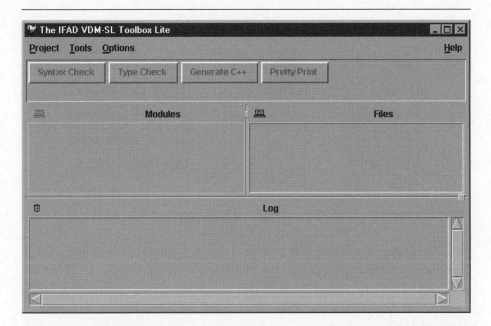

3.2 Installing Toolbox Lite

The CD-ROM contains a `setup.exe` program which can be executed. When this is done it will automatically copy Toolbox Lite onto the hard-disk. The user must choose the desired directory during the installation. In addition the installation copies source files for the examples used in the different chapters into an examples directory. Finally an HTML version of the BNF grammar for the subset of VDM-SL will be installed. Since some of the files we supply have names longer than 8 + 3 characters, we recommend using an installation of Windows®95 which allows long file names or Windows NT.

3.3 Configuring the alarm example

In order to start Toolbox Lite, select it from the programs entry in the Windows setup. The main Toolbox window as shown in Figure 3.1 will appear. In order to understand how the different parts of this window are used it is possible to use a help-facility. At any point when using the Toolbox press the **F1** button to get *help* for that part of the tool the mouse

Figure 3.2 *The pull-down menus*

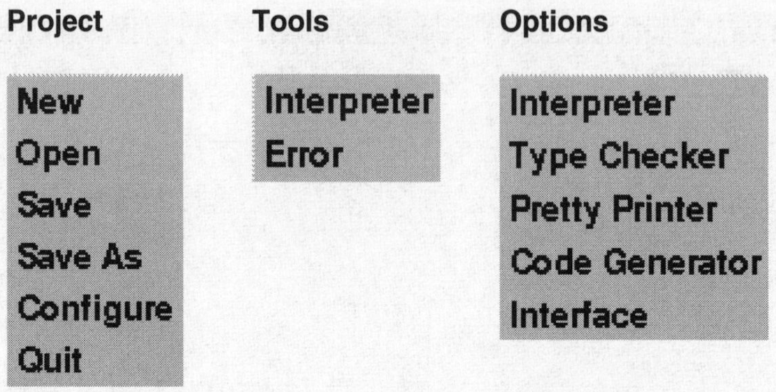

Project	**Tools**	**Options**
New	Interpreter	Interpreter
Open	Error	Type Checker
Save		Pretty Printer
Save As		Code Generator
Configure		Interface
Quit		

is pointing to. The help text is organised in a hypertext format so it is possible to jump around the text and search for information. However, remember that the help text is for the full version of the IFAD VDM-SL Toolbox so it provides help for more functionality than is available in Toolbox Lite.

At the top of the main Toolbox window are three pull-down menus (labelled "Project", "Tools" and "Options"). These three pull-down menus are shown in Figure 3.2. When the Project menu is selected it is possible to configure the choice of files for the current project by selecting the config-ure item in the Project menu. A project is simply a collection of specifica-tion files which belong together. When this item is selected, the window in Figure 3.3 will appear. For the chemical plant alarm example we select alarm.vdm by clicking it with the mouse in the left-hand side menu and then pressing the Add to project button. This has the consequence that alarm.vdm will appear in the Files in the project list. Pressing Ok will update the startup window (Figure 3.1) with alarm.vdm in the list of files as shown in Figure 3.4. This completes the configuration of Toolbox Lite to the alarm example file. It is now possible to start analysing the definitions made in this model.

3.4   Syntax and type checking models

Returning to the main window shown in Figure 3.4 we will now consider the facilities in the Toolbox Lite that allow us to analyse the

Figure 3.3 *Configuration of files*

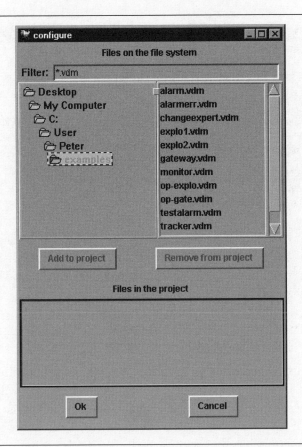

VDM-SL models in the project that has just been configured. Select
`alarm.vdm` by clicking on it. Notice that the Syntax Check button will
turn from grey to black showing that it is available. Pressing this button
will carry out a syntax check on the selected file(s). In the Modules
menu a letter S, three dashes and DefaultMod will now appear. The S
shows that this file has been successfully syntax checked, i.e. that the
definitions presented in the `alarm.vdm` file follow the syntax rules given
for VDM-SL. The dashes indicate that it has not yet been type checked,
code generated or pretty printed. Note that Toolbox Lite does not include
the code generation or pretty printing facilities which are available in
the full VDM-SL Toolbox. The symbol DefaultMod is used to indicate
that the alarm example has been presented as a collection of definitions

Figure 3.4 *After configuration of* `alarm.vdm`

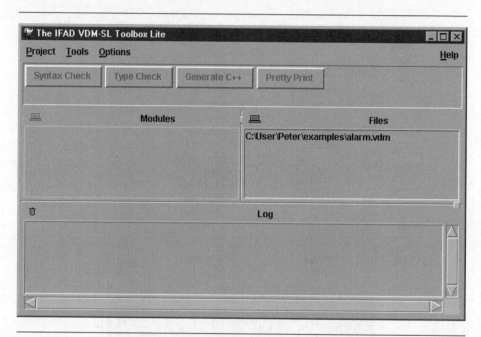

without any use of modular structuring. Unlike the full Toolbox, Toolbox Lite does not include support for modules, so DefaultMod will appear for all the models we will introduce. The module concept is reviewed in Chapter 11.

After successful syntax checking the Type Check becomes available. If this button is pressed the first of the three dashes in the Modules part of the window will change to a T indicating that the model has been type checked without any errors (see Figure 3.5). This means that, in addition to fulfilling the syntax rules of VDM-SL, the use of the different operators etc. in the definitions have satisfied the scope and type rules provided for VDM-SL. In this case the file was both syntactically correct and type correct right from the beginning. This is not surprising because this file has been developed and analysed separately. However, most developers make errors in early versions of models. It is therefore worth examining the facilities for reporting and correcting errors in Toolbox Lite. By way of preparation for this, a file called `alarmerr.vdm`, containing deliberate mistakes, has also been supplied.

In order to examine this file we need to configure Toolbox Lite again.

Figure 3.5 *Having both syntax and type checked* `alarm.vdm`

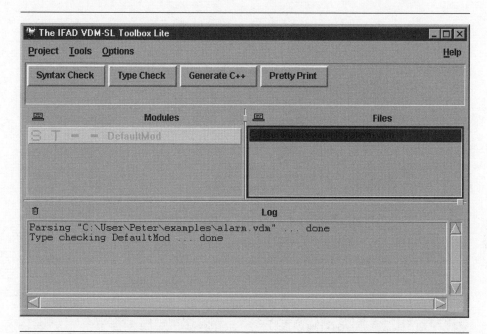

Enter the Projects pull-down menu and select the configure item again. In order to get rid of the definitions from `alarm.vdm`, select it from the Files in the project and press the Remove from project button. Then `alarmerr.vdm` can be selected instead. When Ok is pressed on the configure window the startup window (Figure 3.4) will be updated with `alarmerr.vdm` instead of `alarm.vdm`.

When this file is selected and the Syntax Check button is pressed the Error tool will pop up with four error messages as shown in Figure 3.6. We can traverse through the errors using the $\boxed{>}$ and $\boxed{<}$ buttons. The $\boxed{\gg}$ and $\boxed{\ll}$ buttons are used to go to the last and first messages respectively. In each case the Display part of the window will indicate the precise location of the error indicated in the Errors and Warnings part of the window. In each case the syntax checker explains what kind of construct is expected and provides a qualified guess at how it can be corrected. The suggested corrections are often, but not always, correct.

Exercise 3.1 Use an editor to correct all the errors discovered by the syntax checker on the `alarmerr.vdm` file and syntax check your corrected file again until no syntax errors appear. □

Figure 3.6 *Syntax errors in the error tool*

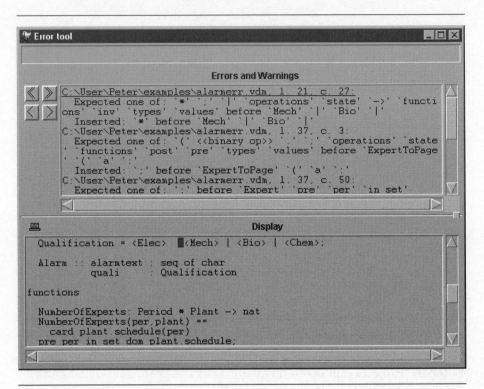

When no more syntax errors are present the model can be type checked. This model contains a number of type errors and the fact that the model is not type correct is shown by a slash through the T in the Modules part of the main window. In addition, the Error tool will appear again with a number of type errors as shown in Figure 3.7. The first one says: Error : Function is applied with wrong number of parameters. This is because QualificationOK has been called with three parameters instead of just two as indicated in its definition. The next one says: Error : Unknown identifier exss. This is due to a typographical error which is easy to correct. Altogether four errors and one warning are reported. The type checker distinguishes between *errors* which are things that are definitely wrong and must be corrected by the user, and *warnings* which are hints about things that could be wrong.

Figure 3.7 *Type errors in the error tool*

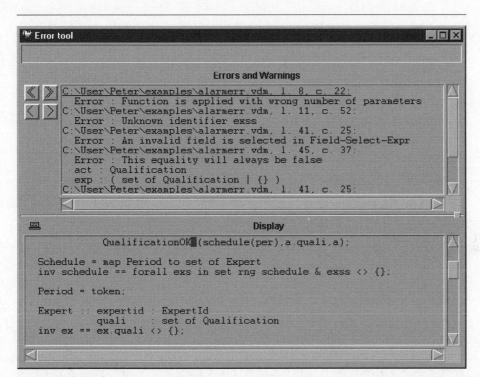

Exercise 3.2 Correct all the errors discovered by the type checker on the `alarmerr.vdm` file and syntax and type check your corrected file again until no syntax and type errors appear. □

3.5   Interpreting and debugging models

In addition to the static kind of analysis presented in the previous section, insight into models can be gained by executing them. We call this *interpreting* the models because they are not compiled as most programming languages are, but instead interpreted by an abstract machine. Toolbox Lite contains such an interpreter which allows execution and debugging of models written in a subset of the VDM-SL notation. Take the second pull-down menu Tools and select the Interpreter item. A window like that shown in Figure 3.8 will appear. Start by pressing the

Figure 3.8 *The Interpreter tool from Toolbox Lite*

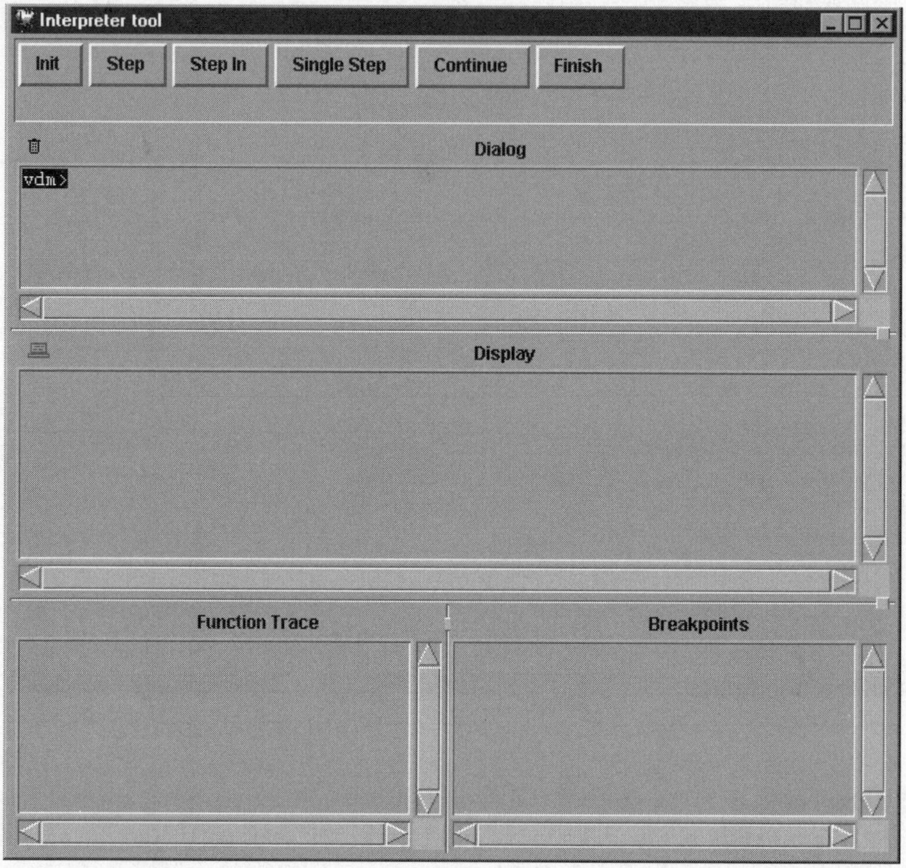

Init button in the top-left corner. This will initialise all the definitions you have read into the Toolbox (using the Syntax Check button from the main window). By initialisation we mean setting up the environment corresponding to the definitions read into the Toolbox. This environment includes type definitions, functions, as well as any value (constant) definitions and global state variables present (we discuss state definitions in Chapter 10). The alarm example only has type definitions and function definitions that are now available for testing.

The dialog part of the window can be used to provide commands to the interpreter and each of the commands will be submitted to the interpreter tool by hitting the return button on the keyboard. Typing `functions` will get a list of explicit functions which have been read into the Toolbox. For the alarm example we actually only provided three explicit function definitions and one implicit function definition. However, the list provided here contains nine function names. The extra ones have special prefixes (`inv_`, `pre_` and `post_`). These functions are automatically generated from the definitions containing invariants, pre-conditions and post-conditions. We will return to such special functions in Chapter 5. Any of these functions returned using the `functions` command can be executed if arguments are provided for them.

The file `testalarm.vdm` contains some value definitions for the alarm example. The schedule used in these definitions reflects the schedule presented in Figure 2.1 on page 20. All components from this figure have been given a name as a value definition in `testalarm.vdm` and below we will refer to these names. In order to get access to these definitions this file must first be included in the configuration in the same way that `alarm.vdm` and `alarmerr.vdm` were. Note here that you should not remove the `alarmerr.vdm` file which you have corrected from your project configuration. Having done this the `testalarm.vdm` file can be selected in the Files part of the main window. Then this file can be syntax checked (and type checked) and we can reinitialise the interpreter by pressing the Init button again. In this way we also get access to the value definitions provided by `testalarm.vdm`. In the dialog part of the window we can type `values` to see the list of value definitions which are available.

To illustrate interpreting, type `print NumberOfExperts(p1,plant)` in the Dialog part of the window and press return. The interpreter responds by printing 3 indicating that three experts are on duty in period `p1` which corresponds to "*Monday day*" from Figure 2.1 and `plant` corresponds to the entire figure represented in VDM-SL.

Exercise 3.3 Use the interpreter to evaluate the following expressions:

```
NumberOfExperts(p2,plant)
NumberOfExperts(p3,plant)
ExpertIsOnDuty(e1,plant)
ExpertIsOnDuty(e2,plant)
ExpertIsOnDuty(e3,plant)
```

□

Sometimes it is not clear why a function is returning a particular result when applied with some input values. In such cases it is valuable to be able to debug the model by setting up *break points*. A break point is a position where we wish the execution to be interrupted during interpretation. Set up a break point by typing `break NumberOfExperts`. The consequence is that `DefaultMod'NumberOfExperts` appears in the Break Points part of the window. Type `debug NumberOfExperts(p3,plant)`. The display part of the window will show where the execution has been stopped as shown in Figure 3.9[2]. Press Single Step a few times to see how the body of the function is evaluated step by step. While debugging an expression, subexpressions can be evaluated by using the `print` command in the Dialog part of the window. When execution does not deliver the expected results, break points provide a useful aid to debugging.

During debugging the trace of functions called is displayed in the Function Trace part of the window. When the arguments to a function become too large to display they are compressed into three dots. Such dots can be expanded by clicking the left mouse button with the cursor on top of the dots; the value can be folded back again by pressing the left mouse button again. Press the Continue button to end debugging and then the interpreter will continue either until the next break point is encountered or until the execution is finished.

Notice that `ExpertToPage` did not appear in the list of functions returned by the `functions` command. This is because it is an implicit function and such functions cannot be executed directly[3]. However, it is possible to execute pre-conditions and post-conditions of implicit functions. These functions return Boolean values as described by the logical expressions inside the pre and post-conditions. We will return to the issue of calling such pre-conditions in Subsection 5.8.3 and post-conditions in Subsection 6.4.3.

3.6   Setting options

In addition to calling automatically-generated functions (with prefixes such as `inv_`, `pre_` and `post_`) directly, these parts of the definitions can be used in other ways in dynamic analysis of models. Options can be set to make use of these constructs using the Options pull-down menu.

---

[2] The only difference between `print` and `debug` is that `debug` will stop when a break point is reached whereas `print` will ignore break points.

[3] The only other kind of construct that cannot be executed by the interpreter is a type binding which we will illustrate in the next chapter.

Figure 3.9 *Debugging the VDM model*

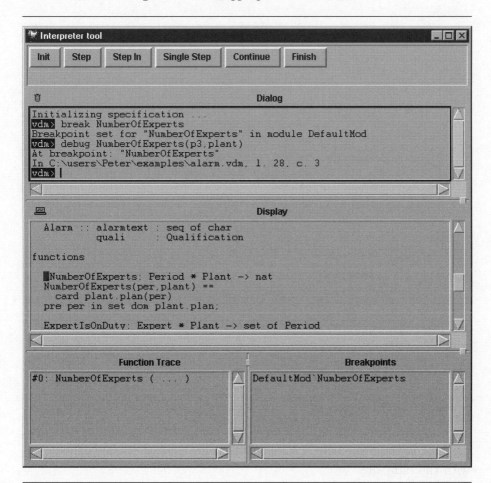

Choose the Interpreter item and the window shown in Figure 3.10 will appear. The options for the interpreter can then be changed by enabling dynamic type checking, invariant checking and pre-condition checking. When this has been done, pressing Ok at the bottom of this window will save these new settings.

Now select the Interpreter item under the Tools menu. Type "print NumberOfExperts(p5,plant)". The response is "Run-Time Error 58: The pre-condition evaluated to false". This indicates that the call of the function NumberOfExperts has violated the pre-condition from its definition.

Figure 3.10 *The interpreter options*

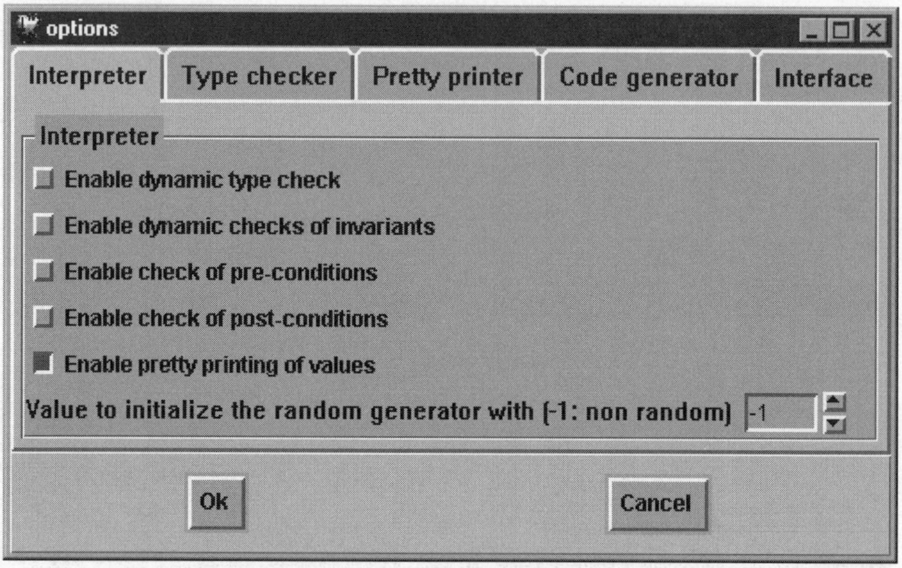

Such dynamic checks of properties can be used to gain more confidence in the correctness of a model.

In the Options pull-down menu there is also an entry for the Interface and here it is possible to set your preferred editor. If this has been done it is possible to click the editor icons present over the Files and the Modules parts of the main Toolbox window to automatically start up the editor with the right file.

Summary

In this chapter the different features of Toolbox Lite have been introduced:

- Configuration of selected VDM-SL files;
- syntax checking of VDM-SL models;
- type checking of VDM-SL models;
- the notion of error messages;
- executing and debugging VDM-SL models; and
- setting options for the different components.

In addition it has been illustrated that tool support may be valuable in providing insight in the consequences of a model.

Exercise 3.4★ Imagine an extension to the alarm example which would enable experts to swap duties. This function is called `ChangeExpert`. Given a plant, two experts and a period it will yield a new plant where the plan has been changed such that the first expert will be replaced by the second expert in the given period. A first version of this function could be formulated as:

```
ChangeExpert: Plant * Expert * Expert * Period -> Plant
ChangeExpert(mk_Plant(plan,alarms),ex1,ex2,per) ==
   mk_Plant(plan ++ {per |-> plan(per)\{ex1} union {ex2}},alarms)
```

where the \ symbol removes the `ex1` value from the schedule for the given period `per` and `union` adds the `ex2` value.

Do you see any problems with this function? This definition is placed in the file `changeexpert.vdm` so you should configure your project once again by adding this file. When it has been syntax checked and type checked (not strictly required) the interpreter can be initialised again. Now use the interpreter to inspect the plant returned from call such as:

```
ChangeExpert(plant,e4,e7,p3)
ChangeExpert(plant,e3,e7,p3)
```

Will the invariant on the `Plant` data type be violated? Test this by setting the option for the invariant checking. In case the invariant is broken it is possible to make a break point for the invariant `inv_Plant` itself and call that with a `Plant` value which possibly satisfies the invariant. By single stepping inside this it becomes easier to discover how the invariant is broken. If necessary, add the pre-condition needed to complete the function. □

4

Describing System Properties Using Logical Expressions

Aims

The aim of this chapter is to introduce the use of logic for stating the properties of data and functions in system models. The logic used in VDM-SL models is introduced via a temperature monitor example. On reaching the end of the chapter, the reader should be able to state and analyse logical expressions in Toolbox Lite.

4.1 Introduction

An important advantage of building a model of a computing system is that it allows for analysis, uncovering misunderstandings and inconsistencies at an early stage in the development process. The discovery of a possible failure of the `ExpertToPage` function in the previous chapter was the result of just such an analysis. The ability to reason about the types and functions in a model depends on having a *logic* in which to describe the properties of the system being modelled and in which to conduct arguments about whether those properties hold or not.

This chapter introduces the language of logical expressions used in VDM-SL, based on *Predicate Logic*. It begins by introducing the idea of a predicate, then examines the basic operators which allow logical expressions to be built up from simpler expressions. Finally, we examine the mechanisms for dealing with mis-application of operators and functions in the logic of VDM-SL.

4.2 The temperature monitor

The example running through this chapter continues the chemical plant theme. Suppose we are asked to develop the software for a temperature monitor for a reactor vessel in the plant. The monitor is connected to a temperature sensor inside the vessel from which it receives a reading (in degrees Celsius) every second.

Figure 4.1 *Sample temperature variations and last five readings*

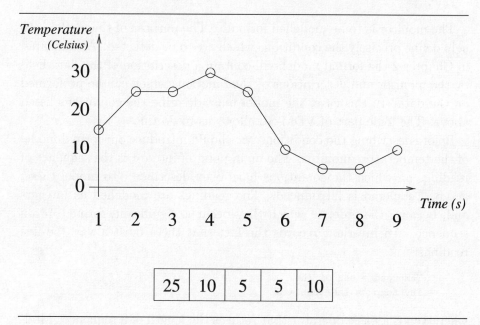

<table>
<tr><td>25</td><td>10</td><td>5</td><td>5</td><td>10</td></tr>
</table>

The monitor records the five most recent temperature readings in the order in which they were received from the sensor. For example, suppose the temperature at a sensor has varied as shown on the graph in Figure 4.1. The last five temperatures recorded in the monitor are shown as a sequence in the lower part of the figure.

In order to keep the reactor under control, the monitor should be able to detect and warn of certain conditions such as steady, wildly fluctuating or excessively high temperatures. It can do this by examining the changes over the last five temperature readings.

Suppose the following conditions are to be detected:

Rising temperature: the last reading in the sample is greater than the first;

Over limit: there is a reading in excess of 400°C;

Continually over limit: all the readings in the sample exceed 400°C;

Safe: if the readings exceed 400°C by the middle of the sample then the reactor is still safe provided the reading is less than 400°C by the end of the sample; and

Alarm: an audio alarm is to be sounded if and only if the reactor is not safe.

The monitor is to be modelled formally. The purpose of the model is to help define precisely the conditions which are to be detected. As indicated in Chapter 2 the formal model will contain a description of the data held by the monitor and descriptions of the functions which can be performed on the data. In this case, the model must describe the conditions listed above. The logic part of VDM-SL allows us to do this.

Before describing the conditions, we should introduce our formal model of the temperature monitor. The main point of interest is the sequence of readings on which the conditions have been described. To model these, a type `TempRead` is introduced. The readings are modelled as integers and, because the order in which they occur is significant, formed into a sequence. An invariant records the fact that there must always be five readings:

```
TempRead = seq of int
inv temp == len temp = 5
```

where `len` is a basic operator that returns the length of a sequence. Modelling using sequences will be presented in Chapter 7.

4.3   Logical expressions

4.3.1   *Simple predicates*

The simplest kind of logical expression in VDM-SL is a *proposition*. A proposition describes some property of specific values and is built up from the values using operators which return Boolean results i.e. operators which return either `true` or `false` when applied to values. For example, in the world of numbers, the operators < (read "is less than"), > (read "is greater than") and = (read "is equal to") allow propositions to be built up from values. For example:

```
3 < 27
```

is a proposition asserting that 3 is less than 27. Propositions can be true or false. For example, the proposition just given is true, but the following proposition is false:

```
5 = 9
```

Both are perfectly valid propositions.

Propositions have rather limited value in specifying realistic computing systems. For example, in our reactor monitor, we have to be able to deal with any arbitrary sequence of readings, not just some specific values. Using propositions to describe the conditions is impractical: we would have to describe every possible sequence of readings and say whether it exhibited a condition or not. For that reason, we allow *variables* to stand for values in expressions, in just the same way as variables are allowed to stand for values in conventional applied mathematics, where a mass might be termed *m* and a velocity *v*. If we allow the variable x to stand for an arbitrary number then it is possible to write:

    x < 27

This expression will be true if x is 3, but false if x is 82.

A logical expression containing a variable is termed a *predicate* in VDM-SL. Here are some other examples of predicates in VDM-SL:

    x < 23   The variable is x. If x is 3 then the pred-
                          icate is true, if x is 29, then it is false.

    (x ** 2) + x - 6 = 0 The variable is x. The symbols + and –
                          are arithmetic addition and subtraction;
                          ** raises a number to a power (in this case
                          x is squared). The predicate is true if x
                          is 2 or x is -3.

Predicates can have more than one variable. For example, the predicate

    (x ** 2) + y = 3

has two variables (x and y). It is true when x is 0 and y is 3; also when x is 1 and y is 2.

Returning now to the reactor monitor, predicates can be used to describe the conditions which must be detected. We introduce a variable which can stand for any sequence of five readings. Call the variable temp. To refer to a reading in temp, we index into the sequence, as one might index into an array in a program. Thus, the oldest reading in the list is written formally as

    temp(1)

while the most recent reading is

```
temp(5)
```

These readings are integers, so we can compare them using the conventional numerical comparison operators < (less than), <= (less than or equal to) etc. For example, if we want to say that the temperature has increased over the sample period, we can formally write

```
temp(1) < temp(5)
```

To state that the temperatures at the beginning and at the end of the sample period are the same, we can write

```
temp(1) = temp(5)
```

The two formulae above are logical: they are either true or false, depending on the readings in the variable **temp**. For example, if **temp** holds the sequence of values shown in Figure 4.1, the following are **true**:

```
temp(1) >= temp(5)
temp(3) = temp(4)
```

but the following three predicates are **false**:

```
temp(1) = temp(5)
temp(4) > temp(2)
temp(1) < temp(3)
```

Condition 1: Rising temperature The temperature is said to be rising if the last reading in the sample is greater than the first. To be able to use this predicate in a model (and in Toolbox Lite), we incorporate it into a Boolean function:

```
Rising: TempRead -> bool
Rising(temp) ==
  temp(1) < temp(5)
```

4.3.2   *Building more complex predicates: connectives*

Simple predicates are very limited in their capabilities. It is often necessary to build more complex predicates out of simpler ones by using logical *connectives*. In this section, each connective is introduced with an example.

Negation – "not" Negation allows us to state that the opposite of some logical expression is true. For example, if the monitor needs to detect the condition that the initial temperature in a sample is not over 350°C, the condition could be recorded as follows:

```
not temp(1) > 350
```

The property above could equally well be stated positively as `temp(1)` `<= 350`. It is usually the case that properties have several equally valid representations. The symbol `not` represents the negation of a logical expression. The expression `not A` is `true` only when `A` is `false`. The operator's behaviour can be represented using a *truth table* as follows:

A	not A
true	false
false	true

The column headed "`A`" gives each possible truth value of an arbitrary logical expression `A`. The column headed "`not A`" gives the corresponding truth value of the expression `not A`.

Disjunction – "or"

Condition 2: Over limit A sequence of readings is over limit if one of the readings exceeds 400°C. There are five possibilities:

> `temp(1)` exceeds 400°C or `temp(2)` exceeds 400°C or
> `temp(3)` exceeds 400°C or `temp(4)` exceeds 400°C or
> `temp(5)` exceeds 400°C

The "or" is represented in VDM-SL using the logical disjunction operator "`or`". The condition above is formulated as follows[1]:

> `temp(1) > 400 or temp(2) > 400 or`
> `temp(3) > 400 or temp(4) > 400 or`
> `temp(5) > 400`

---

[1] The line breaks in these logical expressions do not affect their meaning, but it is a good discipline to space expressions out in order to make them easier to read.

The Boolean function incorporating this predicate is defined as follows:

```
OverLimit: TempRead -> bool
OverLimit(temp) ==
   temp(1) > 400 or
   temp(2) > 400 or
   temp(3) > 400 or
   temp(4) > 400 or
   temp(5) > 400
```

Exercise 4.1 Try evaluating the following expressions by hand:

```
OverLimit([350,365,421,390,380])
OverLimit([350,390,320,395,330])
OverLimit([345,341,433,321,314])
```

Configure Toolbox Lite to work on the file **monitor.vdm** which contains the definition of **OverLimit**. Initialise the interpreter and use it to evaluate the expressions above, comparing the tool's answer with those you expected. □

The truth table for disjunction makes it clear that disjunction is an "inclusive or", i.e. the disjunction is true if any or all of its components (called disjuncts) are true:

A	B	A or B
true	true	true
true	false	true
false	true	true
false	false	false

The truth table defines the disjunction of a pair of logical expressions, even though disjunction has been used with longer lists of expressions above when defining the "over limit" condition. The extension from a binary disjunction to a longer one is straightforward: the disjunction is true if any of the disjuncts are true. Strictly, we regard a disjunction of the form

```
E1 or E2 or E3 or ... or En
```

as the following series of binary disjunctions:

```
(...((E1 or E2) or E3) or ...) or En
```

Parentheses indicate the order in which subexpressions should be evaluated.

Conjunction – "and" Conjunction allows us to say that more than one predicate is true at a time. For example, if we want to state formally that the first three readings in `temp` are decreasing, we can say

```
temp(1) > temp(2) and temp(2) > temp(3)
```

Condition 3: Continually over limit A sequence of readings is continually over limit if all of the readings exceed 400°C.

> `temp(1)` exceeds 400°C and `temp(2)` exceeds 400°C and
> `temp(3)` exceeds 400°C and `temp(4)` exceeds 400°C and
> `temp(5)` exceeds 400°C

The **and** symbol represents the logical conjunction of logical expressions called *conjuncts*. Formally, in VDM-SL, the condition is

```
temp(1) > 400 and temp(2) > 400 and
temp(3) > 400 and temp(4) > 400 and
temp(5) > 400
```

This gives the following Boolean function:

```
ContOverLimit: TempRead -> bool
ContOverLimit(temp) ==
  temp(1) > 400 and
  temp(2) > 400 and
  temp(3) > 400 and
  temp(4) > 400 and
  temp(5) > 400
```

Exercise 4.2 Evaluate the following expressions by hand and compare your results with those obtained by evaluating the same expressions using Toolbox Lite configured on the file `monitor.vdm`.

```
ContOverLimit([450,465,421,590,480])
ContOverLimit([350,390,420,395,430])
ContOverLimit([345,341,433,321,314])
```

□

The truth table for the expression `A and B` indicates that it is **true** only when both conjuncts are **true**:

A	B	A and B
true	true	true
true	false	false
false	true	false
false	false	false

Implication – "if"

Condition 4: Safe The sample is still considered safe if the readings exceed 400°C by the middle of the sample as long as they fall to less than 400°C later. To express this formally, it would be convenient to have some notion of "if ... then ..." in the logic. This is embodied in the implication operator "=>".

The reactor is safe when the following condition holds:

> **if** the readings exceed 400°C by the middle of the sample **then** the reading should be less than 400°C by the end of the sample.

The condition that the readings exceed 400°C by the middle of the sample can be expressed by the simple predicate:

```
temp(3) > 400
```

The condition that the readings exceed 400°C by the end of the sample can be expressed by the simple predicate:

```
temp(5) < 400
```

The safety condition is formally expressed:

```
temp(3) > 400  =>  temp(5) < 400
```

and the Boolean function for checking safety is:

```
Safe: TempRead -> bool
Safe(temp) ==
   temp(3) > 400 => temp(5) < 400
```

The reactor should be safe if the middle temperature is lower than 400°C. The only possibility we should exclude here is the case where the temperature exceeds 400°C by reading 3, but does not fall to less then 400°C by reading 5. This is reflected in the truth table for implication. The left-hand side of the implication is called the *antecedent* and the right-hand side is called the *consequent*.

A	B	A => B
true	true	true
true	false	false
false	true	true
false	false	true

Biimplication – "if and only if"

Condition 5: Alarm Having expressed all the conditions required in the model, the remaining requirement is that an alarm should be raised *if and only if* the reactor is not in the safe condition. We have already formulated the safe condition as `Safe(temp)`.

The alarm should therefore be raised if and only if the negation of the safe condition is true:

    not Safe(temp)

If the Boolean variable `alarm` stands for the state of the alarm, either `true` (alarm is sounding) or `false` (alarm is not sounding). We could try to formulate the condition as

    not Safe(temp) => alarm

This asserts that the `alarm` should be sounded when the reactor is not safe, but does not prevent the alarm from going off when the reactor is perfectly cool. The requirement said that the alarm should go off if and only if the reactor is unsafe, so we introduce the *biimplication* symbol "<=>" to stand for "if and only if". This can be considered a double implication because it works as a conjunction of two implications: one in each direction. Thus, the biimplication shown below

    not Safe(temp) <=> alarm

is equivalent to the following conjunction of implications:

    not Safe(temp) => alarm and
    alarm => not Safe(temp)

The Boolean function for stating the alarm can be expressed as an implicit definition as follows:

    RaiseAlarm(temp: TempRead) alarm: bool
    post not Safe(temp) <=> alarm

The truth table for biimplication makes it clear that the two sides of the <=> must have the same logical value for the biimplication to be true:

A	B	A <=> B
true	true	true
true	false	false
false	true	false
false	false	true

4.4   Presenting and evaluating predicates

The predicates presented so far in this chapter have been comparatively simple. When evaluating more complex predicates, using parentheses to bracket subexpressions helps to reduce confusion. Consider a complex logical expression such as:

```
(Rising(temp) and (ContOverLimit(temp) or OverLimit(temp))) =>
    not Safe(temp)
```

The parentheses tell the reader how to evaluate the expression, starting with the most deeply nested parts. For example, if temp has the value [453,345,400,387,401] the predicate is evaluated by first replacing the value for temp all places and then evaluating each of the function calls. The evaluation goes from the bracketed subexpressions from the most deeply nested outwards:

```
(false and (false or true)) => false
(false and true) => false
false => false
true
```

This detailed evaluation seems very tedious, but, with practice, short cuts become apparent: for example, the fact that one conjunct is false is enough to make the whole expression false. Indeed, Toolbox Lite evaluates just enough sub-expressions (working from left to right) to determine the overall value of a logical expression.

Operator Precedence

In VDM-SL, the logical connectives have a precedence relation which tells the reader how to evaluate expressions when parentheses have been omitted. The precedence relation is as follows:

Highest   not

                and

                or

                =>

Lowest   <=>

In order to evaluate an expression, work from left to right, first bracketing every **not** with the expression following it. Then work left to right again, bracketing each **and** with the expressions on either side of it. Carry on down the precedence relation.

To see how this works suppose we are presented with the complex expression above, but this time without any parentheses:

```
Rising(temp) and ContOverLimit(temp) or OverLimit(temp) =>
   not Safe(temp)
```

Bracketing the expression using the rules given above yields the following version:

```
((Rising(temp) and ContOverLimit(temp)) or OverLimit(temp)) =>
      (not Safe(temp))
```

At first glance one may think that this gives the same result as before.

Exercise 4.3 Evaluate the new bracketed version of the expression by hand using the same value of `temp` as was used at the beginning of the section. Check your result using Toolbox Lite. □

The result is different from the original version because the bracketing is different. Notice that the precedence relation causes the **ands** to be evaluated before the **ors**, whereas the bracketing in the original version of the expression encouraged the **or** to be evaluated before the **and**. The moral of the story is simple: when in doubt, use parentheses to make clear the order of evaluation you want – the default order based on the precedence relation may not be exactly what was required.

4.5   Using quantifiers

Some of the predicates used in Subsection 4.3.2 to represent conditions on the reactor temperature are rather long-winded. For example, the reactor is over limit if there is a reading in excess of 400°C. This was formulated as follows:

```
OverLimit: TempRead -> bool
OverLimit(temp) ==
   temp(1) > 400 or
   temp(2) > 400 or
   temp(3) > 400 or
   temp(4) > 400 or
   temp(5) > 400
```

This is acceptable for a short sequence of five readings, but suppose one was modelling a system with hundreds of readings to compare, or one with an unknown or variable number of readings. In this case, it would be much more convenient to use a variable for the index into the sequence, referring to

```
temp(i)
```

for the ith element of the sequence. It is straightforward to state that temp(i) exceeds 400°C:

```
temp(i) > 400
```

However, we need to be able to say that this should hold for some value of i in the range {1,...,5}. In the formal language of VDM-SL, we do this by using an *existential quantifier*. We assert that *there exists* an element i of the set {1,...,5} such that temp(i) > 400. Formally, this is written as follows:

```
exists i in set {1,...,5} & temp(i) > 400
```

The existential quantifier allows us to construct a logical expression about a whole collection of values of the variable i in one go, but it is equivalent to forming a long disjunction out of all the possible instances of i.

The equivalent to taking a long conjunction of formulae is the *universal quantifier* forall. The following formula states the "continually over limit" condition that all the recorded temperatures exceed 400°C:

```
forall i in set {1,...,5} & temp(i) > 400
```

The variable which is constrained by a quantifier to range across a set of values is called the *bound* variable (it is said to be bound to the elements of the set of values). Variables which are not bound in a formula are said to be *free*, e.g. temp in the formula above.

Quantifiers allow us to express properties of whole collections of values at once, rather than just one at a time. For example, in real models we need to describe properties such as the following:

- *All reactors hotter than 500 degrees Celsius should have the heating switched off.*
- *There are no two users with the same identifier.*
- *There is only one user with root access.*

These logical expressions range over whole groups of values (e.g. *all reactors, users*).

The syntax for expressions using the two quantifiers is:

`forall` *binding* & *predicate*

`exists` *binding* & *predicate*

The *binding* part names the bound variables and gives the collection of values (called the range) they belong to. If the range is a type, the binding is called a *type binding* and we use a colon notation e.g.:

```
forall x:nat1 & x>0
```
"All numbers in nat1 are greater than 0"

If the range is a set, the binding is called a *set binding* and we use the **in set** notation, e.g.:

```
exists x in set {1,2,6,7} & x>0
```
"There is a number in the set {1,2,6,7} which is greater than 0"

The main difference between types and sets is that types can have infinitely many elements whereas sets are always finite in VDM-SL. This also means that the interpreter from Toolbox Lite will be able to execute quantified expressions with set bindings, but not those with type bindings. Notice that for sets, we are using the $\{\_,\_,\_,\_\}$ notation to list members. We can also represent a range of numbers in a set using the ... notation, e.g. $\{5,\ldots,15\}$ which represents the integers from 5 to 15 inclusive. For example, the following expression asserts that all the readings in `temp` are over 400:

```
forall i in set {1,...,5} & temp(i) > 400
```

The following expression asserts that every reading is less than its successor:

```
forall i in set {1,...,4} & temp(i) < temp(i+1)
```

Notice that the set $\{1,\ldots,4\}$ is used in the expression above to avoid comparing `temp(5)` with `temp(6)`, which would involve indexing out of range on the sequence of readings.

The name of a bound variable is not important, as long as it does not interfere with the names of free variables in the predicate part of a quantifier, causing confusion. Thus, the following expression is equivalent to the previous one:

```
forall fred in set {1,...,4} & temp(fred) < temp(fred+1)
```

Several variables may be bound at once by a single quantifier. Consider, for example, a logical expression which states that no two readings are equal:

```
forall x,y in set {1,...,5} & not (temp(x) = temp(y))
```

Suppose we had the following value for `temp`:

```
[320, 220, 105, 119, 150]
```

Would the expression above be true? Certainly there are no two distinct readings which have the same value, but let us look carefully at the formula. It asserts that, for any x and any y, the reading at x and the reading at y are not equal. There is nothing to prevent us selecting the same index number for x and for y, say 3, so that `temp(x)` and `temp(y)` are bound to be the same. Thus, the formula above would never be **true**, because we could always find an x and y which have the same reading. The lesson from this example is to be very careful when dealing with quantifiers that introduce several bound variables ranging over the same set of values: the variables could take the same values from the range. In this particular case, we could include a restriction that x is not equal to y and assert that, for any x and y, **if** x and y are distinct, **then** the readings at x and y are different:

```
forall x,y in set {1,...,5} &
       not (x = y) => not (temp(x) = temp(y))
```

Exercise 4.4 Try formulating the following properties using predicate logic:

1. All the readings in `temp` are less than 400 and greater than 50.

2. Each reading in `temp` is greater than its successor by at least 1 and at most 10°C degrees.

3. There are two distinct readings in `temp` which are over 400°C.

□

Mixing Quantifiers Much of the power of quantifiers arises from the ability to mix them in logical expressions. For example, to assert that for any natural numbers between 10 and 20 inclusive, there is a natural number equal to half of the first number, we write the following:

```
forall n in set {10,...,20} & exists p:nat & 2*p=n
```

This logical expression is equivalent to `false` but it is still a valid expression.

In the chemical plant monitor, we might wish to record a condition where there is a "single minimum" in the sequence of readings, i.e. there is a reading which is strictly smaller than any of the other readings. This could be formalised as follows:

```
exists min in set {1,...,5} &
   forall i in set {1,...,5} & i <> min => temp(i) > temp(min)
```

Notice that the order in which quantifiers are used is very important. When mixing quantifiers that the order is which they occur is important. The "single minimum" example is a case in point. If the order of quantifiers is reversed, the expression is:

```
forall i in set {1,...,5} &
   exists min in set {1,...,5} & i <> min => temp(i) > temp(min)
```

Reading this carefully we see that the expression says that, for every reading i, there exists another reading at index `min` which is strictly less than the original reading, providing `min` is a different index from i,

We know that we can always select `min` to be the same as i, making the implication trivially `true`, so this expression always evaluates to `true`, unlike the "single minimum" example.

Exercise 4.5 Debug the two different expressions mixing the `forall` and `exists` quantifications to convince yourself the order is important. Try evaluating the expressions on the value [375,230,230,250,275]. □

4.6   Coping with undefinedness

Very often in modelling critical or high-integrity systems, we wish to model failure and recovery behaviour. Suppose that the temperature sensors in our example are assumed to fail in such a way that they send a special value (called `<ERROR>`) to the monitor when they are unable to send an accurate temperature reading. In this situation, we cannot make comparisons like

```
<ERROR> < 400
```

The "<" operator does not make sense of `<ERROR>` and so the comparison is neither true nor false, but simply meaningless. Our logic and modelling notation are meant to handle realistic computing systems, so they should be equipped with some means of handling undefined applications of operators. Similar situations can arise, for example, when division by zero may occur. Attempts to evaluate undefined expressions can lead to non-termination.

Dealing with undefinedness in logic

The logic in VDM-SL has been designed to cover undefined values. The logic called LPF (Logic of Partial Functions) extends the truth tables to cover undefined values. For example if a logical expression is undefined, so is its negation. We represent an undefined value by * in the truth tables. Thus, the table for negation is:

A	not A
true	false
false	true
*	*

The other tables are considered below.

Disjunction Consider the expression `A or B`. Either A or B or both could be undefined, but it is sometimes possible to evaluate the expression as a whole if we know the value of one of the disjuncts. Suppose we evaluate A and B in parallel. As soon as one of the disjuncts evaluates to `true` we know that the entire disjunction is `true`, regardless of whether the other disjuncts evaluate to `true`, `false` or are undefined. If one disjunct evaluates as `false`, but the other is undefined, we cannot know whether the disjunction as a whole is true or not, so it remains undefined. This approach results in the following truth table:

A	B	A or B
true	true	true
true	false	true
true	*	true
false	true	true
false	false	false
false	*	*
*	true	true
*	false	*
*	*	*

Conjunction If one conjunct is false, we know that the whole conjunction is `false`, regardless of whether the other conjunct is true or false or undefined. If one conjunct is known to be true, but the other is undefined, we cannot determine whether the conjunction as a whole is true or not, so it remains undefined:

A	B	A and B
true	true	true
true	false	false
true	*	*
false	true	false
false	false	false
false	*	false
*	true	*
*	false	false
*	*	*

Implication In the case of implication, we know that `A => B` is `true` if A is `false`, regardless of the truth or undefinedness of B. We also know that `A => B` is `true` if B is `true`, regardless of A. This gives the following table:

A	B	A => B
true	true	true
true	false	false
true	*	*
false	true	true
false	false	true
false	*	true
*	true	true
*	false	*
*	*	*

Biimplication Here we need both values A and B to determine the truth of A <=> B, so in all other cases the result must be undefined.

A	B	A <=> B
true	true	true
true	false	false
true	*	*
false	true	false
false	false	true
false	*	*
*	true	*
*	false	*
*	*	*

Dealing with undefinedness in the interpreter

How can we deal with undefinedness when interpreting logical expressions in Toolbox Lite? The treatment of undefinedness requires sub-expressions to be evaluated in parallel because of the risk of non-termination of one of the sub-expressions. However, this is not a practical approach because of the process management overhead. So we evaluate sub-expressions in a fixed order, from left to right as in most programming languages. Thus, it is necessary to guard against expressions that can yield a run-time error (and thus an undefined value). We have carefully done this in the VDM-SL definitions presented here. Thus, if a value elem must be in the domain of a mapping m and it must be associated with a special value info when it is looked up in the map it must be written as:

```
elem in set dom m and m(elem) = info
```

rather than:

```
m(elem) = info and elem in set dom m
```

because in this way it is guaranteed that `elem` belongs to the domain of m before the partial operation of looking up in the map is carried out.

Consequently the truth tables for the logical connectives implemented in the interpreter in the Toolbox are no longer symmetrical when subexpressions are undefined. For disjunction the truth table becomes:

A	B	A or B
true	true	true
true	false	true
true	*	true
false	true	true
false	false	false
false	*	*
*	true	[*]
*	false	*
*	*	*

where the small box indicates the place where there is a difference from the tables presented earlier. For conjunctions the truth table becomes:

A	B	A and B
true	true	true
true	false	false
true	*	*
false	true	false
false	false	false
false	*	false
*	true	*
*	false	[*]
*	*	*

and again the small box indicates the place where there is a difference. Finally, for implication the truth table becomes:

A	B	A => B
true	true	true
true	false	false
true	*	*
false	true	true
false	false	true
false	*	true
*	true	$\boxed{*}$
*	false	*
*	*	*

The truth tables for negation and biimplication are not affected.

Summary

- *Predicates* are logical expressions with *free variables* which may be instantiated to values in a *binding*.
- Predicates may be composed using the basic logical operators **and**, **or**, **not**, **<=>** and **=>**. The meaning of the basic operators are given via truth tables.
- The *Universal* (**forall**) and *Existential* (**exists**) *Quantifiers* allow logical expressions to be made about collections of values. Bindings in quantifications allow variables to range over types or sets. Universal quantification may be looked on as potentially infinite conjunction; existential quantification as a potentially infinite disjunction.
- A quantifier can bind several variables. Quantifiers can be nested and mixed in a logical expression.
- The Logic of Partial Functions extends the truth tables of basic Predicate Logic to allow for reasoning with undefined values.

Exercise 4.6 Define the functions Xor and Nand with the following truth table:

A	B	Xor(A,B)	Nand(A,B)
true	true	false	false
true	false	true	true
false	true	true	true
false	false	false	true

Test the functions using the interpreter with the different combinations.
□

Exercise 4.7 Construct the truth table for "`(not A) or B`" and take
the undefined element * into account. □

5

The Elements of a Formal Model

Aims

This chapter aims to introduce the reader to the most basic kinds of data value available to the modeller and to show how values can be manipulated through operators and functions. These are introduced using a traffic light kernel control example. On completing this chapter the reader should be able to recognise and use all the basic data types of VDM-SL.

5.1 Introduction

A functional model of a system is composed of definitions of types which represent the kinds of data values under consideration and definitions of functions which describe the computations performed on the data. In order to develop a formal model, we therefore require a means of defining types and values, and ways to construct logical expressions which state the properties of values. This chapter illustrates these features in VDM-SL and introduces the basic types available in VDM-SL using an example based on traffic light control. To make use of a type, we will need:

- a symbol to represent the type, e.g. `nat`;
- a way of writing down values in the type, e.g. `3`, `"John"`;
- value operators to manipulate elements of the type, e.g. `_ + _` where the underscores are used to indicate the positions of the arguments of the constructors; and
- comparison operators, e.g. `_ < _`, to allow expressions of elements of the type to be compared.

This chapter introduces the basic types of VDM-SL (the ones that come "for free" with the language), and the three most basic type constructors: optional types with the `nil` value (`[_]`), union types (`_|_`) and record

72

types (with :: definitions). Such type constructors are used for constructing more interesting types from the basic ones.

For each of the operators that we introduce we will distinguish between *total* and *partial* operators.

An operator op having the following signature:

```
op: A1 * A2 * ... * An  ->  B
```

is said to be *total* if op(a1,...,an) is defined for all possible inputs a1,...,an of types A1,A2,...,An. Numerical addition mentioned above is a total operator because all real numbers can be added to any other real number. However, within a computer, "addition" is normally a partial operator because the computer can only represent a finite range of numbers. VDM-SL allows us to deal with unrestricted numeric values or to introduce restrictions if they are relevant to the model.

An operator op is said to be *partial* if there is some input such that op(a1,...,an) is undefined. For example, the numeric division operator is partial because division by 0 is undefined. In an implementation, division by zero would typically result in a run-time error.

Having introduced these basic definitions we are now ready to look at the ongoing example for this chapter.

5.2   A traffic light control kernel

This example is derived from a model developed by Paul Ammann in the Z notation [Ammann95, Ammann96]. Traffic light control is safety critical because certain failures of traffic signals can lead to hazardous road conditions which can result in accidents. One approach to ensuring that a traffic light controller will not contribute to an accident is to develop a *safety kernel* of the system [Rushby86]. The safety kernel provides the only means of control over the critical functions of the system. Usually the kernel is the only part of the software which has direct access to the controllers of the physical system, so that other software components must use the kernel to interact with the environment. Since the kernel is responsible for maintaining safety, it is worth modelling it at an early stage of development, so that the designers have a clear understanding of how the kernel should behave. A kernel must ensure a desired behaviour for the overall system without making any assumptions about the trustworthiness or proper functioning of the remaining parts of the software system.

Figure 5.1 *Example intersection with traffic lights*

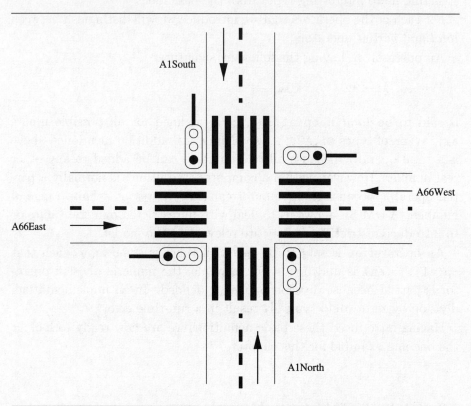

Traffic lights. Where roads cross it may be necessary to regulate the traffic using coloured lights. Each traffic light is responsible for informing drivers whether they can drive through the intersection or whether they must wait. A green light is used to indicate that drivers can continue and a red light is used to indicate that drivers must stop. The amber light is used to indicate that the lights are about to change from green to red. All traffic paths are regulated by lights and some traffic paths conflict in the sense that traffic flowing simultaneously in conflicting paths may result in an accident. A simple intersection with four traffic lights is shown in Figure 5.1.

A *traffic light controller* is responsible for controlling the lights. The aim of the traffic light controller is to ensure that the traffic will flow as smoothly as possible without accidents. The safety kernel for such a controller should ensure that the lights do not permit traffic to flow in conflicting paths simultaneously. A light associated with a particular path may only change according to the transitions shown as arrows in Figure 5.2. For a light on a given path to turn *Red*, it must have been *Amber* for at least *AmberChange* seconds prior to the transition, thereby giving drivers fair warning of the impending *Red*. For a light to turn *Green* all lights in conflicting paths must have been *Red* for at least *RedClearance* seconds, in order to give traffic time to clear the junction. From a functional perspective, for a light to turn *Amber*, the light must be *Green* for at least *MinimumGreen* seconds in order to allow a fair chance for traffic to flow smoothly. However, this requirement may be violated: for example, if an emergency vehicle needs to pass in a conflicting path.

Figure 5.2 *Rules for traffic light transitions*

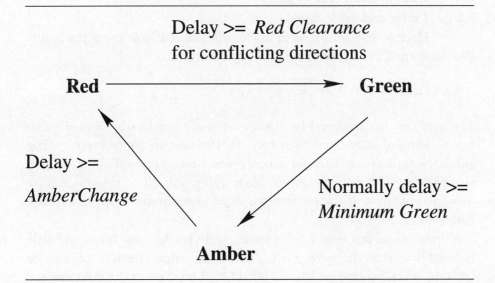

Safety requirements for a traffic light controller. The requirements for the safety kernel of the traffic light controller are as follows:

S1 It must always be the case that if a pair of paths conflict then the lights associated with one of the paths is red.

S2 Before a light is allowed to change from *Red* to *Green*, there must have been a delay of *RedClearance* seconds after the lights in all conflicting paths turn *Red*.

S3 There must be a delay of *AmberChange* seconds after the light turns *Amber* before the light is allowed to change from *Amber* to *Red*.

This example is used to introduce some of the basic types and operators from VDM-SL. We will first develop a model of the kernel, and then review the safety requirements to check that they hold in the model. As always, we will be careful to consider the purpose of the model before constructing it, as this purpose will be our guide in determining which aspects of the system to include in the model. In this case, the model is being built to help define the functionality of the safety kernel. We therefore concentrate on those issues which affect the safety of the lights system at the junction.

5.3   Union and basic types

5.3.1   *Union and quote types*

First we consider how to model the different colours of the lights. We can introduce this by making a type definition:

```
Light = <Red> | <Amber> | <Green>
```

The symbols distinguished by the use of angle brackets are called *quote types*. Vertical bars have been used to separate the quote types. The bar is the type constructor for *union types*, which are used for expressing alternatives. The combination of union types and quote types is similar to what is known as an enumerated type in a number of programming languages.

A quote type has only one element, and this has the same syntactic representation as the type itself. Thus, the value `<Green>` belongs to the type `<Green>` and to the type `Light`. The type `Light` contains the union of the types `<Red>`, `<Amber>` and `<Green>` and hence only the values `<Red>`, `<Amber>` and `<Green>`.

5.3.2   *The numeric types*

As it will be necessary to model periods of time passing (e.g. the delays *RedClearance* and *AmberChange*), we must introduce a type to model time. A numeric type seems appropriate. However, there is a choice to make because a number of numeric types exist. They are:

Natural numbers incl. 0	`nat`	0,1,2,...
Natural numbers excl. 0	`nat1`	1,2,3, ...
Integers	`int`	..., -2,-1,0,1,2,...
Reals	`real`	...-3.7, ..., 0, π ..., 5.8372, ...

Here it is worth noting that only a finite number of real numbers can be represented in the Toolbox. For example, π cannot be represented because it has an infinite number of digits so, as usual, it must be approximated. The modeller here has chosen to use the real numbers and operate in seconds. The type definition is:

```
Time = real
```

An alternative could be to work in, say, milliseconds and use the integers because the resolution at milliseconds would be sufficient. The natural numbers could also be used with this unit, thereby excluding negative times. For numeric types the usual arithmetic and comparison operators are available (see Subsection A.4.2). We will use them when they are required in the following chapters.

5.3.3   *The token type*

Another important concept for the model of the traffic light controller is that of *path* (we will have to model the notion of conflicting paths). For the model of the traffic light control system made here, we are not really concerned about the underlying representation of the paths. In an instantiation of the implementation of a general traffic light controller, paths may be identified using a name of a road (e.g. "A1") and the town the road is leading to (e.g. "towards Washington" or "Northbound"). However, for this model, we need only to be able to compare paths to see whether they are identical and record which paths conflict with one another. In this case we make a type definition like:

```
Path = token
```

The basic type `token` is used whenever the representation of a data type is immaterial to the formal model. As a general guide, the representation is immaterial if the functions do not require access to the values of the type. For example, if a function were required to modify the name of a path, we would have to have defined a more elaborate representation. However, no such function is required, and so `token` is sufficient as a representation for `Path`. The only operation that can be carried out on a token value is a comparison for equality with another token value.

In order to represent the paths shown in Figure 5.2 we could create some value definitions. This is done by prefixing the definitions with the keyword `values`:

```
values

p1 : Path = mk_token("A1North");
p2 : Path = mk_token("A1South");
p3 : Path = mk_token("A66East");
p4 : Path = mk_token("A66West")
```

In order to define a value, we give the name of the value, its type and its actual value. Note that value definitions must be given in such an order that each expression describing an actual value may only make use of other value identifiers that have already been defined. Otherwise Toolbox Lite would not be able to initialise the model. Token values are written with a `mk_token` constructor and an arbitrary value inside the braces[1]. In this case we have simply chosen to use strings, i.e. sequences of characters.

5.4   Basic type constructors

We have introduced most of the basic types of VDM-SL. However, we would not be able to model many useful computing systems if these were all we had. *Type constructors* build more complex types from simpler ones. For example, strings can be represented as sequences of characters:

```
String = seq of char
```

using the sequence type constructor "`seq of`" applied to the basic character type `char`[2]. In the following sections we will introduce some basic type constructors. Chapters 6, 7 and 8 show how to model systems using the most important type constructors in VDM-SL (sets, sequences and mappings).

---

[1] Strictly speaking, this is an extension to the ISO VDM-SL Standard, which states that values of the `token` type cannot be inspected or constructed.

[2] The different character values which can be used in VDM-SL can be found in Appendix A on page 227.

5.5   Record types

If we wish to model the possibility that paths can be conflicting, we need to consider pairs of paths. This is done by introducing a type `Conflict` which models two paths that are in conflict with each other:

```
Conflict :: path1: Path
            path2: Path
```

This is a *record type* with two fields. Note that this type definition uses ":::" instead of the equality symbol used in the other type definitions above. This notation indicates that all values belonging to the type are extended with a *tag* containing the name of the type. The tag allows us to define a constructor operator on each record type. The constructor is written mk_*tag*, where *tag* is the name in the tag. In this example, the constructor is called mk_Conflict, so one particular conflict value could be written as follows:

```
mk_Conflict(mk_token("A1North"),mk_token("A66East"))
```

Given the value definitions presented for the above paths this conflict could also be written as:

```
mk_Conflict(p1,p3)
```

where p1 is defined to be mk_token("A1North") and p3 is defined to be mk_token("A66East"). This is known as a *record constructor* expression. Given a record it is possible to extract the value of a field using the "dot" notation. For example, given a conflict con, the first path is given by "con.path1". An expression using the dot notation is called a *field selection expression*.

We now make a first attempt at the model for the kernel. There are two components: the current status of the lights and the information about the paths that conflict:

```
Kernel :: lights    : ???
          conflicts : ???
```

Which types could we use for these two fields? The conflicts component is just a set of Conflicts:

```
Kernel :: lights    : ???
          conflicts : set of Conflict
```

while the `lights` component is a mapping relating each `Path` to the `Light` on that path:

```
Kernel :: lights    : map Path to Light
          conflicts : set of Conflict
```

We will discuss in detail sets in Chapter 6 and mappings in Chapter 8.

For the junction shown in Figure 5.2 the set of conflicts can be defined as follows:

```
conflicts : set of Conflict
        = {mk_Conflict(p1,p3),
           mk_Conflict(p1,p4),
           mk_Conflict(p2,p3),
           mk_Conflict(p2,p4),
           mk_Conflict(p3,p1),
           mk_Conflict(p4,p1),
           mk_Conflict(p3,p2),
           mk_Conflict(p4,p2)}
```

and the current setting of the lights for the different paths is defined to be:

```
lights : map Path to Light
       = {p1 |-> <Red>,
          p2 |-> <Red>,
          p3 |-> <Green>,
          p4 |-> <Green>}
```

5.6   Invariants

It is often necessary to express the property that only certain values of a defined type should arise in a model. For example, we may wish to record that a path may not be in conflict with itself. Such additional restrictions on a type are recorded as data type invariants in VDM-SL.

For both of the record types introduced above it would be appropriate to write an invariant. For `Conflict` we would like to record that a path cannot be in conflict with itself. The type definition would then be changed to:

```
Conflict :: path1: Path
            path2: Path
inv mk_Conflict(p1,p2) == p1 <> p2
```

The invariant is defined by giving the properties of a typical element of the type. After the "inv" keyword, we name a typical value and then describe the restrictions on that value as a logical expression. In the example above, the typical value is given by a pattern which matches the structure of the values belonging to the type. The mk_Conflict(p1,p2) part is called a *record pattern* and it can be used whenever we know that a parameter value will have a similar structure. In this case, we know that elements from the conflict type will be tagged by the name Conflict and have two components. The identifiers p1 and p2 can then be used by the right-hand side of the *definition sign* == to formulate the desired logical expression.

An equally good alternative is to give the name for a whole Conflict and use the dot notation to retrieve the fields from it:

```
inv con == con.path1 <> con.path2
```

When invariants are defined, a truth-valued function is automatically generated with a prefix like inv_. In this case we get a function called inv_Conflict which takes as input a value following the structure of the type expression, and returns a Boolean.

Exercise 5.1 The definitions presented in this chapter are present in the file traffic.vdm. Configure Toolbox Lite with this file and check whether all of the values from the conflicts set satisfy the automatically generated invariant function for the Conflict type. **Hint:** use a quantified expression to check this. Remember to initialise your model in the interpreter before executing any functions. □

For the Kernel type we could express the property that, for all conflicting paths, the lights must be known in the lights mapping:

```
Kernel :: lights    : map Path to Light
          conflicts : set of Conflict
inv mk_Kernel(ls,cs) ==
      forall c in set cs &
            c.path1 in set dom ls and
            c.path2 in set dom ls
```

In addition it is required that one of the lights in such a conflicting path must be red. Adding this restriction we get:

```
Kernel :: lights    : map Path to Light
          conflicts : set of Conflict
```

```
inv mk_Kernel(ls,cs) ==
    forall c in set cs &
        c.path1 in set dom ls and
        c.path2 in set dom ls and
        (ls(c.path1) = <Red> or ls(c.path2) = <Red>)
```

A universal quantifier is used to express this here. The dot notation is used to obtain the two different paths from a conflict value c.

Exercise 5.2 Before you read on, strengthen the invariant for Kernel by adding the constraint that the set of conflicting paths is symmetric (i.e. if p1 is in conflict with p2 then p2 is also in conflict with p1.) □

For the Time type it would also be appropriate to introduce an invariant. Under the assumption that we are not interested in negative numbers the type definition should be:

```
Time = real
inv t == t >= 0
```

Thus, any value t which belongs to the type Time is a real number and t satisfies the predicate t >= 0.

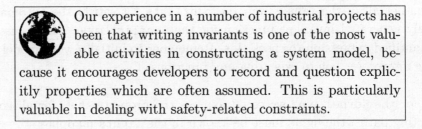

Our experience in a number of industrial projects has been that writing invariants is one of the most valuable activities in constructing a system model, because it encourages developers to record and question explicitly properties which are often assumed. This is particularly valuable in dealing with safety-related constraints.

5.7 Explicit function definitions

Using only the basic operators can be tedious and repetitious, especially in large formal models or with complex data types. It is often desirable to define operators specifically for the model under development. In this section we look at one way of defining such operators – as *functions*.

A function takes a number of arguments and produces a single result. For any set of actual arguments, a function returns only one result. Functions may, however, be partial. An *explicit function definition* in VDM-SL has the following form:

```
f: T1 * T2 * ... -> T
f(p1, p2, ... ) == expression-defining-result
pre logical-expression
```

and it has the following parts:

The signature giving the name of the function, types of arguments and
result (`f: T1 * T2 * ...-> T`);

The parameter list, naming the parameters to the function using patterns
which are usually simply names (`(p1, p2, ... )`);

The function body, which is an expression in terms of the parameters,
evaluating to the result (*expression-defining-result*); and

The pre-condition, which is a logical expression which is true exactly for
those values where the function is defined. The pre-condition may
be omitted when the function is defined for all possible input values
(*logical-expression*).

The rest of this chapter gives examples of explicit function definitions.
Functions can also be defined *implicitly*, i.e. by means of a post-condition
instead of a function body. Implicit function definitions have already been
introduced in Chapter 2. However, we will not discuss implicit functions
further until Chapter 6.

5.8   Functions for changing signals

In our traffic light example it would make sense to define functions
for changing the signals in a given path. We need three different functions
for carrying out such changes. All of them will have a similar signature.
That of the function changing a signal to green is as follows:

```
ToGreen: Path * Kernel -> Kernel
```

This function will change the light to green in the given path and keep all
the other lights unchanged. The function will have a structure such as:

```
ToGreen: Path * Kernel -> Kernel
ToGreen(p,mk_Kernel(lights,conflicts)) ==
  mk_Kernel(ChgLight(lights,p,<Green>),conflicts)
```

using a record pattern in the parameter list and a record constructor
expression in the body. The function `ChgLight` updates the `lights` map-

ping so that the path p now has the colour <Green>. We will defer the definition of ChgLight to later in this section.

Exercise 5.3 Before you read on define similar functions which change lights to amber and to red. □

5.8.1 *Adding pre-conditions*

The purpose of the traffic light kernel is to help avoid accidents, and the light-changing functions have the potential to lead to hazards if they are improperly used. Thus, each function must respect the safety requirements. Restrictions on the proper use of a function are documented using a *pre-condition*. All the functions changing the light should, for example, require that the path is known in the given traffic light controller kernel.

Let us start by considering the most dangerous function: changing a light to green. From *S2* it can be seen that it is only possible to make a transition to green if the signal is already red. In addition we need to ensure that all the conflicting paths are already red (let us not consider the timing requirements for now). A first attempt at defining ToGreen is:

```
ToGreen: Path * Kernel -> Kernel
ToGreen(p,mk_Kernel(lights,conflicts)) ==
  mk_Kernel(ChgLight(lights,p,<Green>),conflicts)
pre p in set dom lights and
    lights(p) = <Red> and
    forall con in set conflicts &
        (con.path1 = p => lights(con.path2) = <Red>) and
        (con.path2 = p => lights(con.path1) = <Red>)
```

The pre-condition has three conjuncts. The first one checks that the path is known about in the traffic light controller. The second states that we can only move to green from red, and the third states that all the conflicting paths must be red. However, since the invariant for the Kernel type should state that the set of conflicting paths is symmetric (see Exercise 5.2) the final conjunct inside the universal quantification is not needed. This simplification will be used at a later stage in this chapter.

Two useful checks can be performed to gain confidence that the pre-conditions and invariants cover the necessary cases:

- If part of a pre-condition is already implied by the invariants on the types of the inputs, that part of the pre-condition can be removed.
- If there is a conjunct which is common to all the pre-conditions of functions using a particular input type, it *may* be worth considering adding that restriction as an invariant on the type rather than repeating it in all the function definitions.

The structures of the functions describing the other two state transitions are the same as that of `ToGreen` except that no check on the status of conflicting paths is required. Thus, we get:

```
ToRed: Path * Kernel -> Kernel
ToRed(p,mk_Kernel(lights,conflicts)) ==
  mk_Kernel(ChgLight(lights,p,<Red>),conflicts)
pre p in set dom lights and lights(p) = <Amber>
```

and

```
ToAmber: Path * Kernel -> Kernel
ToAmber(p,mk_Kernel(lights,conflicts)) ==
  mk_Kernel(ChgLight(lights,p,<Amber>),conflicts)
pre p in set dom lights and lights(p) = <Green>
```

Finally let us consider the auxiliary function `ChgLight`:

```
ChgLight: (map Path to Light) * Path * Light -> (map Path to Light)
ChgLight(lights,p,colour) ==
  lights ++ {p |-> colour}
```

The `++` operator is used for overwriting one mapping with another. In this case the resulting mapping will have the new `colour` for the given path `p`. We will explain the operations on mappings in much more detail in Chapter 8.

Now we have developed a basic model for the key functions of the kernel. However, we have not yet taken the timing constraints into account.

5.8.2   Adding timing constraints

In order to take the timing constraints into account we must assume that we have defined the constants `RedClearance`, `MinimumGreen` and `AmberChange` as value definitions in VDM-SL:

```
RedClearance : Time = 2.6;
MinimumGreen : Time = 1;
AmberChange : Time = 2.6
```

The actual values used here are arbitrarily chosen within the limits provided in the United States standards for traffic lights with the unit of time being seconds. Note that in each value definition the type of the construct is also supplied.

In addition to these definitions we need to add a field called `lastch` to keep track of the last time the light on each path has been changed. Furthermore, the functions for changing the signals in a given path must also take the time as an argument.

The data model of the kernel is as follows:

```
Kernel :: lights    : map Path to Light
          conflicts : set of Conflict
          lastch    : map Path to Time
inv mk_Kernel(ls,cs,lc) ==
      dom ls = dom lc and
      forall c in set cs &
            mk_Conflict(c.path2,c.path1) in set cs and
            c.path1 in set dom ls and
            c.path2 in set dom ls and
            (ls(c.path1) = <Red> or ls(c.path2) = <Red>)
```

where the `lastch` component has been added and the invariant has been expanded slightly, requiring the two mappings to have the same domain. In addition the result from Exercise 5.2 has been incorporated. In the test data we wish to say that the lights in all paths have been changed initially. This can be described by a value definition as:

```
lastchanged : map Path to Time
            = {p1 |-> 0,p2 |-> 0,p3 |-> 0,p4 |-> 0}
```

Thus the full traffic light controller value can be composed of the different components described so far. This looks as:

```
kernel : Kernel
       = mk_Kernel(lights,conflicts,lastchanged)
```

The function which describes changing the light in a path to green now additionally involves ensuring that lights for all conflicting paths have been red for at least the RedClearance interval. The ToGreen function can be changed to:

```
ToGreen: Path * Kernel * Time -> Kernel
ToGreen(p,mk_Kernel(lights,conflicts,lastch),clock) ==
  mk_Kernel(ChgLight(lights,p,<Green>),conflicts,
            ChgTime(lastch,p,clock))
pre p in set dom lights and
    lights(p) = <Red> and
    forall mk_Conflict(p1,p2) in set conflicts &
           (p = p1 => (lights(p2) = <Red> and
                       RedClearance <= clock - lastch(p2)))
```

where the current time has been added as an extra parameter in the function signature and in the parameter list. Here we have introduced another auxiliary function called ChgTime for changing the lastch mapping to the current time clock. This is defined in a way similar to the ChgLight function, but we defer its definition to later in this section. The RedClearance delay has been incorporated in the pre-condition as well. Note that this time we have used a *record pattern* mk_Conflict(p1,p2) directly in the quantified expression. This can be done because elements from conflicts have this structure and thus a pattern matching of each of the elements will take place in the universal quantification expression. In case the value of a field in a record pattern is not relevant to the remaining part of the expression it is possible to use a "don't care" pattern which is written as a dash; see the alarm example on page 27.

The ToRed function is changed in the same way:

```
ToRed: Path * Kernel * Time -> Kernel
ToRed(p,mk_Kernel(lights,conflicts,lastch),clock) ==
  mk_Kernel(ChgLight(lights,p,<Red>),conflicts,
            ChgTime(lastch,p,clock))
pre p in set dom lights and lights(p) = <Amber> and
    AmberChange <= clock - lastch(p)
```

For the ToAmber function it is tempting to make a similar change using MinimumGreen. However, since it should be possible to overrule the requirement about a minimum time for the signal to be green, this timing requirement does *not* belong in the safety kernel and thus ToAmber is only changed for the lastch component. Recall that the purpose of this model is to define the functionality of the safety kernel and that we therefore concentrate on modelling only those areas of functionality relevant to the kernel.

```
ToAmber: Path * Kernel * Time -> Kernel
ToAmber(p,mk_Kernel(lights,conflicts,lastch),clock) ==
  mk_Kernel(ChgLight(lights,p,<Amber>),conflicts,
            ChgTime(lastch,p,clock))
pre p in set dom lights and lights(p) = <Green>
```

Finally let us consider the auxiliary function ChgTime:

```
ChgTime: (map Path to Time) * Path * Time -> (map Path to Time)
ChgTime(lastch,p,time) ==
  lastch ++ {p |-> time}
```

The ++ operator is again used for overwriting one mapping with another. In this case the resulting mapping will have the new time for the given path p.

5.8.3   *Combining the kernel functions*

In the model developed so far, we have defined a separate function for each possible change of colour in the lights. This means that the interface to the traffic light kernel has at least these three functions. It might be considered advisable to limit the size of the interface to the kernel and this could be done by introducing a single function to permit any allowable change of lights. Call this function ToColour. In addition to using the path, controller and time as parameters for the different functions for changing the lights, the ToColour function takes as input an indication of the colour the light should change to. The signature for this function is:

```
ToColour: Path * Kernel * Time * Light -> Kernel
```

Depending upon the value of the Light parameter, we would simply apply the appropriate function already defined. To do this we use a *cases expression*. A first version of the ToColour function definition could be:

```
ToColour: Path * Kernel * Time * Light -> Kernel
ToColour(p,con,clock,light) ==
  cases light:
    <Red>   -> ToRed(p,con,clock),
    <Amber> -> ToAmber(p,con,clock),
    <Green> -> ToGreen(p,con,clock)
  end
```

This cases expression works in a similar way to those in programming languages except that the case alternatives can be patterns (see page 249) and not simply constant values such as <Red>, <Amber> and <Green> as used in the present example. The value of light determines which of the alternatives is chosen. However, ToColour is not always able to deliver an appropriate result. Since it uses the other functions, it is the responsibility of ToColour to ensure that the pre-conditions of the other functions are satisfied. Thus, we need to supply a pre-condition for ToColour which is sufficiently strong to guarantee this. It would be irritating to have to repeat all the logical expressions used for defining the pre-conditions for the other functions. Therefore we use a feature of VDM-SL known as *pre-condition quotation* which provides a convenient means of referring to the pre-conditions for the other functions. The signature for the pre-condition functions is simply the same as the function in which it is defined except that the return type is bool. Thus here we get:

```
pre_ToRed: Path * Kernel * Time -> bool
```

Quoting such pre-conditions of the relevant functions, we get:

```
ToColour: Path * Kernel * Time * Light -> Kernel
ToColour(p,con,clock,light) ==
  cases light:
    <Red>   -> ToRed(p,con,clock),
    <Amber> -> ToAmber(p,con,clock),
    <Green> -> ToGreen(p,con,clock)
  end
pre ((light = <Red>)   => pre_ToRed(p,con,clock)) and
    ((light = <Amber>) => pre_ToAmber(p,con,clock)) and
    ((light = <Green>) => pre_ToGreen(p,con,clock))
```

Notice how a combination of conjunction and implication is used to formulate the pre-condition of ToColour. For large models this is normally a very valuable way of documenting the assumptions made by a function. Notice also the careful use of bracketing to ensure that the pre-condition has the intended meaning.

In this example the different case selectors <Red>, <Amber> and <Green> are constant values. The cases expression in VDM-SL is actually more powerful because each of these can be arbitrary patterns which then are matched against the selector value. We will return to this in Exercise 6.14.

Exercise 5.4 Reconfigure Toolbox Lite to use the `traffic2.vdm` instead of `traffic.vdm` where time was not taken into account. Syntax check the file and start up the `Interpreter` tool. Initialise the example and type `print ToGreen(p1,controller,8)` in the Dialog part of the `Interpreter` window. Activate the pre-condition checking option in the interpreter by choosing the interpreter item in the Options pull-down menu. Execute the same call. What does the result indicate? □

Exercise 5.5 Call the pre-conditions for the different functions with the inputs `(p1,controller,8)` as in the previous exercise. What can you conclude from these results? Try changing `p1` to `p3` in the input and see whether any of the pre-conditions are satisfied. What does the result indicate? □

Exercise 5.6 In order to see how the traffic light controller kernel can evolve over time you can try calling the light changing functions one after each other. In order to refer to the result of the previous call, you can write `$$`. Provide a list of calls which may change the initial traffic light. □

Exercise 5.7 Set the invariant checking option in the interpreter options menu. Can you construct a call to one of the defined functions which breaks an invariant? □

5.9   Reviewing the safety requirements

Having constructed a model for the traffic light kernel we need to analyse whether the model satisfies the safety requirements *S1* to *S3* from Section 5.2. Below we argue, for each of them, why they have been respected in the model. In Chapter 9 we will return to more rigorous ways of validating and verifying such requirements.

S1 If a pair of paths conflict then it must always be the case that the light associated with one of the paths must be red. *This requirement has been considered in the invariant to the* `Kernel` *type.*

S2 Before light is allowed to change from *Red* to *Green*, there must have been a delay of *RedClearance* seconds after the lights in all conflicting paths turn *Red*. *This requirement has been considered in the pre-condition to the* `ToGreen` *function.*

S3 There must be a delay of *AmberChange* seconds after the light turn-
ing *Amber* before the light is allowed to change from *Amber* to *Red*.
This requirement has been considered in the pre-condition to the ToRed
function.

5.10   Optional types: modelling failure behaviour

As we construct a model we use abstraction to suppress details
not relevant to the model's purpose. In the model of the traffic light
controller kernel which we have provided above, we have abstracted away
from failure behaviour of the hardware associated with the system.

If we wanted to be able to represent the condition that, for example,
the light is dark due to a power failure or a broken bulb, an extra quote
type <Dark> could be added as a union to Light in a new type definition
which we call LightFail.

```
Light = <Red> | <Amber> | <Green>;

LightFail = Light | <Dark>
```

Alternatively, it is possible to use a type constructor letting us model the
absence of a physical light value. Then the LightFail type will look like:

```
LightFail = [Light]
```

The square brackets surrounding the previous type definition are the
optional type constructor. Using this adds the special value nil to the
elements from the argument types. In this case we model the fact that the
light is not working by using the special nil value. Thus, it represents
the situation where the light has failed. Equality, inequality and type
membership are defined for nil. For example, the following are true:

```
nil <> <Red>
nil : LightFail
```

> The model of the kernel discussed in the main part of this chapter did not incorporate this kind of failure behaviour because it was not considered to be important for the safety requirements of the kernel in the US standard. However, for safety-critical systems, modelling of failures is often important in order to make the design of such systems so robust that they can deal with certain kinds of failures. Clearly, component failure does have safety implications. Whenever one produces a model of a system it is important to keep the model's limitations in mind.

Summary

- Quote types are written with angle brackets around identifiers. These are used for enumerated types.
- There are four kinds of numeric types: `nat`, `nat1`, `int` and `real`. The usual arithmetic and comparison operators are described in Subsection A.4.2.
- The token type is used as an abstraction for identifiers.
- Record types have a number of fields which can be selected. Records have special constructor expressions and can be decomposed into the fields using record patterns.
- Invariants can be added to all type definitions. These put extra restrictions on the values which belong to a type.
- Explicit function definitions have four parts: a signature with the types of the function, a parameter list, a function body and optionally a pre-condition describing when the function is defined.
- Value definitions are made with a name for the value, its type and its actual value.

6

Sets

Aims

The aim of this chapter is to show how unordered collections of values can be modelled as sets. The set type constructor and set operators in VDM-SL are introduced via an example of a safety-related system. On completion of this chapter, the reader should be confident in the use of sets and the associated operators for modelling systems involving collections of values.

6.1   Introduction

A formal model of a computing system should be sufficiently abstract to model the system properties of interest, and not so concrete that a great deal of irrelevant detail has to be tackled in order to understand or analyse the model. Modelling languages such as VDM-SL contain a number of features supporting such abstraction. One of the most fundamental is the facility to model sets of values without being concerned about the order in which they are stored.

A set is an unordered collection of values. For example, the collection of names:

> John, Peter, Edna, Alison

is a set. The order of presentation is not important, so it is the same set as:

> Alison, Peter, John, Edna

Duplication is also not significant, so another presentation of the same set is:

> Alison, John, Peter, Edna, Peter, Alison, Alison, John

In VDM-SL, collections of values which form a set are presented in braces, so the following expression is a set (of strings of characters) in VDM-SL:

```
{"Alison", "John", "Edna", "Peter"}
```

The empty set is represented as {}.

Sets can contain values of any type, even other sets. For example, the following expression represents a set of sets of numbers:

```
{ {9, 13, 77}, {32, 8}, {}, {77}}
```

When to use sets

Sets are used to model collections of values, but they are abstract in the sense that ordering and duplication of the elements do not affect the set itself. We therefore use sets in situations where ordering and duplication are not relevant for the purposes of the model. Here are some examples of system models where the decision about whether or not to use a set is important:

An air traffic control display This is the display indicating the positions and identifiers of aircraft in a controlled air space. Suppose a model of the display is to be developed in order to clarify the functionality of some software used to plot possible future movement of aircraft and avoid close approaches. For the purposes of the display, the model is a set of aircraft positions, with associated information. Having two identical entries at the same point in the display makes no difference, and the entries are clearly not ordered.

An airport departures display Suppose the purpose of a model of the departures display at an airport is to clarify the rules for updating the display. Here, the order may be deemed to be significant, in that the order of flights should be preserved when the screen is updated. A sequence might be a more appropriate abstraction than a set here.

A secure area controller This controller keeps track of who is in a controlled area. If the model does not involve tracking the order in which people arrive and leave, then the model would contain a set of identifiers for the people in the area. If the order of arrival is important, then a sequence might be more appropriate here too.

6.2 The set type constructor

Given a type T, the *type* of sets of elements of T is written:

`set of T`

Thus, the set of natural numbers {1, 5, 7} belongs to the type `set of nat`.

6.3 Defining sets

There are three ways of defining sets: enumerating the elements; selecting a subrange from the integers; and using set comprehension to generate a set containing all values which satisfy a predicate.

Enumeration A set with just one element, e.g.

`{45}`

is called a *singleton* set. The elements of the set are listed in no particular order, separated by commas, e.g.

`{45, 77, 8, 32, 9, 13}`

Subranges Obviously enumeration is not suitable for large sets. Where the elements of a set come from the integer type `int`, the expression

`{integer1, ..., integer2}`

represents the set of integers greater than or equal to `integer1` and less than or equal to `integer2`. Thus, for example:

`{12, ..., 20}`

represents the integers from 12 to 20 inclusive, i.e.

`{12, ..., 20} = {12, 13, 14, 15, 16, 17, 18, 19, 20}`

Exercise 6.1 What is the value of the subrange

`{integer1, ..., integer2}`

when `integer1 = integer2`, e.g. {12,...,12}? Try evaluating such an expression in Toolbox Lite to see if you are correct. Note that it is possible to interpret expressions such as these which do not use any definitions from a VDM-SL model directly in the interpreter's Dialog part with the print command.

What happens if `integer2 < integer1`, e.g. `{9,...,3}` ? □

Comprehension This is the most powerful way to define a set. The form of a set comprehension is:

{ *value-expression* | *binding* & *predicate* }

The *binding* binds one or more variables to a type or set, just as with the logical quantifiers. The *predicate* is a logical expression using the bound variables. The *value-expression* is also an expression using the bound variables, but this expression defines a typical element of the set being constructed. A set comprehension represents all the values of the expression for each possible assignment of range values to the bound variables for which the predicate is true. For example, the comprehension:

{x**2 | x:nat & x < 5}

represents the set of all values of x**2, where x is a natural number such that x is less than 5:

$$\{x**2 \mid x:nat \ \& \ x < 5\} = \{0**2,1**2,2**2,3**2,4**2\}$$
$$= \{0,1,4,9,16\}$$

Exercise 6.2 Evaluate the following by hand and check your answer by evaluating them in Toolbox Lite:

{x | x in set {1,...,15} & x < 5}

{y | y in set {1,...,20} &
        exists x in set {1,...,3} & x*2 = y}

{x+y | x,y in set {1,...,4}}

□

As mentioned in Chapter 4, expressions with type bindings cannot be executed by Toolbox Lite because of the need to range over a potentially infinite class of values. As a result, set comprehensions with type bindings generate Run-Time error messages in the interpreter.

Comprehension is a valuable technique for expressing collections of values. Further examples of set comprehension will occur in the main part of this chapter, along with advice on how to build comprehension expressions.

A note on finiteness: All sets in VDM-SL are finite. However, the predicate in a set comprehension might be satisfied by infinitely many values. If this is the case, the set comprehension expression is not well-defined. For example, the following comprehension expression contains a predicate satisfied by all the natural numbers greater than 10:

```
{x | x:nat & x > 10}
```

To define an infinitely large collection of values, define a type rather than a set and define an invariant to restrict the type as required, e.g.

```
BigNats = nat
inv x == x > 10
```

6.4 Modelling with sets

6.4.1 *The explosives store controller example*

In this chapter, the basic features of sets are introduced by means of a case study inspired by the work of Paul Mukherjee and Victoria Stavridou [Mukherjee&93] who formulated a VDM-SL model for the control of explosives stores, based on United Nations regulations. Their model describes the structure of an explosives store consisting of a range of different buildings containing explosive objects. The positions, orientations and strength of the buildings are modelled, as are the positions and explosive characteristics of the objects. Here we will look at a simplified part of the problem: positioning objects in stores. An informal requirements description is given below.

> The system to be modelled is part of the controller for a robot which positions explosives such as dynamite and detonators in a store.
> The store is a rectangular building. Positions within the building are represented as coordinates with respect to one corner which is designated the origin. The store's dimensions are represented as maximum x and y coordinates.
> Objects in the store are rectangular packages, aligned with the walls of the store (see Figure 6.1). Each object has dimensions in the x and y

Figure 6.1 *Example store with rectangular objects*

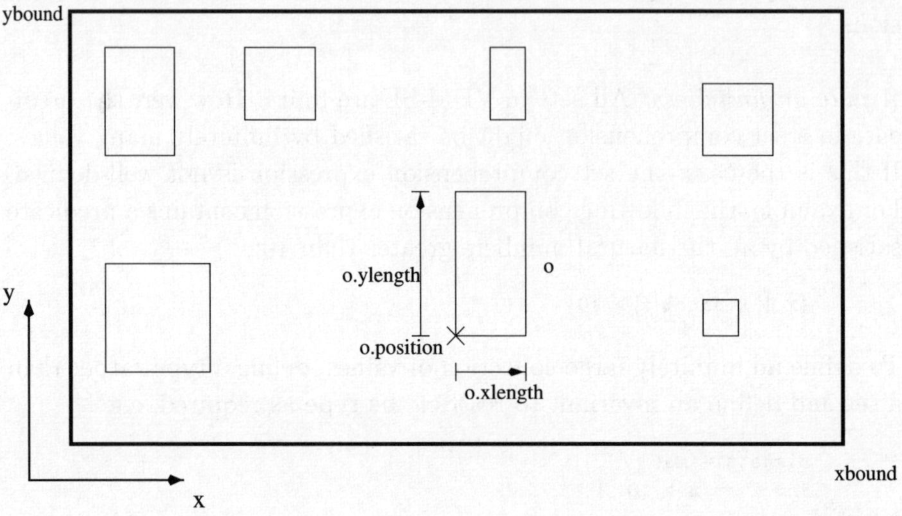

directions. The position of an object is represented as the coordinates of its lower-left corner. All objects must fit within the store and there must be no overlap between objects.

The positioning controller must provide functions to:

1. return the number of objects in a given store;

2. suggest a position where a given object may be accommodated in a given store;

3. update a store to record that a given object has been placed in a given position;

4. update a store to record that all the objects at a given set of positions have been removed.

The purpose of the formal model to be developed here is to help fix the rules for the safe positioning of objects within the store. The model therefore concentrates on representing objects, positions and the bounds of the store.

6.4.2 The explosive store controller's data model

The description suggests that a store has various component parts: its contents and upper bounds in x and y directions. This leads us to consider modelling stores by means of a record type:

```
Store :: contents : ???
         xbound   : ???
         ybound   : ???
```

Consider each component in turn. The contents are a collection of objects. We are not concerned about any ordering among the objects, so a set would appear to be an appropriate abstraction:

```
Store :: contents : set of Object
         xbound   : ???
         ybound   : ???
```

Carrying on with Store, the distances are all measured to the nearest whole unit, so we shall model the bounds as natural numbers:

```
Store :: contents : set of Object
         xbound   : nat
         ybound   : nat
```

Now we take the type Object further. We can tell from the problem requirements that an object has a position (a point in space) and that it has dimensions in the x and y directions. Again, this suggests a record type definition:

```
Object :: position : ???
          xlength  : ???
          ylength  : ???
```

The position is a point in two-dimensional space. We could model points as records with x and y coordinates (natural numbers):

```
Point :: x : nat
         y : nat
```

Then an object is modelled as follows:

```
Object :: position : Point
          xlength  : nat
          ylength  : nat
```

As usual, it is necessary to ensure that any additional restrictions on the types defined are recorded in invariants. Two conditions relate to the store: that all the objects are within the bounds of the store and that no objects overlap. Both of these restrictions relate to the **contents** of a store, and so they should be recorded in an invariant on the **Store** type. **Store**'s type definition then takes the following form:

```
Store :: contents : set of Object
         xbound   : nat
         ybound   : nat
inv mk_Store(contents, xbound, ybound) ==
    objects fit within bounds of the store
    and
    no two distinct objects overlap
```

where a record pattern has been used to define the typical element in the invariant. It is not immediately clear how the clauses of the invariant will be expressed. In such a situation, it is often best to break the modelling task down by formalising the main concepts used in each part of the invariant as auxiliary functions. Here, for example, one could define a function (called **InBounds**, say) returning a Boolean value **true** if a given object fits within the bounds of a given store, and a function (called **Overlap**, say) which returns **true** if two objects overlap. Given these functions, the invariant could be defined as follows:

```
Store :: contents : set of Object
         xbound   : nat
         ybound   : nat
inv mk_Store(contents, xbound, ybound) ==
    (forall o in set contents & InBounds(o,xbound,ybound))
    and
    not exists o1, o2 in set contents &
            o1 <> o2 and Overlap(o1,o2)
```

Note the "o1 <> o2" conjunct which ensures we are checking two distinct objects for overlap, and not comparing an object with itself. In Section 4.5 we discussed why this is necessary.

Now we look in more detail at the auxiliary functions, starting with **InBounds**. The function's definition has the following form:

```
InBounds: Object * nat * nat -> bool
InBounds(o,xbound,ybound) == ???
```

The object o will be within the **xbound** if its position's x component plus the length is less than or equal to the bound. The comparison on the y bound is similar and so the completed function definition is:

```
InBounds: Object * nat * nat -> bool
InBounds(o,xbound,ybound) ==
    o.position.x + o.xlength <= xbound and
    o.position.y + o.ylength <= ybound;
```

The second auxiliary function (**Overlap**) assesses whether or not two objects overlap. It would be possible to define a calculation on the coordinates and dimensions of the two objects in order to determine if they have any points in common. However, this is an abstract formal model and so the objects can be treated simply as sets of points. If two objects have any points in common, then they overlap. We can first formalise the notion of the set of points associated with an object. A suitable auxiliary function would have the following signature:

```
Points: Object -> set of Point
```

If we have two objects o1 and o2, they could be said to overlap if the two sets **Points(o1)** and **Points(o2)** had any elements in common. To test for this commonality, we use the *intersection* operator. Given two sets

```
s1, s2 : set of A
```

The set

```
s1 inter s2
```

is the collection of elements common to both **s1** and **s2**. If there are no elements in common, then

```
s1 inter s2 = {}
```

Exercise 6.3 Evaluate the following, checking your answers using Toolbox Lite:

```
{89, 33, 5} inter {2, 9, 5}

{{<RD>, <RA>, <RB>}, {<RA>, <RB>}} inter {{<RB>}, {<RA>, <RC>}}

{x**x | x in set {10,...,15} & 2*x < 26} inter
    {x**x | x in set {8,...,12} & 2*x < 25}
```

□

Returning now to the definition of two overlapping objects, o1 and o2 will overlap if they have any points in common:

```
Points(o1) inter Points(o2) <> {}
```

The completed function definition is

```
Overlap: Object * Object -> bool
Overlap(o1,o2) ==
    Points(o1) inter Points(o2) <> {}
```

It is worth noting that this definition embodies a major abstraction. Typically, an implementation for this function would include an algorithm which checks whether the edges of objects cross one another. Here, however, the model is sufficiently abstract for its purpose: it defines the notion of overlapping without giving algorithmic detail which could complicate the model's analysis and certainly make it more difficult to understand.

It remains to complete the definition of Points. The set of points in an object is precisely the set of points with coordinates within its bounds. A set comprehension will allow us to describe the set of all points satisfying the constraint that they are within the bounds of the object. A point mk_Point(x,y) is in the object mk_Object(pos,xlen,ylen) if its x coordinate is between pos.x and pos.x + xlen inclusive and its y coordinate is between pos.y and pos.y + ylen inclusive. Using set ranges, we can conveniently express this as follows:

```
x in set {pos.x ,..., pos.x + xlen} and
y in set {pos.y ,..., pos.y + ylen}
```

The set of all the points in an object is given by a comprehension:

```
{mk_Point(x,y) | x in set {pos.x ,..., pos.x + xlen},
                 y in set {pos.y ,..., pos.y + ylen}}
```

and the overall function definition is

```
Points: Object -> set of Point
Points(mk_Object(pos,xlen,ylen)) ==
    {mk_Point(x,y) | x in set {pos.x ,..., pos.x + xlen},
                     y in set {pos.y ,..., pos.y + ylen}}
```

A useful technique in forming a set comprehension is to begin by thinking of the collection (set or type) of values one wishes to quantify over. Record this collection in a binding. Then ask whether it is necessary to limit consideration to certain values drawn from the collection. Describe the characteristics of the desired values in a predicate. Finally, form the value expression to get the desired elements in the resulting set. In this example, the quantification is over x and y drawn from the dimensions of the object, and there is no predicate. The value expression is just the `Point` made from the x and y coordinates.

6.4.3   *The controller's functionality*

Four main functions are required for this example:

1. to return the number of objects in a store;
2. to suggest a free space large enough to accommodate an object;
3. to record the placing of an object in a store; and finally
4. to update a store by removing a collection of objects.

First, consider the function to return the number of objects in a store. A store contains a set of objects, so this function simply returns the number of objects in that set. The skeleton of the function is:

```
NumObjects: Store -> nat
NumObjects(store) == ???
```

The number of elements in a set, called its *cardinality*, is obtained by applying the `card` operator.

Exercise 6.4   Evaluate the following expressions by hand, comparing your answers with those produced by Toolbox Lite:

```
card {1, 5, 7, 5, 3}
```

```
card {}
```

```
card {x*x | x in set {-5,...,3}}
```

□

The number of objects in **store** is given by the expression:

```
card store.contents
```

The completed function definition is as follows:

```
NumObjects: Store -> nat
NumObjects(store) == card store.contents
```

The next function should suggest a position in a store where there is enough space to house an object. The system description is not specific about which point is to be suggested – any point with sufficient space available will do. Since we need not be specific about exactly which result is returned, an *implicit* function definition is appropriate here. Recall from Chapter 2 that an implicit function definition characterises the result without giving a particular mechanism for calculating it. An implicit function definition has three parts:

The function heading with the function name, the parameters and the result identifier, each accompanied by their types;

The pre-condition which is a logical expression stating what assumptions are made about the inputs to the function being defined; and

The post-condition which is a logical expression stating the relationship between the input parameters and the result which must hold after application of the function.

A suitable function might have the following header (note how it is possible to abbreviate the parameter list when more than one parameter has the same type):

```
SuggestPos(xlength,ylength:nat, s:Store) p:Point
```

This does not take account of the possibility that there is no suitable position in the store. We modify the header using an optional type constructor to allow the function to return the value `nil` in this case:

```
SuggestPos(xlength,ylength:nat, s:Store) p:[Point]
```

The body of the function has the following form:

```
SuggestPos(xlength:nat, ylength:nat, s:Store) p:[Point]
post if there is room at a point
     then p is a point where there is room
     else p = nil
```

This is an example of looseness. We are not interested in which position is chosen, as long as there is enough room at that position for the added object. This leaves freedom to an implementer to optimise the choice of position in different ways. Recall that our purpose in developing this abstract model is to help fix the rules for safe positioning within the store, not optimise the choice of positions. Hence the loose specification where several functionally different implementations will satisfy this post-condition.

This suggests that an auxiliary function could usefully be defined to model the idea of there being sufficient room at a point:

```
RoomAt: nat * nat * Store * Point -> bool
```

The function could return `true` if a point `p` is within the bounds of a store `s` and an object with the dimensions `xlength` and `ylength` could be placed there without overlapping any other object in `s`. Let `new_o` be the object placed at the position `p`. Then `new_o` is within the bounds of the store if

```
InBounds(new_o,s.xbound,s.ybound)
```

There is overlap if there exists an object in the store which overlaps with `new_o`, i.e.

```
exists o1 in set s.contents & Overlap(o1,new_o)
```

The object will not interfere with anything else as long as there is no object in `s.contents` with which it overlaps, i.e.

```
not exists o1 in set s.contents & Overlap(o1,new_o)
```

So, reusing the auxiliary functions defined earlier, it is possible to complete the definition of `RoomAt`:

```
RoomAt: nat * nat * Store * Point -> bool
RoomAt(xlength,ylength,s,p) ==
  let new_o = mk_Object(p,xlength,ylength) in
    InBounds(new_o,s.xbound,s.ybound) and
    not exists o1 in set s.contents & Overlap(o1,new_o)
```

Here we have used a *let expression* to introduce an identifier `new_o` as a local name. The structure of this construct is:

```
let pattern = defining-expression
in
  use-expression
```

and this construct is evaluated as follows:

1. evaluate the *defining-expression* and match the result of that against the *pattern* (in this case simply the identifier `new_o`); and

2. evaluate *use-expression*, replacing each occurrence of the identifiers from the pattern (in this case simply new_o) in *use-expression* with the value obtained in step 1.

Such *let expressions* can be used anywhere that expressions can be used – not just in function bodies, but also places such as set comprehension expressions.

It is now possible to complete the definition of SuggestPos. For the condition in the if expression, it is necessary to state that there exists a position which has room for the object:

```
exists pt:Point & RoomAt(xlength,ylength,s,pt)
```

The then part states that there is room at p, giving the completed function definition as follows:

```
SuggestPos(xlength,ylength:nat, s:Store) p:[Point]
post if exists pt:Point & RoomAt(xlength,ylength,s,pt)
     then RoomAt(xlength,ylength,s,p)
     else p = nil
```

In Chapter 5 the use of *pre-condition quotation* was illustrated. In the same way it is possible to make *post-condition quotation*. However, for post-conditions it is necessary to provide both the input and the suggested output; then the predicate in the post-condition will be calculated using these values. Thus the signature for post_SuggestPos is:

```
post_SuggestPos: nat * nat * Store * [Point] -> bool
```

This function is automatically produced and can be used in the interpreter of Toolbox Lite.

The third function records the placement of an object at a position in the store, returning the updated store:

```
Place: nat * nat * Store * Point -> Store
Place(xlength,ylength,s,p) == ???
```

The store is to be updated by adding the new_o mentioned above to the set of store contents. To add a value to a set we use the union operator. Given two sets

```
s1, s2 : set of A
```

the set

```
s1 union s2
```

contains exactly all the elements of `s1` and `s2`.

Exercise 6.5 Evaluate the following expressions by hand and test your results using Toolbox Lite:

```
{{1,5,6}, {1,3,3}} union {{12, 7}, {1,3,3}}

{x | x in set {2,...,5} & x*x < 12 } union
   {x | x in set {-2,...,-5} & x*x < 12 }

{2, ..., 10} union {}
```

□

The contents of the new store, with `new_o` added, are given by the following expression:

```
s.contents union {new_o}
```

The complete `Place` function returns the modified store, with the new contents, leaving the bounds unchanged. The function has a pre-condition requiring that there should be room at the chosen point:

```
Place: nat * nat * Store * Point -> Store
Place(xlength,ylength,s,p) ==
   let new_o = mk_Object(p,xlength,ylength) in
   mk_Store(s.contents union {new_o},
            s.xbound,
            s.ybound)
pre RoomAt(xlength,ylength,s,p)
```

The final function to be described models the removal of the objects at a given set of points in the store. A possible signature is:

```
Remove: Store * set of Point -> Store
```

The *set difference* operator is used to describe removal of elements from sets. Given sets:

```
s1,s2 : set of A
```

the set

```
s1 \ s2
```

is the set consisting of those elements of s1 which are not in s2. Elements of s2 which do not occur in s1 have no effect. If there are no elements in common between s1 and s2, the set difference evaluates to s1.

Exercise 6.6 Try evaluating the following expressions by hand and then check your answers with the Toolbox Lite:

```
{89, 33, 5} \ {5}

{89, 33, 5} \ {43, 5, 22}

{20,...,40} \ {2*x | x in set {10,...,20}}
```

□

Exercise 6.7 Set difference can be defined in terms of a set comprehension. Complete the following definition of the function SetDiff, which returns s1\s2, using set comprehension rather than the "\" operator in the definition. Test your answer using Toolbox Lite:

```
SetDiff: set of nat * set of nat -> set of nat
SetDiff(s1,s2) == ???
```

□

Returning to the Remove function:

```
Remove: Store * set of Point -> Store
Remove(mk_Store(contents,xbound,ybound),sp) == ???
```

In order to define this function we need to be able to check whether a given point belongs to the given set of points. This kind of check can be carried out using a *set membership* operator. If a point p belongs to a set of points sp the expression "p in set sp" will be true. Otherwise it will be false. The set of objects represented by the given points can be described by a set comprehension using the membership operator as a restricting predicate[1]:

```
{o | o in set contents & o.position in set sp}
```

---

[1] Note that the first "in set" operator is a part of the binding whereas the second "in set" is a logical operator which takes two expressions as input where the second one must be a set value.

These are the objects to be removed from `contents`, so the `Remove` function can be defined as follows:

```
Remove: Store * set of Point -> Store
Remove(mk_Store(contents,xbound,ybound),sp) ==
    let os = {o |o in set contents & o.position in set sp} in
    mk_Store(contents \ os, xbound, ybound)
```

If some points in the input set `sp` do not correspond to the positions of objects, then no objects for these points will make their way into `os` and so will not be removed. Having some spurious points in `sp` therefore appears to be harmless. Nevertheless, spurious points could be excluded by a pre-condition. We have a *subset* operator for comparing two sets which can be used for this purpose. This operator returns a Boolean result. A set `s1` is a subset of another set `s2` if all the elements of `s1` are also elements of `s2`. Thus, `{} subset s` holds for any set `s`, and a set is always a subset of itself, i.e. `s subset s`. For `Remove` we add the pre-condition giving the following:

```
Remove: Store * set of Point -> Store
Remove(mk_Store(contents,xbound,ybound),sp) ==
    let os = {o |o in set contents & o.position in set sp} in
    mk_Store(contents \ os, xbound, ybound)
pre sp subset {o.position | o in set contents}
```

Exercise 6.8 Try evaluating the following expressions by hand and then check your answers with the Toolbox Lite:

```
{89, 33, 5} subset {5}

{89, 33, 5} subset {43, 89, 5, 22, 33}

{20,...,40} subset {19,...,39}
```

□

Exercise 6.9 Configure Toolbox Lite with the file `explo1.vdm`, syntax and type check it and initialise the interpreter. Construct a store value `mk_Store({},7,15)` which can be used to test the different functions. Remember that in order to refer to the result of the previous call you can write `$$`. Note that, since `SuggestPos` is defined implicitly, it cannot be called directly, but its post-condition can be quoted. In this case the post-condition itself is defined using a type binding so as explained in Section 4.5, it will not be able to execute it with the Toolbox in this case. □

6.5   Distributed set operators

So far, we have seen how sets can be used to model collections of objects where ordering among values is not important. The means of expressing sets (enumeration, subranges and comprehension) have been described, and we have seen the basic set operators (intersection, union, cardinality, difference, membership and subset) in use in the explosives store controller example. In this section, we examine some of the more powerful, and more rarely used, operators on sets which, instead of dealing with one or two sets, deal with whole collections of sets at once. These are called *distributed operators* and we introduce them by considering an extension to the controller.

> Rather than dealing with a single store, the system is to be extended to provide information on a *site*. A site is a collection of stores, each of which has a unique name. The following additional functionality is to be provided to allow an inventory to be taken over the whole site:
>
> > 5. For a given site, provide a listing, in no particular order, of all the objects in the site. For each object, give the label of the store in which it is to be found and the object details already recorded.

This extension requires some modification to the data types defined so far (adding names to stores, for example) and the addition of new types such as one describing a site.

The `Store` data type is extended with a component modelling the name of the store:

```
Store :: contents : set of Object
         xbound   : nat
         ybound   : nat
         name     : StoreName
inv mk_Store(contents, xbound, ybound, -) ==
    (forall o in set contents & InBounds(o,xbound,ybound))
    and
    not exists o1, o2 in set contents &
            o1 <> o2 and Overlap(o1,o2)
```

The type `StoreName` models the names given to stores. Note that, in the record pattern used to define the typical element in the invariant, we introduced a "don't care pattern" for the `name` component. This is to indicate to the reader that this component has no effect on the predicate in the invariant.

For the purposes of modelling the functionality described, the details of the particular representation of store names are immaterial, i.e. we abstract away from their actual representation. Thus, the `token` type can be used:

```
StoreName = token
```

A new type is needed to represent a site. As no special ordering is required among the stores, we can use sets:

```
Site = set of Store
```

The store names are all required to be unique, so an invariant to this effect must be added to the type definition. This states that, for any two stores, if their names are the same, then they must be the same store:

```
Site = set of Store
inv site ==
    forall st1, st2 in set site &
           st1.name = st2.name => st1 = st2
```

An inventory is to be taken, consisting of a collection of items, each consisting of the name of a store and the details of an object in the store. Observe from the system description that the ordering of the items is not important, so the inventory can be modelled as a set:

```
Inventory = set of InventoryItem;

InventoryItem :: store : StoreName
                 item  : Object
```

The required functionality is to return the inventory for the whole site:

```
SiteInventory: Site -> Inventory
```

We will model the inventory for a single store and then consider its extension to the collection of stores which constitutes a site.

Consider a function `StoreInventory` which returns the inventory for a given store:

```
StoreInventory: Store -> Inventory
StoreInventory(store) == ???
```

The inventory here is the set of items formed from the name of the store (`store.name`) and each object in `store.contents`. This set is expressed as a set comprehension:

```
StoreInventory: Store -> Inventory
StoreInventory(store) ==
    {mk_InventoryItem(store.name,o) | o in set store.contents}
```

It is possible to construct the inventory for each store, but how can these be combined to form the inventory for the whole set of stores in the site? The **union** operator already introduced allows two sets to be combined, but here it is necessary to gather a set of sets. The operator used for this purpose is a *distributed union*, written **dunion**. Given a set of sets:

```
ss: set of (set of A)
```

The set

```
dunion ss
```

is the single set containing all the elements of the sets in `ss`. If `ss` is empty, `dunion ss` is the empty set.

Exercise 6.10 Try evaluating the following expressions by hand and compare your answers with those Toolbox Lite:

```
dunion {{1, 3, 5}, {12, 4, 3} , {3, 5, 11}}

dunion {{3, 8, 15} inter {4, 9, 23}}

dunion {{x | x in set {1,...,y}} | y in set {3,...,6}}

dunion {{{1}},{1},{2}}
```

☐

Returning to the inventory example, the inventory across the whole site is the distributed union of the individual store inventories:

```
SiteInventory: Site -> Inventory
SiteInventory(site) ==
    dunion {StoreInventory(store) | store in set site}
```

Exercise 6.11⋆ For a given site, provide an inventory in the `Inventory` format described in the requirements for `SiteInventory` above of all items over a certain size, given the minimum size in the x and y directions. A possible signature is:

```
ListBigItems: Site * nat * nat -> Inventory
```

The items returned should be those items in the inventory of the site whose `xlength` exceeds the first natural number argument and whose `ylength` exceeds the second. Write the body of the function as a set comprehension. Test the function using the Toolbox. Here the file `explo2.vdm` can be configured with the Toolbox where `explo1.vdm` is removed from the current project. This file contains the definitions made so far for the distributed operators. □

There is a distributed version of the intersection operator too. Written `dinter`, this forms the intersection of all the sets in a given set of sets. For example:

```
dinter {{1, 3, 5}, {12, 4, 3} , {3, 5, 11}}  =   {3}
```

Notice an important but subtle point: the distributed intersection returns only those elements in *all* of the sets of the collection. It does not return those elements which occur in two or more sets. Distributed intersection is partial: the intersection of an empty set of sets is undefined. The distributed intersection of a set of sets which includes the empty set is the empty set:

```
dinter {{1, 3, 5}, {7, 11}}  =  {}
```

```
dinter {{}, {2, 5, 6}}  =  {}
```

6.6   Summary

- Sets are finite collections of elements. Repetition and order of presentation are not significant.
- Sets can be presented by enumeration, subrange or comprehension.
- Some operators on sets are partial, e.g. the division operator / in numeric expressions.
- Special operators allow for distributed operations on sets of sets.

- In building a formal model, one strategy is to begin with a type representing a "high-level" component of the system and pursue a top-down strategy, making new definitions of types and auxiliary functions as required.

Exercise 6.12 Evaluate the following expressions:

1. `{ x | x in set {2,3,4,5} & x>2 }`
2. `{ x | x in set {2,3,4,5} & x**2 > 22 }`
3. `dunion {{1,2},{1,5,6},{3,4,6}}`
4. `dinter {{1,2},{1,5,6},{3,4,6}}`

□

Exercise 6.13 If `s: set of (set of nat)`, write an expression to state that all the sets in `s` are pairwise disjoint (i.e. if you choose two different sets from `s` they must not be overlapping). □

Exercise 6.14⋆ In reality there is a serious risk associated with placing fuses in close proximity to explosives. In this exercise, the model developed in this chapter is extended to take account of this.

The rule for placement of fuses is that explosives may be placed next to explosives and fuses next to fuses, but fuses must be at least 10 units from explosives. We begin by defining two classes of objects: explosives and fuses. We define a safe space around each object and modify the functions in the model so that an object of one class may not be placed in the safe space around an object of the other class.

1. Define an enumerated type `Class` which contains two quote values: `<Expl>` and `<Fuse>`.
2. Redefine the type `Object` so that it has a field indicating the class of the object.
3. Now we define the function:

```
SafeSpace: Object * Object -> set of Point
SafeSpace(o,s) ==
    ???
```

We could define the safe space around the object `o` as the set of points with x coordinate starting from `o.position.x - 10` up to `o.position.y + 10`. Here we will use a *let expression* as introduced on page 105 in order to give a name to two rather complex sub-expressions:

```
let xrange = {o.position.x - 10,...,o.position.x + 10},
    yrange = {o.position.y - 10,...,o.position.y + 10}
in
  {mk_Point(x,y) | x in set xrange,
                   y in set yrange}
```

Take some time to consider this model before reading on.

A problem arises if the object o is within 10 units of the wall of the store. For example, if o is at mk_Point(5,3) then some points in the safe space would have negative coordinates, but we defined positions as having natural number coordinates.

The modeller has a choice here. One approach would be to modify the types of the coordinates to int in order to allow negative values. Here we will follow a different approach which is to define functions to "cut off" the safe space.

Given the function:

```
Bottom: nat -> nat
Bottom(n) ==
  if n < 10
  then 0
  else n - 10
```

Define the function SafeSpace, so that the points returned are non-negative.

4. Modify the definition of the function Overlap, so that it returns true if the points in o1 and o2 have different classes and the SafeSpace of o1 overlaps with the points in o2.

When all these types and functions have been defined, use Toolbox Lite to check them. Use debugging, for example with objects such as

```
mk_Object(<Fuse>,mk_Point(3,1),3,3)
```

and

```
mk_Object(<Expl>,mk_Point(12,4),5,4))
```

to check whether the definition of the function of the Overlap is adequate.

□

7

Sequences

Aims

The aim of this chapter is to show how ordered collections of values can be modelled as sequences. The sequence type constructor and sequence operators in VDM-SL are introduced via an example of a security-related message processing system. On completion of this chapter, the reader should be confident in the use of sequences and the associated operators in models of systems involving ordered collections of values.

7.1 Introduction

In Chapter 6 finite sets were introduced as a way of modelling collections of values in which ordering and the presence of duplicate values is not significant. In this chapter, finite sequences are introduced as a way of modelling collections where these two factors are relevant.

A sequence is a collection of values which are ordered in some way. In VDM-SL, sequences are presented in brackets, with elements separated by commas. The following expression shows a sequence of values:

        [<Red>, <Amber>, <Green>]

The order and duplication of elements is significant, so

        [<Red>, <Amber>, <Green>] <> [<Red>, <Green>, <Amber>]

and

        [<Red>, <Amber>, <Green>] <> [<Red>, <Green>, <Red>, <Amber>]

When to use sequences

Sequences are used to order collections of values where the order in which the values are recorded is significant for the purposes of the

116

model. We typically use sequences in cases where values have to be dealt with in a certain order, or have some order in their presentation, which must be preserved. Here are some examples of system models where the decision about whether or not to use a sequence is important:

Email addresses An Email address such as `J.Bloggs@newcastle.ac.uk` typically contains domain information (the user name, the area, the network and the domain) which has to be presented in the correct order. A model of an Email router could have to treat these components in order, and hence the ordering is significant. We could model Email addresses as sequences of user or domain names.

Railway signalling If a model of a railway signalling system is to be developed, the order in which trains encounter signals may be of significance and so sequences may be needed to model train paths. As usual, this depends on the purpose of the analysis. If we wish to record the fact that trains may leave one sequence of signals and join another, a more complex network representation might be appropriate.

Text processing A text processing system, such as one which searches through text for key strings, should model the text as a sequence, since the order in which symbols arise is significant when matching against a search string. This is the case with the trusted gateway example shown later in this chapter.

7.2 The sequence type constructor

Given a type T, the *type* of sequences of elements of T is written:

```
seq of T
```

For example, strings could be modelled as sequences of characters:

```
String = seq of char
```

7.3 Defining sequences

The three definition mechanisms used for sets (enumeration, subrange and comprehension) are also available for sequences. Below, we briefly examine each in turn.

Enumeration The empty sequence is represented as []. A sequence of length 1 is called a *singleton sequence*. Sequence enumeration is just a matter of listing the elements of the sequences in the way shown above. The elements of a sequence can be sequences themselves, e.g.

```
[ [ 2, 5, 4, 5 ],
  [ 2, 5, 4, 5 ],
  [ 3 ]
]
```

Subrange Given a finite sequence of values, it is possible to extract a subsequence by giving the positions of the first and last elements of the subsequence required. In VDM-SL, sequence indexing starts with position 1. Given a sequence s, the subsequence from position i to position j inclusive is given by

```
s(i,...,j)
```

This is a sequence itself. If i>j the subsequence is empty, and if j lies beyond the end of s, the subsequence goes up to the end of s. If both i and j are beyond the end of the sequence, the subsequence is empty.

Exercise 7.1 Evaluate the following expressions, checking your answer with Toolbox Lite:

```
[4, 5, 3, 3, 9, 3, 2, 3](2,...,5)

[4, 5, 3, 3, 9, 3, 2, 3](5,...,12)

[4, 5, 3, 3, 9, 3, 2, 3](5,...,5)

[4, 5, 3, 3, 9, 3, 2, 3](5,...,2)
```

□

Comprehension Sequences can be defined by comprehension. This construction can provide a concise way of describing filters on sequences of values. Sequence comprehension takes the following form:

```
[ expression | set-binding & predicate ]
```

The set binding must be satisfied by a collection of *numeric* values. The values satisfying the binding are considered in order, smallest first. Those which do not satisfy the predicate are ignored. The expression is evaluated on those which do satisfy the predicate, yielding a sequence as a result.

For example, suppose we have a sequence of natural numbers and wish to filter out all the even numbers in the sequence. Given the input sequence

```
[6, 7, 4, 9, 3, 3]
```

We would want to return the result

```
[7, 9, 3, 3]
```

This could be achieved by the following comprehension:

```
[s(i) | i in set inds s & not Even(s(i))]
```

where **inds** returns the set of indices of a sequence (here $\{1,\dots,6\}$) and **Even** is an auxiliary function checking the evenness of natural numbers using a simple sequence index application to get hold of a specific element.

The comprehension works as follows: The values satisfying the binding are $\{1,\dots,6\}$. Those which satisfy the predicate are $\{2,4,5,6\}$. These are taken in order resulting in the sequence `[s(2), s(4), s(5), s(6)]`, namely `[7,9,3,3]`.

Exercise 7.2 The following function takes the sequence s and the number n as inputs. It filters out the elements of s which are greater than n. Complete its definition and test it using Toolbox Lite.

```
FilterBig: seq of int * int -> seq of int

FilterBig(s,n) == ???
```

□

A note on finiteness As with sets, sequences in VDM-SL are finite. However, since sequence comprehensions can only be described using set bindings, their use does not entail a risk of violating the finiteness constraint.

Using recursion to traverse data structures For data structures such as sets, sequences and mappings, a common approach to traversing the structures is recursion. Function definitions in VDM-SL are allowed to be recursive, i.e. the definition of a function f can include a call to f, operating on a new input.

In order to define recursive functions over sequences we need to be able to split a sequence up. This can be done by two operators called *head* and *tail*. The first element in a non-empty sequence s is called the *head* of the sequence, written hd s. By convention, the head of a sequence is written at its left-hand end. The hd operator is partial in that the head of the empty sequence (hd []) is undefined. The remainder of the sequence after the head has been removed is called the *tail* of s, written tl s. Again, the tail of the empty sequence is undefined.

Using the head and tail functions, and an *if expression*, the function SeqSum produces the sum of a sequence of natural numbers:

```
SeqSum: seq of nat -> nat
SeqSum(s) ==
    if s = []
    then 0
    else hd s + SeqSum(tl s)
```

A recursive function is defined only if the recursion is guaranteed to terminate on every valid input (i.e. inputs of the correct type satisfying any relevant invariants and pre-conditions). In this case, the function is applied to the tail of s, then the tail of its tail, and so on until the empty sequence [] is reached, when the "then" part of the conditional applies and the function delivers 0 (the neutral element of addition). To guarantee termination, a recursive function requires a *base case* where there is no recursive call, and all recursive calls in the function body have to be on values which take us closer to the base case until eventually the base case is reached. In the SeqSum function, this constraint is satisfied because the recursive call is always applied to the tail of a non-empty sequence, which is shorter that the sequence itself. Eventually, we reach the empty sequence and the base case.

Exercise 7.3 Type the definition of SeqSum into a file using an editor and configure the Toolbox with this file. Initialise the interpreter and make a breakpoint in SeqSum. Debug SeqSum([2,8,5,6]) and pay attention to the recursive calls recorded in the function trace part of the interpreter window. □

Figure 7.1 *Overview of the trusted gateway*

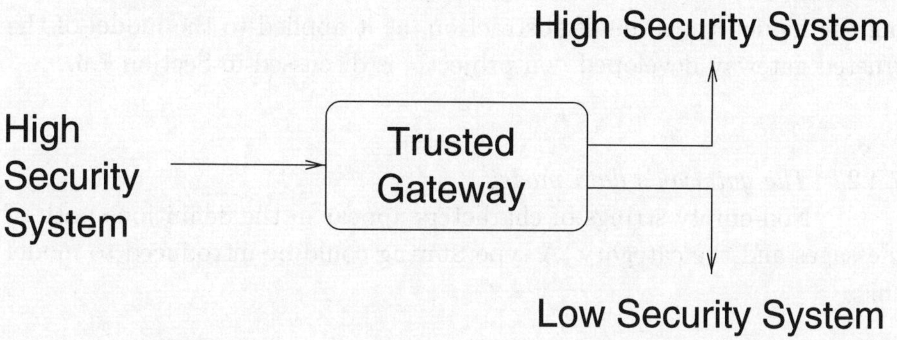

High Security System

**High
Security
System** ⟶ ⟶ Trusted
Gateway

Low Security System

7.4   Modelling with sequences

7.4.1   *The trusted gateway example*

The example used to introduce operators on sequences in this chapter is inspired by the trusted gateway model developed as part of the ConForm project at British Aerospace Systems & Equipment Ltd. (BASE) [Fitzgerald&95, Larsen&96].

> A trusted gateway is a device for processing messages which may contain confidential information. It is typically used to prevent secret messages from entering computer systems which are not authorised to process such messages securely.
>
> A message is a stream of 1 to 100 characters. A sequence of messages arrives at the gateway's input port. The messages are then assessed to determine their security classification, either high or low. Messages which are high-security are passed to a high-security output port. Messages which are low-security are passed to a low-security output port.
>
> A message is deemed to have a high classification if it contains any occurrences of special marker strings. The set of marker strings is called a *category*. Marker strings have minimum length 1.
>
> The gateway provides one major function: to take an input stream of messages and category and produce the streams of messages at the output ports with the messages classified.

The purpose of the trusted gateway model is to define the security level of messages and fix the security policy which the gateway must respect. The model therefore concentrates on the definition of messages, their security classification and the allocation of messages to output ports. Other aspects of the gateway, such as the details of particular communications protocols, are not relevant to the analysis of the model. After introducing the model, the issue of abstraction, as it applied to the model of the trusted gateway developed "on project", is discussed in Section 7.6.

7.4.2   The gateway's data model

Non-empty strings of characters appear in the definitions both of messages and the category. A type `String` could be introduced to model this:

```
String = seq of char
```

Non-emptiness could be modelled by a simple invariant:

```
String = seq of char
inv s == s <> []
```

A message can be viewed as a string of characters. A type `Message` is defined to model this:

```
Message = String
```

The system description also indicates that messages are restricted to a maximum length of 100 characters. This could be recorded as an invariant, provided we have a means of obtaining the *length* of a sequence. The operator `len`, given a sequence, returns the number of elements of the sequence, zero if the sequence is empty. The completed definition of `Message` is therefore:

```
Message = String
inv m == len m <= 100
```

A message classification is simply high or low. We could model this as a Boolean:

```
Classification = bool
```

However, this suffers from a few deficiencies. First, it does not reflect the high/low naming used in the system description and it is not clear what `true` and `false` means in the context of classification. Second, it does not provide the flexibility to allow any additional classifications to be introduced without substantially revising the type definition and all its points of use. Finally, a type checker will allow Boolean operators such as not, and, or, => to be applied to classifications, which we would be surprised to see in the model. Rather, we prefer to use an enumerated type, built up from a union of quote types as described in Subsection 5.3.1:

```
Classification = <HI> | <LO>
```

This can be extended if, at a later stage, one wishes to add a new classification, e.g.

```
<HI> | <LO> | <TOPSECRET>
```

The category of marker strings could simply be modelled as a set of strings:

```
Category = set of String
```

Finally, the output ports can be modelled as a record with two ports, each a sequence of messages:

```
Ports :: high: seq of Message
         low : seq of Message
```

7.4.3 *The gateway's functionality*

Having modelled the principal data types for the gateway, we can now consider the functionality. We will call the main function Gateway and it will have a signature as follows:

```
Gateway: seq of Message * Category -> Ports
```

Since the input sequence of messages could be empty we must consider what the result should be in this case. A port value with two empty output ports seems like a reasonable choice. As a general rule, it is wise to consider empty data values when using collections such as sets, sequences and mappings, especially since operators on these collections are often undefined when applied to the empty structure. A first sketch of the function is thus:

```
Gateway: seq of Message * Category -> Ports
Gateway(ms,cat) ==
```

```
    if ms = []
    then mk_Ports([],[])
    else process list of messages one by one
```

It is appropriate to use recursion to complete the definition. A recursive call of `Gateway` with the tail of the sequence of messages will give us a `Ports` value for all messages except the first one. We could define an auxiliary function `ProcessMessage` which will be responsible for adding the result of the first message to the `Ports` value from the rest of the sequence. `Gateway` can thus be completed as:

```
Gateway: seq of Message * Category -> Ports
Gateway(ms,cat) ==
  if ms = []
  then mk_Ports([],[])
  else let rest_p = Gateway(tl ms,cat)
       in
         ProcessMessage(hd ms,cat,rest_p)
```

We have now reduced the problem to processing a single message. If the message has a high classification it must be passed to the high-security output port. Otherwise, the message must be passed to the low-security output port. We can record this by using an *if expression*. The structure of `ProcessMessage` is:

```
ProcessMessage: Message * Category * Ports -> Ports
ProcessMessage(m,cat,ps) ==
  if the message has a high classification
  then add message to high output port
  else add message to low output port
```

From the test here, it appears we need to be able to work out the classification of a message and so we will develop a suitable auxiliary function for this purpose:

```
Classify: Message * Category -> Classification
Classify(m,cat) == ???
```

If there is a string from the set `cat` which occurs inside the message m, then the classification is `<HI>`. Otherwise the classification is `<LO>`. This can be modelled as:

```
Classify: Message * Category -> Classification
Classify(m,cat) ==
  if exists hi in set cat & Occurs(hi,m)
```

```
then <HI>
else <LO>
```

The function `Occurs` will return the Boolean value `true` if the string `hi` occurs at some point in the string `m`:

```
Occurs: String * String -> bool
Occurs(substr,str) == ???
```

The argument `substr` is a substring of `str` if we can find positions `i` and `j` in `str` such that

```
substr = str(i,...,j)
```

The positions in a sequence are known as its indices. The indices of the sequence [3, 6, 6, 2, 3] are the set {1, 2, 3, 4, 5}. The set of indices of the empty sequence is the empty set {}.

Exercise 7.4 Define a function with the following signature to return the set of indices of a sequence of integers. The body of the function definition should use set subrange and `len`. Test your function using Toolbox Lite, remembering to evaluate it on the empty sequence as well as more complex examples.

```
Indices: seq of int -> set of nat
```

□

The built-in operator `inds` introduced in Subsection 7.3 above will return the set of indices of any given sequence. We can complete the definition of `Occurs`, by quantifying `i` and `j` over the indices of the string `str`:

```
Occurs: String * String -> bool
Occurs(substr,str) ==
  exists i,j in set inds str & substr = str(i,...,j)
```

So the definition of `Classify` has now been completed. Let us now return to the `ProcessMessage` function.

```
ProcessMessage: Message * Category * Ports -> Ports
ProcessMessage(m,cat,ps) ==
  if Classify(m,cat) = <HI>
  then add message to high output port
  else add message to low output port
```

Figure 7.2 *Operation of the trusted gateway*

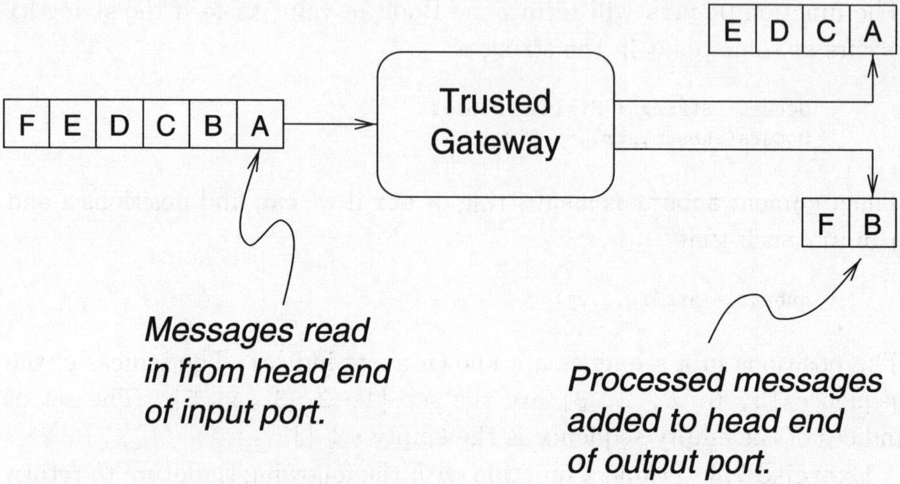

Messages read
in from head end
of input port.

Processed messages
added to head end
of output port.

Consider first high classification output. We need to return a `Ports` value consisting of:

- at the high output, the current message on the front of `ps.high`;
- at the low output, `ps.low`.

The current message is to be placed at the front of this sequence. Here we use the *sequence concatenation* operator. Given sequences `s1` and `s2`, the sequence `s1^s2` is the single sequence obtained by joining the two sequences together. Thus, if `s1` is non-empty, the following expressions are both true:

```
hd (s1^s2) = hd s1
tl s1^s2 = (tl s1)^s2
```

The empty sequence is a neutral element for the concatenation operator i.e. `[]^s = s` and `s^[] = s`.

In the `ProcessMessage` function, we place `m` onto the head end of the result of processing the rest of the input, `ps`. This process is illustrated in Figure 7.2, where the input messages A, C, D and E are high classification and the messages B and F are low classification. We use the head end to ensure that messages appear at each output in the same relative order as they were in the input, although this is not stated as a specific requirement:

```
[m]^ps.high
```

Note that the added value m must be made into a singleton sequence, because ^ only accepts two sequences as its arguments. A common error in using sequences is to forget that concatenation expects sequences as arguments (so, in this case, m^ps.high would not pass a type check).

The output to be returned in the high classification case is the Ports record value consisting of the high port constructed above and the unchanged low port component of ps. This is formulated using a record constructor expression as:

```
mk_Ports([m]^ps.high, ps.low)
```

The completed version of ProcessMessage is as follows:

```
ProcessMessage: Message * Category * Ports -> Ports
ProcessMessage(m,cat,ps) ==
  if Classify(m,cat) = <HI>
  then mk_Ports([m]^ps.high,ps.low)
  else mk_Ports(ps.high,[m]^ps.low)
```

Note how the third input parameter to ProcessMessage is acting as an accumulating parameter gradually constructing the result in reverse order. This approach, with an accumulating parameter which gradually builds up the resulting value, was also shown in the Gateway function and is often used when recursive functions are defined.

This completes the definition of the trusted gateway's functionality using recursion.

Comprehension versus recursion

As the example above illustrates, the use of recursive definitions can be complex. On some occasions it is possible to express the same functionality using comprehension instead. Comprehensions seem to be easier to understand in general, and thus we would recommend their use when possible. The Gateway function can be expressed using two sequence comprehensions with the following form:

```
Gateway2: seq of Message * Category -> Ports
Gateway2(ms,cat) ==
  mk_Ports([ms(i)|i in set inds ms & Classify(ms(i),cat) = <HI>],
           [ms(i)|i in set inds ms & Classify(ms(i),cat) = <LO>])
```

Note that the function `ProcessMessage` is not even needed in this case. When we have data in a set, sequence or mapping we can almost always use comprehensions if the result we wish to get back is also a collection. In the `Gateway` case we wish to get two such collections back whereas in the `SeqSum` case we "reduced" the collection to a single value. Whenever such a compression is carried out recursion is the only way to model the functionality.

7.5   Further operators on sequences

Some useful operators on sequences are not covered by the trusted gateway example, and these are introduced via a number of small examples related to the trusted gateway.

Gathering the elements of a sequence. Suppose it is necessary to analyse a sequence of messages to see whether or not any of them have a high classification. An auxiliary Boolean function could be defined to return **true** if there is a message in the sequence which would be classified as high security:

```
AnyHighClass: seq of Message * Category -> bool
AnyHighClass(ms,cat) == ???
```

To complete the body of the function, we would expect to quantify over all the elements of the sequence, but how can we build the set of such elements? The `elems` operator, given a sequence `s`, returns the set of elements of `s`. If `s` is the empty sequence, `elems s = {}`. The completed definition of `AnyHighClass` is as follows:

```
AnyHighClass: seq of Message * Category -> bool
AnyHighClass(ms,cat) ==
  exists m in set elems ms & Classify(m,cat) = <HI>
```

Exercise 7.5 Evaluate the following expressions, checking your answer with Toolbox Lite:

```
elems [<Red>]
elems [2,5,4,5]
elems tl [2]
elems [tl [2,5,4,5] ]
```

☐

Distributed concatenation: flattening sequences of sequences. Recall from Chapter 6 that there exist distributed versions of the operations for set union and intersection. A useful distributed version of sequence concatenation is also provided. As an example, suppose we were asked to provide a compression utility which takes a sequence of messages and transforms them into a single message. We would need an operator which joins all the messages in the sequence together. Remember that each message is itself just a sequence of characters:

```
FlattenMessages: seq of Message -> Message
FlattenMessages(ms) == conc ms
```

The `conc` operator takes a sequence of sequences and returns the sequence formed by concatenating all the individual sequences.

Although `FlattenMessages` looks simple, it is, in fact, faulty! The function is supposed to return a `Message`, but recall that a `Message` is a sequence of no more than 100 characters. The messages in the input, although individually less than 100 characters long, could add together to give a too long sequence, violating the invariant on `Message`. We restrict the use of the function to those cases where the input messages will add together to a message of no more than 100 characters. This is done by adding a pre-condition stating that the length of `conc ms` is no greater than 100:

```
FlattenMessages: seq of Message -> Message
FlattenMessages(ms) ==
  conc ms
pre len conc ms <= 100
```

Sequence modification. Suppose a facility is to be provided allowing messages to be altered so that certain parts of the contents are removed: some kind of `Censor` function. Let this function take as input a message along with a start index and length of the string we would wish to remove. We would like the `Censor` function to return a message where the described interval has been filled with, for example, blanks:

```
Censor: Message * nat1 * nat1 -> Message
Censor(m,index,length) == ???
```

For this purpose we would like to introduce one final sequence operation: sequence modification.

The sequence modification expression updates a sequence at desired indices. The sequence s ++ {3 |-> <Red>} is the sequence s with the third element changed to the value <Red>. In general we have:

```
_++_ : seq of T * map nat1 to T -> seq of T
```

The first parameter is the sequence we wish to modify, and the second parameter maps indices we wish to change to the new value we wish to place at those indices. The sequence modification operator is partial: the indices from the domain of the mapping must be in inds s, i.e. they must be valid for the sequence being modified.

Exercise 7.6 Evaluate the following expressions, checking your answer with Toolbox Lite:

```
[<Red>] ++ {1 |-> <Green>}
(tl [2,5,4,5]) ++ {3 |-> 6}
[3,8,4,2,3,4] ++ {1 |-> 8, 3 |-> 8}
```

□

Returning to the Censor function we must first describe the modification mapping. The indices we wish to modify must start at index and go up to index + length - 1. Thus we can define a mapping like:

```
{i |-> ' ' | i in set {index,...,index + length - 1}}
```

With this mapping we can produce a first version of our Censor function as follows:

```
Censor: Message * nat1 * nat1 -> Message
Censor(m,index,length) ==
    m ++ {i |-> ' ' | i in set {index,...,index + length - 1}}
```

We should also consider what the pre-condition, if any, should be for this function. Since the sequence modification expression is only well-defined if the indices in the domain of the mapping are indeed proper indices of the sequence, the final version of the function is as follows:

```
Censor: Message * nat1 * nat1 -> Message
Censor(m,index,length) ==
  m ++ {i |-> ' ' | i in set {index,...,index + length - 1}}
pre index + length - 1 <= len m
```

7.6 Level of abstraction

The model of the trusted gateway in this chapter deals with whole streams of input messages at once. However, the real trusted gateway operates in real time, handling individual messages when they arrive at the input port. It would therefore seem natural, faced with the problem of modelling the gateway, to model the classification of messages one at a time in some sort of looping state-machine model. Why then, did we choose to model the system in this more abstract way?

The reason for the abstraction is closely related to the *purpose* of the model. The model was developed primarily in order to analyse the *security policy* of the gateway (the rules for classifying messages and for treating them), not for analysing its design at the level of the order or time limits in which operations are performed. With that in mind, a more complex model with several operations and a loop would have been unnecessary and more difficult to analyse. Had the model been developed for other purposes (for example to determine the characteristics of the input buffering mechanism), a different abstraction would have been appropriate.

In the project which actually developed the gateway, models of other aspects of the system (e.g. the handling of power loss) were developed. It was noted that the first attempt at a model was often at a lower level of abstraction than was necessary. For example, the system engineer's first model of string searching (the `Occurs` definition) was a complicated forward search function working on messages.

An important lesson from the BASE study ConForm was that the first model to be developed may be obvious, but can often be complex to write and analyse. The "life-cycle" of a model often shows increasing complexity in the early drafts of the model as developers incorporate as many aspects of the system as they feel are expressible. There typically comes a point at which simplifying abstractions become apparent and the

Figure 7.3 *A binary tree of natural numbers*

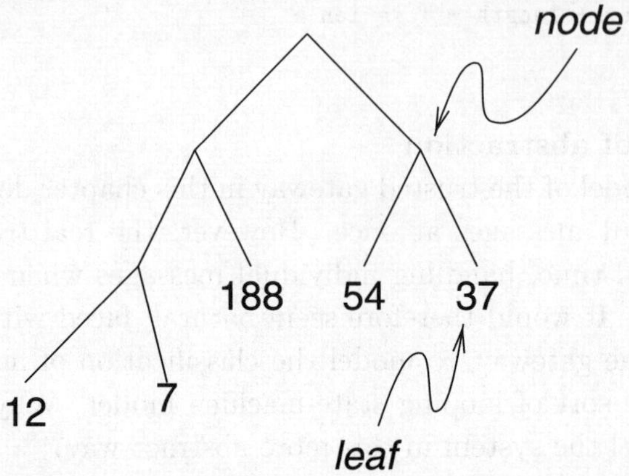

overall size of the model is reduced. Concentration on the *purpose* of the model can often yield significant simplification.

7.7   Recursive data structures

Although this chapter has concentrated on the use of finite sequences to model ordered collections of values, recursion in functions is also significant. We introduced recursion as a means of traversing of large data structures, and illustrated it on sequences. However, recursion is central to an understanding of many other structures, including trees and graphs. This section explores this idea further.

We begin by considering a common data structure: a tree. Suppose we have to build a tree of natural numbers. An example of such a tree is shown in Figure 7.3. Each point in the tree either contains data but has no descendents or else it is a *node* (it has no data but has two subtrees). The most basic kind of tree consists of a single leaf. The more complex kind of tree consists of a node. This leads to the following model of trees:

```
Tree = nat | Node
```

A node consists of two subtrees. These are themselves just trees: they could be a single leaf, or they could be roots of subtrees. The definition of the type `Node` therefore uses the type `Tree`, making for a recursive data structure:

```
Node :: left : Tree
        right: Tree
```

We can define functions to traverse binary trees, collecting data. Since the tree data structure is recursive, it is not surprising that the function to traverse a tree is too.

Suppose we are asked to define a function `MaxTree`, which returns the largest element of a tree. The function has the following signature:

```
MaxTree: Tree -> nat
```

Within the function, given a tree t, we are immediately faced with a choice. If t is a node, say mk_Node(l,r), we will return the greater of the two numbers given by `MaxTree(l)` and `MaxTree(r)`. If t is just a leaf, we return the number at the leaf, as this is certainly the greatest number in t. The function is therefore:

```
MaxTree: Tree -> nat
MaxTree(t) ==
  cases t:
    mk_Node(l,r) -> max(MaxTree(l),MaxTree(r))
    others       -> t
  end
```

where `max` is a simple auxiliary function defined as follows:

```
max: nat * nat -> nat
max(n1,n2) ==
  if n1 > n2
  then n1
  else n2
```

Exercise 7.7 Define a similar function `SumTree`, which returns the sum of the elements in a tree. □

Let us look at a more demanding example. Two trees with different shapes may still store the same numbers in the same order, e.g. Figure 7.4. Suppose we are to define a function `TestTrees` which returns true if the leaves of two trees have the same values in the same order (following left to right traversal of the trees). We can do this by converting each tree to a sequence of numbers and then simply asking if the sequences derived from the two trees are the same. The `TestTrees` function would have the following definition:

Figure 7.4 *Different binary trees can hold the same numbers
in the same order*

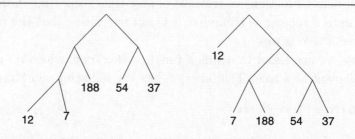

```
TestTrees: Tree * Tree -> bool
TestTrees(t1,t2) ==
  TreeToSeq(t1) = TreeToSeq(t2)
```

Given a tree, the function `TreeToSeq` reduces it to a sequence. In this
case, we need a recursion over the input tree, concatenating the sequences
corresponding to the subtrees as we go:

```
TreeToSeq: Tree -> seq of nat
TreeToSeq(t) ==
  cases t:
    mk_Node(l,r) -> TreeToSeq(l) ^ TreeToSeq(r),
    others       -> [t]
  end
```

Exercise 7.8 Using Toolbox Lite, type in the definitions of `TestTrees`
and `TreeToSeq`. Syntax and type-check the definitions, and use the interpreter to test them. □

Summary
- Sequences are finite ordered collections of elements. In contrast
  to sets, both repetition of elements and the order of presentation
  are significant.
- Sequences can be presented by enumeration, subrange or comprehension.
- Some operators on sequences are partial, such as the numeric division operator **/** in numeric expressions.

- There is one special operator which allows for distributed concatenation of sequence of sequences.
- In building a formal model, one strategy is to begin with a type representing a "high-level" component of the system and pursue a top-down strategy, making new definitions of types and auxiliary functions as required.
- Consideration of the purpose of a model can often lead to the introduction of abstractions that simplify the model and make its analysis simpler.
- Recursion is often used in functions designed to traverse sequences. In addition, data structures such as trees can be defined recursively.

Exercise 7.9⋆ We have explored the relationship between trees and sequences, noting that many different trees can represent the same sequence of node values. However, trees need not be binary in the sense that each node leads to precisely two subtrees. We could generalise trees by allowing a node to point to an entire collection of subtrees. This collection of subtrees must be ordered so as to allow traversal in a given direction. Each node is therefore represented as a (non-empty) sequence of subtrees. This is summarised in the following type definitions. The type `GenTree` models generalised trees of natural numbers:

```
GenTree = nat | Node;
Node = seq of GenTree
inv node == node <> []
```

Define the functions `MaxGenTree` and `SumGenTree` which return the maximum number in a generalised tree and the sum of the numbers in a generalised tree respectively.

Hint: The structure of the function definitions reflects the structure of the data. We used binary operators such as `max` in the function `MaxTree` and + in `SumTree`. Now however, we have to obtain the maximum value or sum of values from a sequence of numbers. Define auxiliary functions to perform these computations and use them in your answer. □

Exercise 7.10⋆   In this exercise, you are asked to model a simple calculator for basic arithmetic expressions represented as trees. First define a type for expressions using a tree representation. An expression is either a value (an integer), a binary expression, or a unary expression. A binary expression has three components: a binary operator, which can be addition, subtraction, multiplication or division, and two subexpressions, which are themselves expressions. A unary expression is a unary operator, either minus or plus, and an expression. The representation used in these type definitions is called the *abstract syntax*. Where the concrete syntax representation could be 3+2 the abstract syntax presentation could be mk_BinaryExpr(3,<PLUS>,2). Then define an evaluation function and test your definition; for instance, try to evaluate the following expressions:

```
(+5 + (--3)) -(- 7 * (--2))
5*3 + (+10)/0
```

The first expression should evaluate to 22 and the second should be undefined and give a run-time error. Remember to translate the expressions into your abstract syntax in order to evaluate them. □

Exercise 7.11⋆ Define SetSum: set of nat -> nat as a recursive function which defines the sum of a set of elements. **Hint:** here you can make use of a *let be* expression to extract an element from a set (instead of the **hd** operator for sequences). A let be expression is structured as:

```
let pattern in set set-expression be st predicate
in
   use-expression
```

This expression is evaluated as follows:

1. evaluate the *set-expression* (which should result in a set value) and match the elements of this set against the *pattern*;
2. evaluate the optional *predicate*, replacing each occurrence of the identifiers from the pattern for each possible binding of elements from the set;
3. evaluate *use-expression*, replacing each occurrence of the identifiers from the *pattern* in *use-expression* with one of the values obtained in the binding from 1. This construct can introduce looseness in the sense that different functional implementations are valid. When the interpreter from Toolbox Lite executes this construct, an arbitrary value is chosen (but the same one will be chosen every time).

□

8

Mappings

Aims

The aim of this chapter is to show how relationships between data values can be modelled as mappings. The mapping type constructor and operators in VDM-SL are introduced through an example from the nuclear industry. On completing this chapter, the reader should be confident in modelling and analysing systems involving mappings.

8.1 Introduction

Computing systems frequently involve relationships between sets of values. Such relationships can often be modelled as mappings from elements of one set, known as the *domain*, to elements of the other set, known as the *range*. Mappings can be thought of as tables in which one can look up the domain element and read across to see the range element to which it is related. We will say that each domain element *maps to* the corresponding range element. Each line of the table, being a small part of the mapping, is called a *maplet*. Each domain element can have only one maplet in a mapping, so there is no ambiguity about which range element it points to. For example, the following table represents a mapping from names (strings of characters) to bank balances (integers) consisting of three maplets:

John	-500
Peter	-750
Susan	1025

In VDM-SL, mappings are presented as sets of maplets, with each maplet consisting of the domain element and an arrow pointing to the value of the corresponding range element. For example, the table above would be represented as follows:

```
{ "John" |-> -500, "Peter" |-> -750, "Susan" |-> 1025 }
```

Since a mapping is shown as a set of maplets, the order of presentation of the maplets is not important. Thus:

```
{ "John" |-> -500, "Peter" |-> -750, "Susan" |-> 1025 } =
{ "Susan" |-> 1025, "John" |-> -500, "Peter" |-> -750 }
```

Two mappings are equal only when they have the same domain elements pointing to the same range elements. Thus:

```
{ "John" |-> -500, "Peter" |-> -750, "Susan" |-> 1025 } <>
{ "Susan" |-> 1025, "Peter" |-> 0, "John" |-> -500 }
```

because the domain value **"Peter"** maps to a different value in the two mappings.

It is possible for different domain elements to map to the same range element. Thus the following is a perfectly good mapping:

```
{ "John" |-> -500, "Peter" |-> 1025, "Susan" |-> 1025 }
```

However, each domain element must map to exactly one range element. Thus, the following is not a mapping:

```
{ "John" |-> -5, "Peter" |-> 1, "Susan" |-> 1, "Peter" |-> 63 }
```

When to use mappings

The special characteristic of a mapping is that each domain element points to exactly one range element. We therefore often use mappings to describe relations between identifiers and the records they identify. Two examples are as follows:

Patient records In models of clinical systems, a patient identifier such as a health service or insurance number normally points to a record which contains patient details. The details, such as name, address and blood group would be modelled as a record, while the overall collection is a mapping from patient identifiers to records. Such models are idealised in the sense that patients may develop several separate records, e.g. through movement between care providers or regions. If this is relevant to the analysis of the model, we could use a mapping from patient identifiers to sets of patient records.

Symbol tables Computer language processors such as compilers and editors keep track of the attributes of variables declared in computer programs. This information is often stored in a *symbol table* which is modelled in compiler design as a mapping from variable names to information about the variable such as its type and initial value.

The characteristics of mappings make them at least as useful in system modelling as functional dependencies are in the field of database design. Indeed, mappings often arise in models of systems which have a database aspect.

8.2 The mapping type constructor

A mapping records a relation between two sets of values: the *domain* and the *range*. The type constructor is **map _ to _**; for example, the type:

```
map AccountNo to int
```

represents mappings from account numbers to (possibly negative) balances.

In a mapping, each element of the domain must map to only one range element (each account has exactly one balance; no account can have two or more balances at once). In this respect, a mapping is like a mathematical function. Of course, two different domain elements may map to the same range element (two accounts can have the same balance).

8.3 Defining mappings

Mappings can be defined either by enumeration or by comprehension. Below we briefly examine both.

Enumeration The empty mapping is represented as {|->} with the arrow showing the direction from the domain on the left to the range on the right. A mapping can be enumerated as a set of maplets.

For example, the mapping (from account numbers to balances)

```
{"9311290" |-> -500,
 "1392842" |-> 3129,
 "445829n" |-> 0}
```

is a mapping enumeration. Each maplet is written as a domain value followed by an arrow and a range value. Each maplet is separated with a comma. The domain elements and the range elements can be any kind of value and thus they could be mappings themselves e.g.:

```
{'a' |-> {2 |-> 7}, 'b' |-> {|->}}
```

Comprehension Just as with sets and sequences, we can also describe mappings by means of a powerful comprehension notation. This is very similar to set and sequence comprehension, except that we must quantify over maplets rather than single values. For example, the mapping of numbers from 1 to 5 to their squares can be enumerated as follows:

```
{1 |-> 1, 2 |-> 4, 3 |-> 9, 4 |-> 16, 5 |-> 25}
```

The same mapping can be described by a mapping comprehension using a type binding:

```
{n |-> n*n | n:nat1 & n <= 5}
```

or with a set binding:

```
{n |-> n*n | n in set {1,...,5}}
```

Recall from Section 4.5 that type bindings cannot be executed using the interpreter from Toolbox Lite.

Exercise 8.1 Evaluate the following expressions by hand and check your answers in Toolbox Lite:

```
{x |-> 2 * x | x in set {1,...,15} & x < 5}

{y |-> true | y in set {1,...,20} &
              exists x in set {1,...,3} & x*2 = y}

{x+y |-> x+y| x,y in set {1,...,3}}
```

What happens if one of the addition symbols "+" from the last expression is changed to a minus sign? □

8.4   Modelling with mappings

8.4.1   *The nuclear tracker example*

The example used in this chapter to introduce mappings and mapping operators concerns a system for tracking the movement of containers of hazardous material between phases of processing in a nuclear plant. It is inspired by the formal model of a plant developed by Manchester Informatics Ltd in collaboration with British Nuclear Fuels (Engineering) Ltd. (BNFL) in 1995 [Fitzgerald&98].

A tracker monitors the position of *containers* of material as they pass through the various stages of processing in the plant. A typical plant would consist of a number of *phases* corresponding to physical processes. For example, crates could arrive at an initial unpacking phase where they are opened and the packages inside removed and sorted into different baskets on the basis of the types of material they contain (e.g. glass, metal, plastic, liquid). A subsequent phase could measure the radioactivity and recoverable material content of each basket before passing on to other processes which might involve dissolving metal contents or crushing glass. Finally, the products of the process can be packaged and returned to the customer or put into storage. Figure 8.1 shows an overview of a typical plant.

Each container has a unique identifier. It contains a certain *fissile mass* (quantity of radioactive material) and contains material of only one kind (glass, metal, liquid etc.).

Each phase has a unique identifier. It has a certain collection of containers in it at any time. These containers should all contain a certain kind of material (e.g. the crushing phase accepts only containers with glass in them). Each phase also has a maximum *capacity*: the maximum number of containers which can be in the phase at any time.

Obviously, when dealing with dangerous materials, it is very important to ensure that no material goes missing and that care is taken to avoid too much material getting into a phase, in case there is a build-up of dangerous substances in one area. The tracking manager is responsible for giving permission for movements of containers between phases of processing in order to avoid dangerous situations.

The purpose of the formal model of the tracker is to define the rules for the addition, removal and movement of containers in the plant. The model is therefore concerned with modelling enough information about containers and phases to allow the rules for movement to be fixed. The model is not concerned with other aspects such as the timing of movement between phases.

Figure 8.1 *Overview of typical tracker plant*

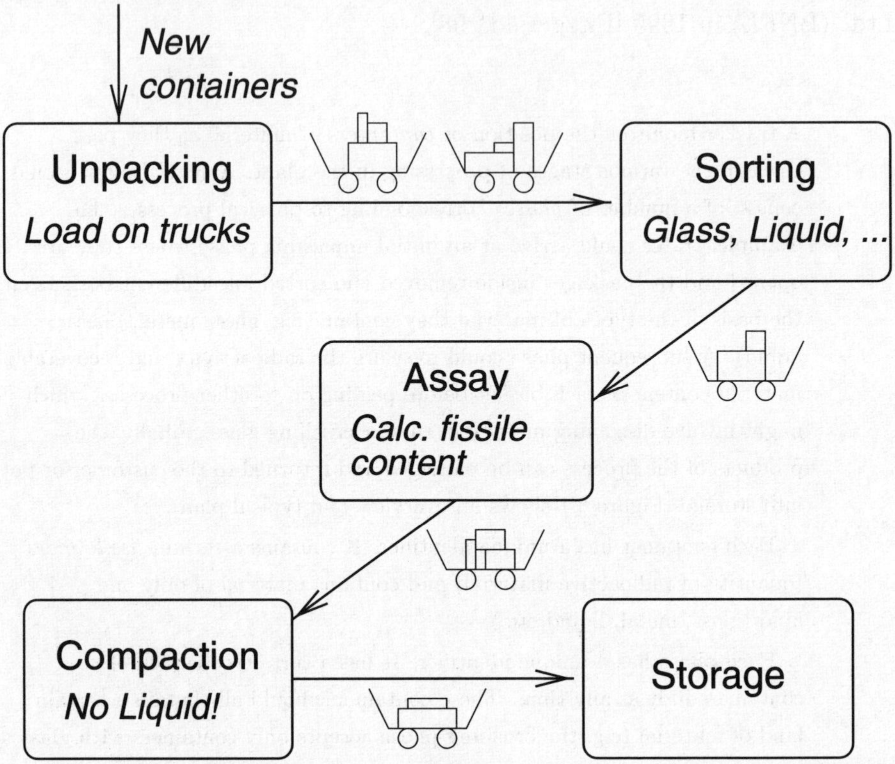

8.4.2 *Basic data types in the tracker model*

The tracker must keep a record of the whereabouts of containers, so it needs to model the contents of phases as well as details of the containers themselves. This suggests that we could model the tracker as a record type with two components containing information about containers and phases:

```
Tracker :: containers : ContainerInfo
           phases     : PhaseInfo
```

How will containers and phases be modelled? The requirements indicate that containers have a unique identifier, so this implies a mapping relationship between container identifiers and information about each container.

Each container identifier maps to a record containing a description of the container: the amount and type of material it contains. Thus we get:

```
ContainerInfo = map ContainerId to Container
```

Similarly for phases, we can have a mapping from phase identifiers to descriptions of the contents of the phase.

```
PhaseInfo = map PhaseId to Phase
```

The details of how identifiers are represented (as serial numbers, time-stamps etc.) are not relevant to the abstract tracker model, so the token type representation is appropriate here:

```
ContainerId = token;
PhaseId = token
```

For each container, we must record the fissile mass of its contents (a real number) and the kind of material it contains. This suggests we use a record type for Container:

```
Container :: fiss_mass : real
             material   : Material
```

The particular materials accepted by a given plant are not of concern here, so Material can be modelled with token:

```
Material = token
```

That deals with containers; it remains to model the phases of the plant. Each phase houses a number of containers, expects certain material types and has a maximum capacity. Again, this suggests a record type:

```
Phase :: contents            : collection of containers
         expected_materials: material types
         capacity            : number of containers
```

The requirements do not suggest any particular ordering among the containers in a phase, so we shall model the contents of the phase as a set of container identifiers. The expected material is an unordered collection of materials and the number of containers is a natural number:

```
Phase :: contents            : set of ContainerId
         expected_materials: set of Material
         capacity            : nat
```

In the tracking manager project with Manchester Informatics,[1] domain experts from BNFL were closely involved in the development of the formal model. These experts were able to point out to the modelling experts the main safety properties which had to be respected by the tracker. Among these was the important requirement that the number of containers in a given phase should not exceed the phase's capacity. This was recorded as an invariant on the type `Phase`:

```
Phase :: contents           : set of ContainerId
         expected_materials: set of Material
         capacity           : nat
inv p == card p.contents <= p.capacity and
         p.expected_materials <> {}
```

In addition the invariant here expresses the requirement that a phase cannot have an empty set of expected materials.

 The domain experts from BNFL often commented that this ability to record constraints formally as invariants which had to be respected by all the functions in the model was extremely valuable.

8.4.3   *The tracker invariant*

Having modelled the basic types representing identifiers, materials, containers and phases, we return to the model of the tracker itself:

```
Tracker :: containers : ContainerInfo
           phases      : PhaseInfo
```

The `containers` mapping represents our knowledge of the contents of each container known to the tracker. The `phases` mapping represents our knowledge of the locations of containers in phases. Here too, a number of invariant properties were identified:

1. all of the containers present in phases are known about in the `containers` mapping;
2. no two distinct phases have any containers in common;

[1] When we refer to the Manchester Informatics project, the reader should bear in mind that the formal model developed on the project was much more complex than that developed in this tutorial book, since it had to cope with nesting of phases, buffering, storage and recording container histories.

3. in any phase, all the containers have the expected kind of material inside them.

We must incorporate these conditions in an invariant on the `Tracker` type. The conditions themselves appear a little complex at first reading, so we will consider them separately by defining an auxiliary Boolean function for each of them. The definition of `Tracker` can then be completed as follows (using auxiliary functions to stand for each of the three invariant properties):

```
Tracker :: containers : ContainerInfo
           phases     : PhaseInfo
inv mk_Tracker(containers,phases) ==
   Consistent(containers,phases) and
   PhasesDistinguished(phases) and
   MaterialSafe(containers,phases)
```

The first condition states that all the containers mentioned in the `phases` mapping should appear in the `containers` mapping. In order to say this formally, we need to be able to extract all the container identifiers in the `phases` mapping and all the container identifiers from the `containers` mapping. We will therefore need to be able to get all the phase descriptions in the range of `phases` and all the container identifiers in the domain of `containers`. To extract the domain of a mapping, we use the `dom` operator. Given a mapping m of type `map A to B`, the expression `dom m` represents the set of values of type A present in the domain of m. Thus:

```
dom containers
```

represents the domain of the containers mapping: a set of container identifiers – in fact the set of container identifiers of all containers known to the tracker.

The operator `rng` extracts the range of a mapping. If m is of type `map A to B`, the expression `rng m` represents the set of values of type B present in the range of m, i.e. those values pointed to by some element of `dom m`. So, to get all the phase descriptions in the range of `phases`, we write:

```
rng phases
```

Exercise 8.2 Evaluate the following by hand and then try evaluating them in Toolbox Lite:

```
dom {3 |-> 8, 7 |-> 4, 4 |-> 8}
rng {3 |-> 8, 7 |-> 4, 4 |-> 8}
dom {|->}
```

□

Exercise 8.3 Express the following as set enumerations and check your answer using Toolbox Lite:

```
rng {x |-> x + 3 | x in set {6,...,12}}
dom {x**x |-> x + 1 | x in set {1,...,5}}
```

□

Given a particular phase description `ph`, i.e.

```
ph in set rng phases
```

the set of containers in the phase description is given by

```
ph.contents
```

We require that `ph.contents` should be a subset of `dom containers`. Thus, the first part of the invariant is stated formally as follows:

```
Consistent: ContainerInfo * PhaseInfo -> bool
Consistent(containers, phases) ==
    forall ph in set rng phases &
        ph.contents subset dom containers
```

The second condition to be recorded in the invariant states that no two phases have any containers in common. The basic form of this condition is:

```
not exists p1, p2 in set dom phases &
        p1 <> p2 and
        Phase p1's contents intersect with Phase p2's contents
```

How can we formalise the notion of the contents of the phase identified by `p1` or `p2`? This is done by "looking up" the identifier in the mapping and seeing what phase it points to. This "looking up" is called *mapping application* because we apply the mapping to the domain element to get the corresponding range element. Given a mapping

```
m : map A to B
```

and a value

        a : A

such that `a in set dom m`, the expression

        m(a)

represents the value of type B pointed to by `a` in `m`. Note that mapping application is partial: if `a` is not in the domain of `m`, `m(a)` is undefined.

In the tracker model, the phase information pointed to by the phase identifier p1 is written `phases(p1)`. The invariant condition is formalised as follows:

```
PhasesDistinguished: PhaseInfo -> bool
PhasesDistinguished(phases) ==
    not exists p1, p2 in set dom phases &
              p1 <> p2 and
              phases(p1).contents inter phases(p2).contents <> {}
```

The final invariant clause requires that all phases have only containers of the type permitted for the phase. To express this, we need to consider each phase and each container in the phase. We need to look each container up in the `containers` mapping to get its material type and check this against the material types of the phase under consideration:

```
MaterialSafe: ContainerInfo * PhaseInfo -> bool
MaterialSafe(containers, phases) ==
    forall ph in set rng phases &
        forall cid in set ph.contents &
            cid in set dom containers and
            containers(cid).material in set ph.expected_materials
```

This completes the formal data model of the tracker, which introduced the mapping type constructor and the operators for domain, range and mapping application. We can now consider the functions to be defined in the model.

8.4.4   *The tracker's functionality*

The tracker is required to provide certain functionality. Functions are to be provided for:

1. introducing a new container to the tracker, giving its identifier and contents;
2. giving permission for a container to move into a given phase;
3. removing a container from a phase;
4. moving a known container to a given phase from another phase;
5. deleting a container from the tracker.

Introducing a new container. This function adds a new container to the tracker, given the new container's identifier, its fissile mass and the kind of material contained. The signature and the beginning of the function body are as follows:

```
Introduce: Tracker * ContainerId * real * Material -> Tracker
Introduce(trk, cid, quan, mat) == ???
```

Somehow we must add a new maplet which relates the container identifier cid to the information about the container. New elements are added to mappings by using a *mapping union* operator written **munion**. For example, if we wanted to add the mapping

```
{5 |-> 22, 7 |-> 11}
```

to the mapping

```
{3 |-> -7, 12 |-> 0, 44 |-> -7}
```

we would write:

```
{3 |-> -7, 12 |-> 0, 44 |-> -7} munion {5 |-> 22, 7 |-> 11}
```

and the expression would evaluate to

```
{3 |-> -7, 12 |-> 0, 44 |-> -7, 5 |-> 22, 7 |-> 11}
```

Mapping union is a partial operator. An expression using it is undefined if the mapping union would lead to ambiguity about a domain element. For example, the following expression:

```
{3 |-> -7,  12 |-> 0} munion {12 |-> 4}
```

is undefined because it is not clear what 12 would point to in the result: it could be 0 or 4. Notice that we can add a new maplet {x |-> y} to a mapping m even if x occurs in the domain of m, provided the x in m points to the value y. Two mappings are said to be *compatible* if every element present in both of their domains points to the same range value in both mappings.

Exercise 8.4 Define a Boolean function `Compatible` with the following signature which returns `true` if two mappings m and n are compatible. Try out your function in the Toolbox Lite interpreter.

```
Compatible: (map nat to nat) * (map nat to nat) -> bool
```

☐

Exercise 8.5 Evaluate the following by hand and then try evaluating them in the Toolbox:

```
{3 |-> 8, 7 |-> 4, 4 |-> 8} munion {1 |-> 3, 2 |-> 4}
{3 |-> 8, 7 |-> 4, 4 |-> 8} munion {3 |-> 8, 5 |-> 4}
{|->} munion {8 |-> true, 9 |-> false}
```

☐

Returning now to the `Introduce` function, we can see that we need to take the existing `containers` mapping and add a new maplet with `cid` pointing to a new `Container` record made up of the `quan` and `mat` values given as input:

```
trk.containers munion {cid |-> mk_Container(quan, mat)}
```

The result of `Introduce` is a `Tracker`, so we need to complete the function definition by making a `Tracker` from the new `containers` component and the old, unchanged, `phases` component:

```
mk_Tracker(trk.containers munion
           {cid |-> mk_Container(quan, mat)},
           trk.phases)
```

This function requires a pre-condition: if the given container identifier `cid` is already used, it will appear in the domain of `trk.containers` and the mapping union could be undefined. We add a pre-condition to ensure that the new container identifier is indeed new (the operator used here is "`not in set`" which stands for the negation of the "`in set`" membership operator). The completed function definition is as follows:

```
Introduce: Tracker * ContainerId * real * Material -> Tracker
Introduce(trk, cid, quan, mat) ==
    mk_Tracker(trk.containers munion
                    {cid |-> mk_Container(quan, mat)},
                    trk.phases)
pre cid not in set dom trk.containers
```

Permission to move a container. The next function returns a Boolean
value which is **true** if permission can be granted for a given container to
move to a given phase. This function needs to check that the **Tracker**
invariant will be respected by the move, i.e. that the destination phase
has room to accommodate an extra container, and that the container to
be moved has a material type which is expected for the destination phase.
A first version of this function can be defined as follows:

```
Permission: Tracker * ContainerId * PhaseId -> bool
Permission(mk_Tracker(containers, phases), cid, dest) ==
    card phases(dest).contents < phases(dest).capacity and
    containers(cid).material in set phases(dest).expected_materials
```

Note one problem with this definition: mapping application is used multiple times (**phases(dest)** and **containers(cid)**), so care must be taken
to ensure that it is defined. We therefore add two more conjuncts to
guarantee this:

```
Permission: Tracker * ContainerId * PhaseId -> bool
Permission(mk_Tracker(containers, phases), cid, dest) ==
    cid in set dom containers and
    dest in set dom phases and
    card phases(dest).contents < phases(dest).capacity and
    containers(cid).material in set phases(dest).expected_materials
```

Removing a container. The third function describes the removal of a container from a phase. Given a container identifier and the identifier of the
phase from which it is to be removed, we modify the **phases** component
of the tracker to reflect the change. The signature and beginning of the
function body are as follows:

```
Remove: Tracker * ContainerId * PhaseId -> Tracker
Remove(mk_Tracker(containers, phases), cid, pid) == ???
```

The **phases** component is to be modified so that **pid** points to a phase
record which has **cid** deleted from the **contents** component and is otherwise unchanged. The following maplet must be added to **phases**:

```
{pid |-> mk_Phase(phases(pid).contents \ {cid},
                  phases(pid).expected_materials,
                  phases(pid).capacity)}
```

If we use `munion`, the function will be undefined, because `pid` already occurs in the domain of `phases`. In order to modify a mapping rather than just add a brand new maplet, we need a new map operator: *mapping override*. This operator, written `++`, is total, unlike `munion` and, where the domains of the two mappings overlap, the mapping on the right of the `++` symbol prevails. Thus:

```
{3 |-> -7, 12 |-> 0} ++ {12 |-> 4} = {3 |-> -7, 12 |-> 4}
```

Where the domains do not overlap, the operator behaves in the same way as `munion`.

Exercise 8.6 Evaluate the following by hand and then try evaluating them in Toolbox Lite. Compare your answers those of Exercise 8.5.

```
{3 |-> 8, 7 |-> 4, 4 |-> 8} ++ {1 |-> 3, 2 |-> 4}
{3 |-> 8, 7 |-> 4, 4 |-> 8} ++ {3 |-> 3, 5 |-> 4}
{8 |-> true, 9 |-> false} ++ {|->}
```

☐

In the definition of `Remove`, we use the override operator. The new `phases` mapping is the old mapping updated at `pid`:

```
phases ++ {pid |-> mk_Phase(phases(pid).contents \ {cid},
                            phases(pid).expected_materials,
                            phases(pid).capacity)}
```

The overall function definition is as follows, including the pre-condition necessary to ensure that the container is being removed from a known phase and that the container is actually present in the phase:

```
Remove: Tracker * ContainerId * PhaseId -> Tracker
Remove(mk_Tracker(containers, phases), cid, source) ==
   let pha = mk_Phase(phases(source).contents \ {cid},
                      phases(source).expected_materials,
                      phases(source).capacity)
   in
      mk_Tracker(containers, phases ++ {source |-> pha})
   pre source in set dom phases and
       cid in set phases(source).contents
```

Notice how we have used a let expression to make the function definition easier to read.

Moving a container. The fourth function describes the movement of containers between phases. The movement involves both removing the container from its current phase and adding it to its new phase. For the removal, the `Remove` function can be used. For the addition, we can take over the structure of the definition of `Remove`. The only difference is that instead of removing using the set difference operator we must add using the set union operator. Here we get:

```
Move: Tracker * ContainerId * PhaseId * PhaseId -> Tracker
Move(trk, cid, ptoid, pfromid) ==
    let pha = mk_Phase(trk.phases(ptoid).contents union {cid},
                       trk.phases(ptoid).expected_materials,
                       trk.phases(ptoid).capacity)
    in
       mk_Tracker(trk.containers,
                  Remove(trk,cid,pfromid).phases ++ {ptoid |-> pha})
pre Permission(trk, cid, ptoid) and pre_Remove(trk,cid,pfromid)
```

The pre-condition ensures that there is permission to move the container into the phase identified by `ptoid` and that the container can currently be found in the phase identified by `pfromid`. The latter is done using the pre-condition quotation technique introduced in Subsection 5.8.3. It is also worth noting that, in the definition of `Move`, we have used record selection throughout rather than splitting the tracker value using a record pattern as was done for `Remove`. There is a tradeoff between these two different ways of formulating record manipulation. In this case the function body had to refer several times to the entire record value `trk`. It seems therefore to be more economical to use a single variable to stand for the whole record and then use record selection when individual fields were needed.

Deleting a container. The final function to be considered deletes a container from the plant entirely, given the container's identifier and the identifier of the phase in which it occurs. Two things need to be done: the `containers` mapping must be updated so that the container's identifier is removed from the domain and the container's record is removed from the range; and the `phases` mapping must be updated so that the container is removed from the relevant phase. We have seen how the removal of the container can be accomplished in the definition of the `Remove` function, but the removal of the container from the `containers` mapping allows us to introduce some new concepts.

The skeleton of the function definition is as follows, including the removal of the container from the nominated phase:

```
Delete: Tracker * ContainerId * PhaseId -> Tracker
Delete(mk_Tracker(containers, phases), cid, source) ==
   let pha = mk_Phase(phases(source).contents \ {cid},
                      phases(source).expected_materials,
                      phases(source).capacity)
   in
      mk_Tracker(containers with cid removed,
                 phases ++ {source |-> pha})
   pre source in set dom phases and
       cid in set phases(source).contents
```

The pre-condition is identical to the one from `Remove`.

We need to describe a mapping which is the same as `containers`, except that `cid` is not in the domain. We can use a map comprehension for this:

```
{c |-> containers(c) | c in set dom containers & c <> cid}
```

The function definition so far is therefore:

```
Delete: Tracker * ContainerId * PhaseId -> Tracker
Delete(mk_Tracker(containers, phases), cid, source) ==
   let pha = mk_Phase(phases(source).contents \ {cid},
                      phases(source).expected_materials,
                      phases(source).capacity),
       con = {c |-> containers(c) | c in set dom containers &
                                    c <> cid}
   in
      mk_Tracker(con, phases ++ {source |-> pha})
   pre source in set dom phases and
       cid in set phases(source).contents
```

This appears rather unwieldy, but there are some features in VDM-SL which we can use to simplify it.

The *domain subtraction* operator, written "`<-:`", reduces a mapping to another mapping by removing maplets with designated elements in their domain parts. Formally, given a mapping `m: map A to B` and a set of elements `as: set of A`, the mapping obtained by subtracting `as` from the domain of `m` is written using the *domain subtraction* as:

```
as <-: m
```

and is defined as follows:

```
as <-: m = {x |-> m(x) | x in set dom m & x not in set as}
```

Thus, `as <-:  m` is the mapping which is left when we have removed all the maplets from `m` which have an element of `as` in their domain.

Instead of subtracting maplets from a mapping one can alternatively restrict a mapping by moving the other entries. This *mapping restriction* operator, written "`<:`", reduces a mapping to a sub-mapping by removing the maplets which are not identified in the restricting set. Thus:

```
as <: m = {x |-> m(x) | x in set dom m & x in set as}
```

holds.

Exercise 8.7 Subtraction and restriction operators on the ranges of mappings are also available. Thus, the *range subtraction* operator is written "`:->`" and the *range restriction* operator is written "`:>`". For example, the expression `m :-> as` represents the mapping obtained by removing from `m` all maplets with a range value in the set `as`. Define "`m :-> as`" and "`m :> as`" in the same way as the domain operators are defined above. □

Domain subtraction is exactly what is required for the `Delete` function, giving the following definition:

```
Delete: Tracker * ContainerId * PhaseId -> Tracker
Delete(mk_Tracker(containers, phases), cid, source) ==
  let pha = mk_Phase(phases(source).contents \ {cid},
                     phases(source).expected_materials,
                     phases(source).capacity)
  in
    mk_Tracker({cid} <-: containers,
               phases ++ {source |-> pha})
pre source in set dom phases and
    cid in set phases(source).contents
```

The update to the `phases` component has already been described in the `Remove` function, so why not use that function instead of repeating its definition? This gives us the final version of the `Delete` function, with the pre-condition necessary to ensure the removal is defined:

```
Delete: Tracker * ContainerId * PhaseId  ->  Tracker
Delete(tkr, cid, source) ==
  mk_Tracker({cid} <-: tkr.containers,
             Remove(tkr, cid, source).phases)
pre pre_Remove(tkr,cid,source)
```

Note that we have made the definition easier to read by quoting the pre-condition of the `Remove` function. Pre-condition quotation was introduced in Subsection 5.8.3.

Note also that we have extracted the `phases` component of the result of the `Remove` function. A single variable `tkr` has been used instead of a pattern for brevity.

8.5 Summary

- Mappings model function-like relationships between finite sets of values called the *domain* and *range* respectively.
- Mappings may be represented by enumeration or comprehension.
- Operators exist to extract the domain and range sets of a mapping, update the mapping by mapping union (partial) or override (total), and reduce the mapping by cutting the domain or the range.

Exercise 8.8 Locating a container: The tracker model allows for the possibility that some containers are recorded in the `containers` mapping but are not present in any phase. How can you test that the opposite case is excluded by the invariant using the debugger in Toolbox Lite? □

Exercise 8.9 The following implicit function finds a container, returning the phase identifier where it is located, or the value `<NotAllocated>` if the container is not allocated to a phase. Modify the function to return a further error value if the container is not even known in the `containers` component.

```
Find(trk:Tracker, cid:ContainerId) p: PhaseId | <NotAllocated>
pre cid in set dom trk.containers
post if exists pid in set dom trk.phases &
            cid in set trk.phases(pid).contents
     then p in set dom trk.phases and
          cid in set trk.phases(p).contents
     else p = <NotAllocated>
```

□

Exercise 8.10 With the knowledge about how to model systems using mappings, revisit the extensions to the explosives example presented in Section 6.5. Make use of the fact that the names of stores on the site are unique. Redefine the `Store` and `Site` data types and redefine the functions. □

Exercise 8.11⋆ Defining distributed override: Define a distributed version of map override, i.e. a function with the following signature:

```
Over: seq of (map A to B) -> map A to B
```

Hint: Use a recursive function definition. Use the interpreter from the Toolbox to evaluate:

```
Over([{1 |-> -1}, {2 |-> 7,3 |-> 8}, {4 |-> -1, 2 |-> 6}])
```

□

Exercise 8.12⋆ Defining distributed merge: The distributed version of the map union operator, `Merge`, has the following signature: it takes a set of mappings and merges them all into one map.

```
Merge: set of (map A to B) -> map A to B
```

Define distributed merge as a map comprehension. If `s:  set of (map A to B)`, state formally the condition required to ensure that `Merge s` is defined. **Hint:** You need to use recursion here again. Try to use the interpreter from the Toolbox to evaluate:

```
Merge({{1 |-> -1}, {2 |-> 7,3 |-> 8}, {4 |-> -1, 2 |-> 7}})
```

Compare the result of this with the result obtained by using the built-in operator `merge`. □

9

Validating Models

Aims

An important aspect of the analysis of a model is gaining confidence that the model is an accurate reflection of the informally stated requirements. This chapter aims to provide an awareness of the techniques through which such confidence can be gained. The idea of model validation is introduced: checks for internal consistency are discussed; techniques of visualisation, testing and proof are illustrated. On completion of this chapter, the reader should be equipped to choose appropriate validation techniques for a given modelling task.

9.1 Introduction

In previous chapters we have introduced a large number of models in VDM-SL. In several cases (e.g. the alarm example in Chapter 2) we started from an informal collection of requirements and built up a model in stages. But just how confident can one be that the formal model really describes the system the customer wanted? This problem arises continually in industry. When the imprecision of the customer requirement is replaced by the precision of a model, how can the modeller be sure that those areas of incompleteness and ambiguity in the original requirement have been resolved in a way that satisfies the customer? There is a further complication: requirement documents often state the client's intentions incorrectly. Such errors can only be resolved by somehow presenting a model of the system to the client in order obtain feedback which may lead to modifying the model.

Any checks which can be performed on a formal model to improve the modeller's confidence in its soundness and the customer's confidence that it has captured the real requirements would be of great benefit in resolving errors before they become extremely expensive to correct. Models written in VDM-SL can, of course, be subjected to inspection just as informal models or programs may be. However, models in VDM-SL have the advantage of being written in a language with a very clearly defined syntax and semantics, and are therefore amenable to checking with the aid of a machine. Readers using Toolbox Lite will already have some experience of investigating models using the debugger. However, this is not the only way to get more confidence in a model.

This chapter presents techniques for the *validation* of formal models. We use the term validation to mean those activities which increase the modeller's and customer's confidence in a model. There are two aspects to this:

- checking that the model is internally consistent, i.e. that the definitions are meaningful (for example, that expressions are not undefined and that functions do not allow invariants to be broken);
- checking that the model accurately represents the required behaviour of the system being modelled.

With respect to internal consistency, we have seen how machine support, such as that available in Toolbox Lite, can be used for syntax and type checking. Such facilities are very useful, but just as with programming languages, they do not allow us to detect all the errors – readers will know from experience how easy it is to write a type-correct program which still crashes for some inputs! There are still more subtle faults which we would like to be able to identify. For example, functions should return results of the correct type. For a result to be of the correct type, it must respect any invariant defined on the result type. As another example, a function definition may use a partial operator, and therefore risk being undefined for some inputs. However, if the function's pre-condition prevents inputs that cause undefinedness, the function is perfectly good.

In order to check automatically that an invariant is respected, we would have to be able to construct a machine which could verify the invariant on all possible result values from the function, and this is not possible in general. Likewise, we cannot develop a machine which ensures that the application of any partial operator is satisfactory for all possible input values satisfying a pre-condition.

In this "grey area", in which it is difficult to decide automatically whether a model contains such subtle errors or not, we use a technique based on *proof obligations* to help us determine whether or not a model is sound. Much of the research in tool support for modelling is aimed at reducing the size of this grey area by developing tools that can perform more and more subtle checks automatically. We introduce the concept of proof obligations in Section 9.2.

The other aspect of validation is checking whether the model accurately records the intended behaviour of the system. So far, we have only used the interpreter in Toolbox Lite for this purpose, but in Sections 9.3 to 9.5 we will present three different systematic approaches which can be used to analyse whether the customer's requirements for the system are captured by the VDM model. The first of these approaches illustrates how models can be visualised for the benefit of people who are not familiar with the VDM-SL notation. The second approach utilises systematic testing with additional features such as test coverage and test case generation. The third approach exploits mathematical proof to ensure that the intended behaviour is captured. These three approaches can be seen as gradually providing more and more confidence in the model. The choice between the different validation techniques and the costs involved in using them are discussed in Section 9.6.

9.2 Internal consistency: proof obligations

Partial operators (i.e. operators which produce an undefined result when applied to certain inputs) were introduced in Section 5.1. We cannot develop a completely general tool which, given any model, can automatically check whether any application of any partial operator is correct. To understand why this is so, let us consider a small example. Suppose a function `SumSeq` is defined as follows:

```
SumSeq: seq of int -> int
SumSeq(l) ==
  if l <> []
  then hd l + SumSeq(tl l)
  else 0
```

Here we have used the partial operators `hd` and `tl`. A human reader can see that they have both been used consistently because they are only going to be applied to non-empty sequences. The test in the `if-then-else` expression acts a guard against applying them to a non-empty sequence. In this case the test is simple. However, in general, the test could be an arbitrarily complex logical formula and this makes it much more difficult to check automatically whether the operator applications are always defined or not. In addition, there are other ways of protecting applications of partial operators: the soundness of an operator application could rely on values respecting a pre-condition on the function, or it could rely on the invariants of the inputs' data types.

In order to check the internal consistency of a model we need to check that the types of inputs are acceptable (including invariant restrictions) and that partial operators and user-defined functions are applied within their defined domain. When we have an expressive language such as VDM-SL we always have checks we would like to perform which cannot be automated. An option in the IFAD VDM-SL Toolbox[1] enables the type checker to detect all uses of a construct where there *might* be a risk of having an inconsistency e.g. violating an invariant or getting a run-time error. If one wants to be confident of a model's internal consistency, it is a valuable feature.

9.2.1   *The idea of a proof obligation*

If a check cannot be performed completely automatically, the techniques of mathematical proof are required to complete it. For this reason, the collection of all checks to be performed on a VDM model to ensure internal consistency are called *proof obligations*. Some of these can be dealt with automatically, but others put an obligation on the modeller to carry out manual proofs. Such a proof obligation is a logical expression which *must be proved to hold* before a VDM model can be regarded as formally internally consistent. Often simply inspection of such proof obligations may indicate situations which have not yet been taken into account. If one wishes to be more rigorous it is also possible to prove these obligations. We return to the idea of proof in Section 9.5.

The following subsections will define proof obligations for models in VDM-SL. The obligations largely ensure that function definitions do not break data type invariants and that operators and user-defined functions only are applied within their defined domains. We will use the tracker example from Chapter 8 to introduce these different kinds of proof obligations.

---

[1] This option is not available in Toolbox Lite.

9.2.2   *Domain checking*

Although the Logic of Partial Functions (LPF) introduced in Section 4.6 allows us to reason with undefined values, the use of a partial operator outside its defined domain usually indicates an error on the part of the modeller. We should therefore perform checks to identify potential cases of operator misapplication. Two kinds of construct are impossible to check automatically:

- applications of functions having a pre-condition;
- applications of partial operators.

The difference between these is that functions are defined by the user whereas partial operations are built into the notation.

Functions with pre-conditions. In the tracker example, the only time a function is applied, is within the definition of `Delete` (it is the case of the `Remove` function):

```
Delete: Tracker * ContainerId * PhaseId  ->  Tracker
Delete(tkr, cid, source) ==
    mk_Tracker({cid} <-: tkr.containers,
               Remove(tkr, cid, source).phases)
pre pre_Remove(tkr,cid,source)
```

Since `Remove` does have a pre-condition it is the responsibility of the calling function (in this case `Delete`) to ensure that its pre-condition is satisfied when `Remove` is applied. In this example we would get a proof obligation like:

```
forall tkr:Tracker, cid:ContainerId, source:PhaseId &
       pre_Delete(tkr,cid,source) =>
          pre_Remove(tkr,cid,source)
```

The obligation states that, for all possible combinations of input to `Delete` which satisfies its pre-condition, it must be guaranteed that `Remove` is applied within its defined domain.

In this particular case it is very easy to meet this proof obligation because the pre-condition of `Delete` is defined to be identical to the pre-condition for `Remove`.

Partial operators. In the tracker example the only partial operators used are mapping union and mapping application. The `munion` operator is used in the `Introduce` function:

```
Introduce: Tracker * ContainerId * real * Material -> Tracker
Introduce(trk, cid, quan, mat) ==
   mk_Tracker(trk.containers munion
                 {cid |-> mk_Container(quan, mat)},
                 trk.phases)
pre cid not in set dom trk.containers
```

Here the proof obligation which would be generated is:

```
forall trk:Tracker, cid:ContainerId, quan:real, mat:Material &
   pre_Introduce(trk,cid,quan,mat) =>
   forall c1 in set dom trk.containers,
          c2 in set dom {cid |-> mk_Container(quan,mat)} &
          c1 = c2 => trk.containers(c1) =
                     {cid |-> mk_Container(quan,mat)}(c2)
```

At first glance this may look very complicated, but it simply states that for all possible inputs to **Introduce** satisfying its pre-condition we can ensure that the two mappings used as arguments to the **munion** operator are compatible, i.e. if they have overlapping domain elements they must map to the same range values. In this case the pre-condition for **Introduce** is actually stronger than strictly necessary: the use of the **munion** operator would still be valid if **cid** did belong to the domain of the container map provided it mapped to the **mk_Container(quan,mat)** value already. However, it is often the case that the pre-condition is intentionally more strict than required for the sound application of the operators. In this case we would not like to introduce a new container if it already exists in the system.

In the tracker example there are many places where mapping application is used. For each of these places there is a proof obligation on the modeller to ensure that the mapping is applied to values belonging to its domain. This is ensured either by including an explicit check in the body of the function that the value belongs to the domain, or by recording this requirement as a part of the pre-condition for the function. In **Permission** the first approach is taken whereas the second approach is taken, for example, in **Move**.

The **Permission** function is defined as follows:

```
Permission: Tracker * ContainerId * PhaseId -> bool
Permission(mk_Tracker(containers, phases), cid, dest) ==
   cid in set dom containers and
   dest in set dom phases and
   card phases(dest).contents < phases(dest).capacity and
   containers(cid).material in set phases(dest).expected_materials
```

Here the proof obligation which would be generated as a consequence of the boldfaced mapping applications is expressed as follows:

```
forall mk_Tracker(containers, phases): Tracker,
       cid: ContainerId, dest:PhaseId &
       (cid in set dom containers and
        dest in set dom phases) => dest in set dom phases
```

The left-hand side of the implication comes from the part of the function body placed before the map applications that cause this proof obligation to be generated.

Exercise 9.1 Proof obligation for Move: The Move function is defined as follows:

```
Move: Tracker * ContainerId * PhaseId * PhaseId -> Tracker
Move(trk, cid, ptoid, pfromid) ==
    let pha = mk_Phase(trk.phases(ptoid).contents union {cid},
                       trk.phases(ptoid).expected_materials,
                       trk.phases(ptoid).capacity)
    in
      mk_Tracker(trk.containers,
                 Remove(trk,cid,pfromid).phases ++ {ptoid |-> pha})
    pre Permission(trk, cid, ptoid) and pre_Remove(trk,cid,pfromid)
```

What is the proof obligation generated for the map application expression `trk.phases(ptoid)`? □

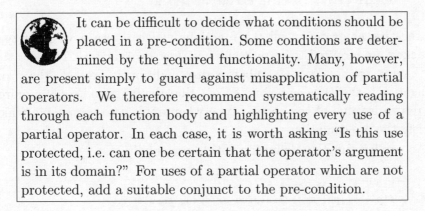

It can be difficult to decide what conditions should be placed in a pre-condition. Some conditions are determined by the required functionality. Many, however, are present simply to guard against misapplication of partial operators. We therefore recommend systematically reading through each function body and highlighting every use of a partial operator. In each case, it is worth asking "Is this use protected, i.e. can one be certain that the operator's argument is in its domain?" For uses of a partial operator which are not protected, add a suitable conjunct to the pre-condition.

9.2.3 *Respecting invariants in explicit definitions*

The proof obligation for a plain explicit function definition (without a pre-condition) requires that the function should produce an output of the correct type for any input of the correct type. Recall that a type's definition may contain an invariant of a function. For the output of a function to be of the correct type, it must respect that type's invariant. Much of the work in checking a function definition lies in ensuring that the output respects the invariant. An explicit function definition:

```
f: T1 * ... * Tn -> R
f(p1,...,pn) == expression defining result
```

is said to *respect the invariant* of R if, for all inputs

```
a1:T1,..., an:Tn
```

the function application

```
f(a1,...,an)
```

is of type R (and therefore obeys the invariant on R). Recall that membership of a data type means that a value respects the invariant for that type; so the values a1,...,an are known to respect any invariants on the types T1,...,Tn respectively.

The obligation is stated formally as follows[2]:

```
forall a1:T1,...,an:Tn & f(a1,...,an):R
```

In the tracker example, all the functions which return a value of type Tracker are required to respect the invariant on Tracker. They do this by having pre-conditions. When a pre-condition is present, the proof obligation is the same as before, except that the function is only required to return a value of the correct type when applied to arguments which satisfy the pre-condition.

An explicit function definition with a pre-condition:

```
f: T1 * ... * Tn -> R
f(p1,...,pn) == expression defining result
pre logical expression
```

---

[2] Note that the proof obligation does not form part of the model – it is a logical formula derived from the model. The modeller has to provide an argument that the obligation is true.

is said to *respect the invariant* of R if, for all arguments

```
a1:T1, ..., an:Tn
```

satisfying the pre-condition, the function application

```
f(a1,...an)
```

is of type R (and therefore obeys the invariant on R).

The obligation is stated formally as follows:

```
forall a1:T1,...,an:Tn & pre_f(a1,...,an) => f(a1,...,an):R
```

For example, the Remove function was defined as follows:

```
Remove: Tracker * ContainerId * PhaseId -> Tracker
Remove(mk_Tracker(containers, phases), cid, source) ==
   let pha = mk_Phase(phases(source).contents \ {cid},
                      phases(source).expected_materials,
                      phases(source).capacity)
   in
      mk_Tracker(containers, phases ++ {source |-> pha})
pre source in set dom phases and
   cid in set phases(source).contents
```

Here the proof obligation would be stated as follows:

```
forall tkr:Tracker, cid:ContainerId, source:PhaseId &
      pre_Remove(tkr,cid,source) =>
         Remove(tkr,cid,source):Tracker
```

The type checker is able to check that the body of Remove looks like a Tracker value but it cannot guarantee that the invariant for Tracker is satisfied. Thus, it must be the responsibility for the modeller of the system to ensure this whether by inspection, testing or proof.

9.2.4 *Satisfiability of implicit definitions*

So far, we have concentrated on explicit definitions of functions. There are proof obligations for implicit function definitions as well. Remember that an implicit function definition does not define how to compute a result for a function: it simply characterises the result by giving its essential properties.

The syntax for an implicitly defined function is as follows:

```
f(p1:T1,...,pn:Tn) r:R
pre logical expression
post logical expression
```

The implicit function definition states that, for any inputs satisfying the pre-condition, the result of the function application is any value r which satisfies the post-condition.

The proof obligation for an implicit definition is given a special name: the *satisfiability proof obligation*. This obligation defines two checks. For any set of arguments satisfying the pre-condition, the writer of the model must show that there exists *at least one result* and the *result is of type* R, and therefore that it respects the invariant on R, if any. Recall that, for the first definition made for the ExpertToPage from Section 2.8 there did *not* exist any results in certain situations.

The implicit function definition of f is said to be *satisfiable* if, for all a1,...,an of types T1,...,Tn for which pre_f(a1,...,an) is true, there is some value r of type R (respecting the invariant), such that the logical expression post_f(a1,...,an,r) is true.

Presented formally:

```
forall a1:T1,...,an:Tn &
      pre_f(a1,...,an) => exists r:R & post_f(a1,...,an,r)
```

In the tracker example the Find function is defined implicitly in Exercise 8.9. The definition is:

```
Find(trk:Tracker, cid:ContainerId) p: (PhaseId | <NotAllocated>)
pre cid in set dom trk.containers
post if exists pid in set dom trk.phases &
            cid in set trk.phases(pid).contents
     then p in set dom trk.phases and
          cid in set trk.phases(p).contents
     else p = <NotAllocated>
```

Here the proof obligation for its satisfiability can be expressed as:

```
forall trk:Tracker, cid:ContainerId &
     pre_Find(trk,cid) => exists p:PhaseId | <NotAllocated> &
                               post_Find(trk,cid,p)
```

Suppose the post-condition of Find had simply been defined as:

```
post p in set dom trk.phases and
     cid in set trk.phases(p).contents
```

In this case it would not have been possible to meet the proof obligation above because it is not guaranteed that a phase `p` satisfying this post-condition can be found for all input values satisfying the pre-condition. However, the way the function has been defined using an `if-then-else` structure takes care of this situation. Without this, we would have the same situation as for `ExpertToPage` because no phase identification can be returned if the container is not allocated to any phase.

9.3 Visualisation of a model

Remember that the goal of validating a formal model is to increase confidence that the model accurately reflects the customer's stated or unstated intentions. Checking for internal consistency of the model is not enough on its own to achieve this. It is possible to write a perfectly syntax- and type-correct, internally consistent model which describes something other than what the customer actually wanted!

In order to check this correspondence with the customer's wishes, we assess the system behaviour described by the model in collaboration with the customer and/or other domain experts. One valuable approach is *visualisation* of the model. The model is usually expressed in a special notation, be it mathematics, data flow diagrams or VDM-SL, with which the customer may be unfamiliar. One way of communicating the content of the model is to execute it, using an interface which hides the details of the model, but which allows the functions to be *invoked* in an intuitive way. This allows the customer to assess the behaviour described in the model and give feedback leading to its improvement. The dynamic link feature of the IFAD VDM-SL Toolbox (not available in Toolbox Lite) supports visualisation. This feature enables the modeller to interpret a model where parts are described using VDM-SL as usual and parts are described directly in C++ code. This code is compiled into a library which is dynamically linked into the Toolbox and the parts of the system described in VDM-SL. This combination enables a prototype of the system to be demonstrated using a heterogeneous model. Typically the part which is implemented in C++ is a relatively simple piece of code used to visualise the system in the form of a user interface.

For the tracker example we can imagine creating a simple user interface directly in C++. This might be as presented in Figure 9.1. The dynamic link feature can only be used when the model is structured into a collection of modules (for more information on modular structuring see Chapter 11).

Figure 9.1 *User interface for the tracker example*

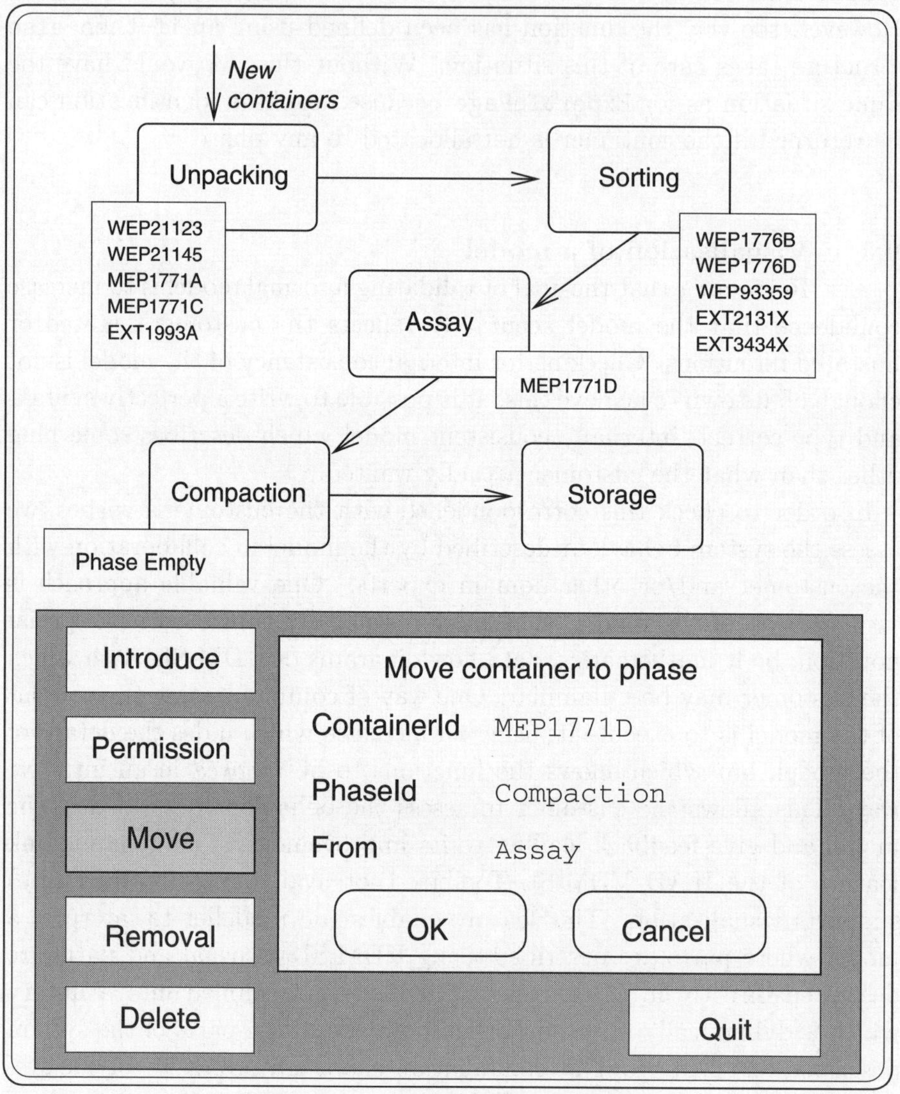

In order to use the C++ code, the interface of each of the C++ functions must be described as signatures for each of the functions at VDM-SL level. This kind of information is recorded in a dynamic link module which also provides a file name reference to the compiled C++ code. Here one could for example declare:

```
SelectFun: () -> <Intro>|<Perm>|<Move>|<Rem>|<Del>|<Stop>;
GetMove: () -> ContainerId * PhaseId * PhaseId;
ShowErr: seq of char -> bool;
ShowTracker: Tracker -> bool
```

where `SelectFun` is used to indicate the button selected by the user; `GetMove` is used to display and handle a pop-up window for assigning a container to a phase; `ShowErr` is a general function used to show an error display for the user; and `ShowTracker` is used to update the overview of the tracker system for the user. All these declarations would appear in the dynamic link module and each of them would then be defined directly in C++.

At the VDM level one would then also define a function gathering the entire system (corresponding to `main` in C). This function would repeatedly call the `SelectFun` function and use a case analysis on the selected function coming from the user interface. This `Main` function would have the following form:

```
Main: Tracker -> Tracker
Main(trk) ==
  cases SelectFun():
    <Intro> -> EvalIntro(trk),
    <Perm>  -> EvalPerm(trk),
    <Move>  -> EvalMove(trk),
    <Rem>   -> EvalRem(trk),
    <Del>   -> EvalDel(trk)
    <Quit>  -> trk
  end
```

and, for example, `EvalMove` could be defined as follows:

```
EvalMove: Tracker -> Tracker
EvalMove(trk) ==
  let mk_(cid,ptoid,pfromid) = GetMove() in
    if pre_Move(trk,cid,ptoid,pfromid)
    then if ShowTracker(Move(trk,cid,ptoid,pfromid))
         then Main(trk)
         else trk
    elseif ShowErr("Permission for assignment not granted")
         then Main(trk)
         else trk
```

Figure 9.2 *Function hierarchy in the tracker example*

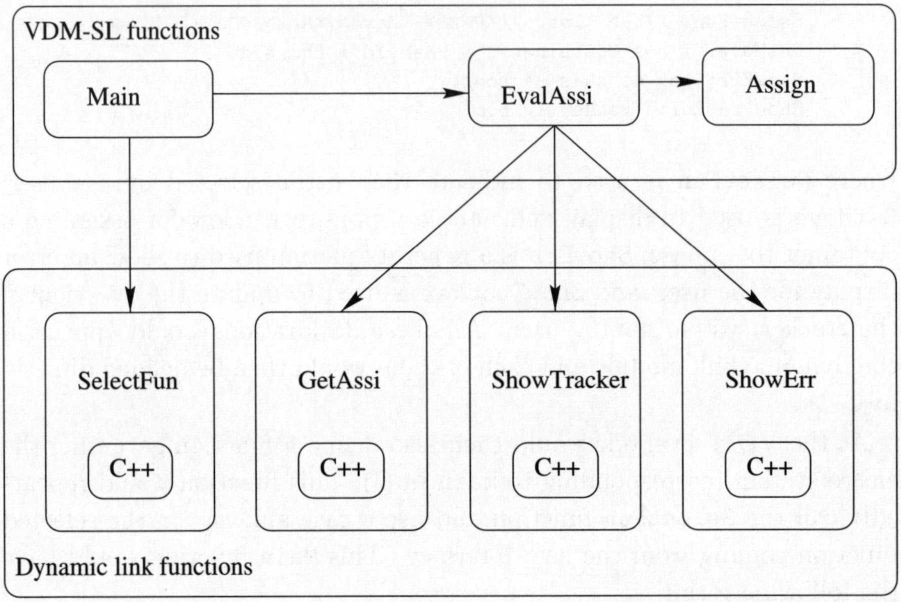

Here we have emphasised the functions provided by the dynamically linked C++ code by typesetting them in a bold face. Note how the functionality present in C++ (e.g. **GetMove**) can be combined with functions modelled in VDM-SL. In this example the `Main` function is called recursively, but if one had used an explicit operation this would be more naturally expressed using iteration with a loop inside `Main`. Similar functionality can naturally be defined for the remaining functionality in the tracker example. An indication of the function hierarchy at the different levels is presented in Figure 9.2.

9.4   Systematic testing

Validation through visualisation involves executing scenarios on the formal model through the dynamically linked interface. The confidence gained in the model is only as good as the particular scenarios used. We can gain confidence that a model accurately reflects informally stated requirements by more systematic testing on the formal model itself. For each test case the result obtained by interpreting the formal model can be inspected. If the result is not as expected the model must be adjusted. Otherwise our confidence in its correctness is increased whenever new test cases are applied.

The production of separate test cases can be done manually or automatically. The main problem about automating the generation of test cases is to keep their number sufficiently low to allow the tests to be carried out within a reasonable time and cost.

Given a test environment with a collection of inputs and a script that automatically executes them and compares the results to the one expected, it is possible to obtain information about the coverage of the tests. Techniques for assessing test coverage are widely known for programming languages but can also be used on the executable subset of VDM-SL.

Suppose we would like to test the `Permission` function. We could, for example, run the following:

```
Permission(mk_Tracker({|->},{|->}),mk_token(1),mk_token(2))
```

This test yields `false`. The test coverage information available for this function after evaluating this single argument is able to show which subexpressions have not yet been evaluated. We illustrate this by changing the font of those parts of the function which have not yet been evaluated:

```
Permission: Tracker * ContainerId * PhaseId -> bool
Permission(mk_Tracker(containers, phases), cid, dest) ==
    cid in set dom containers and
    dest in set dom phases and
    card phases(dest).contents < phases(dest).capacity and
    containers(cid).material in set phases(dest).expected_materials
```

Users of Toolbox Lite will also be able to see how expressions such as this are evaluated. Because the first conjunct `cid in set dom containers` yields `false` the other parts of the function are never evaluated.

Exercise 9.2 Test coverage of `Permission`: Define test inputs for the `Permission` function which cover the first two conjuncts, the first three conjuncts and finally the entire `Permission` function. Debug each of the applications to convince yourself that all parts have been evaluated or, if you have access to the IFAD VDM-SL Toolbox, use the test coverage feature to display the coverage. **Hint:** Introduce some value definitions and use the newly defined values in the debugging of the function. □

9.5   Using proofs

While systematic testing provides a thorough way of exercising a model, the confidence gained is only as good as the particular test sets used. Proof is a technique which allows the modeller to assess the behaviour of the model for whole classes of inputs at once. When using proof to determine if a model reflects the informally expressed intentions, the customer must express certain properties he or she wishes to hold for the system. Each property must then be formalised in terms of a logical expression. A logical expression describing a property which is expected to hold in a model is called a *validation conjecture*. The techniques of mathematical proof allow the property to be verified as a consequence of the definitions in the model.

Proofs can be time-consuming. Machine support for formal proof is rather limited at present, and some considerable additional skill is required to construct a proof. However, a successful proof does give a high degree of confidence that all the possible cases have been considered.

A proof based on a formal model can be carried out at various levels of rigour. Three are identified in particular:

"Textbook" Proof: This is the level of rigour found in most general mathematics texts. The argument is made in English, supported by formulae, justifications for steps in the reasoning often appealing to human insight. This is the easiest of the three styles of proof to read, but the reliance on intuition means that such proofs can only be checked by other human beings.

Formal Proof: At the other extreme, a formal proof (of the kind discussed in [Bicarregui&94]) is a highly structured sequence of assertions in a well-defined logical language. Each step is justified by appealing to a formally-stated rule of inference. A formal proof is so detailed that it can be checked mechanically. It is possible to be very confident about such a proof, but construction of one is very laborious. Formal proof is most frequently employed in safety- or security-critical applications.

Rigorous Proof: This refers to a proof which borrows the ideas of careful structuring and line-by-line justification from formal proof, but relaxes some of the strictures which make the production of a formal proof so costly. Obvious hypotheses may be omitted, abbreviations may be used, justifications may appeal to general theories rather than to specific rules of inference.

For the tracker example we can consider a validation conjecture which states that any phase holds only those containers which contain the correct kind of material for that phase.

When this requirement is formalised it looks like:

```
forall trk: Tracker &
    forall phase in set rng trk.phases &
        forall cid in set phase.contents &
            trk.containers(cid).material in set phase.expected_materials
```

This expression contains three universal quantifications nested inside each other. It states that for any tracker phase inside the tracker's **phases** mapping, and any container identifier inside the contents of that phase, the material inside the container identified must be a kind of material expected from the phase.

A "textbook" proof of this property could be formulated as:

> The invariant for the `Tracker` type includes a call of the auxiliary function `MaterialSafe` and `Consistent` and these two ensure that the validation conjecture holds. `MaterialSafe` is formulated in exactly the same way as the body of the outermost universal quantified expression. `Consistent` ensures that the containers inside a phase are known in the `containers` mapping.

A rigorous proof of the same validation conjecture could be:

```
from trk:Tracker
1 from phase in set rng trk.phases, cid in set phase.contents
  1.1    inv_Tracker(trk)                              Tracker-defn(h)
  1.2    Consistent(trk.containers,trk.phases)     and-E(Unfold(1.1))
  1.3    phase.contents subset dom trk.containers
                                              forall-E(Unfold(1,2),1.h1)
  1.4    MaterialSafe(trk.containers,trk.phases)    and-E(Unfold(1.1)
  1.5    cid in set dom trk.containers and
         trk.containers(cid).material in set
         phase.expected_materials     forall-E(Unfold,1.4,1,h1,1.h2)
    infer trk.containers(cid).material in set
          phase.expected_materials                        and-E(1.5)
  infer forall phase in set rng trk.phases &
           forall cid in set phase.contents &
             trk.containers(cid).material in set
             phase.expected_materials           forall-forall-I(1)
```

A fully formal proof would be too long and detailed to include here. Detailed discussion of the form and content of proofs is beyond the scope of this book. However, note the main characteristics of the proof presented above. Each line is numbered and a justification of each step in the proof is given by referring to different proof rules (e.g. `and-E`). Proof rules describe the inferences which are permitted from previous lines in a proof.

It is possible to increase confidence that a validation conjecture holds true by applying tests, for example using the debugger in Toolbox Lite. However, there are limitations to testing. For example, using the debugger one would quickly discover that it is impossible to create a `tracker` value (satisfying the invariant) which does not satisfy this validation conjecture. However, one cannot conclude from a finite number of tests that the property would always hold. Proof, which uses symbols to stand for arbitrary values instead of selected test cases, gives a higher degree of confidence in the truth of the conjecture provided, of course, that the proof is itself correct!

9.6   Choosing a validation technique

The validation techniques discussed in this chapter each have their own costs and benefits. For a given modelling problem, the developer faces a choice about which technique, or combination of techniques, to use.

To some extent, the choice of technique is related to the level of confidence required in the model and this in turn is related to the purpose for which the model is developed. If a model has been developed in an *ad hoc* way to serve as a means of clarifying some small aspect of a system, it may be sufficient merely to inspect the model visually. At the other extreme, the model might be developed in order to provide an analysis of operating rules related to the safety of a system. In this case, rigorous or even formal proof may be desirable. In some cases, where the production of a formal model is an integral part of the development process, the validation mechanism may be mandated by an external design authority.

The desired level of confidence must be tempered with an appreciation of the costs of particular approaches. Proof, at whatever level of rigour, requires specialist skills and can be time-consuming, whereas testing can be, to a large extent, automated. The cost of a validation technique is in turn determined to a large degree by the quality of available tool support. Tool support for proof is very limited, while the execution and coverage of tests are better supported. This situation is continually changing as new forms of tool support are developed. For example, in areas of hardware design, fast search techniques have made automated model-checking a widely-used technique in industrial applications.

Summary

- A number of checks can be performed to help improve confidence that a formal model is internally consistent and does indeed describe the customer's original requirements. Performing these checks is a process called model *validation*.

- Some of the internal consistency checks can be performed by software tools while others require human-guided proof. All the checks are called *proof obligations*.

- The main proof obligation for an explicit definition is to show that it *respects* data type invariants.

- The main proof obligation for partial operators is to show that they are applied within their defined domain.

- The main proof obligation for an implicit definition of a function is called the *satisfiability proof obligation*.

- Three techniques for increasing confidence that a model accurately records the behaviour desired by the customer: visualisation, systematic testing and proof of validation conjectures.

- Models can be visualised through use of dynamic link modules which can be valuable when customers do not understand the modelling notation.

- Systematic testing can be exploited in conjunction with generation of test cases and measuring of test coverage of the models.

- Proofs can be used for both proof obligations and for validation conjectures to improve the confidence in a model.

Exercise 9.3 There is no initialisation or "setup" button in the tracker interface shown in Figure 9.1. Define a function Setup for the tracker which produces an initialized tracker. Choose your own values for the initialised tracker's components. □

10

State-Based Modelling

Aims

The aim of this chapter is to show how systems with "persistent state" can be modelled. On completion of the chapter, the reader should be able to develop models of systems which contain persistent state components. The difference between this style and the functional modelling style used so far in this book will be highlighted by revisiting the explosives controller and the trusted gateway examples.

10.1 Introduction

Using formal modelling techniques, computing systems may be described at many different levels of abstraction. The models presented so far in the book have been set at a relatively high level of abstraction. This is reflected both in the data types used and in the way functionality is described through mathematical functions which take some data representing the system as input and return a result which describes the system after the computation has been performed. In some cases, the function can be characterised without explicitly expressing the result (e.g. see Subsection 6.4.3).

This functional modelling style has its limitations. Few computing systems are actually implemented via pure functions. More often, systems have persistent variables holding data and these variables are modified by operations invoked by some outside user. In case the purpose of a model to be developed is to document design decisions about the split between ordinary parameters and *persistent* variables it is necessary to use operations in VDM-SL. These operations take inputs and return results, but they also have some effect (often called a *side-effect*) on the persistent variables. For example, in a C++ class, the persistent data is represented by the private variables. The "member functions" act as operations, taking inputs and returning results while possibly modifying the private variables. We will refer to the persistent variables as the *state* of the system.

Our modelling formalism allows for the representation of persistent state and operations on state variables. It is quite natural to model many computing systems in a state-based way, including some of those already used as examples in this book. This chapter introduces the facilities for state-based modelling in VDM-SL and illustrates them by revisiting the explosives store example from Chapter 6 and the trusted gateway from Chapter 7.

10.2 State-based modelling

If a model obviously has a system state, then it may be appropriate to make this clear by differentiating that state from other definitions and the state-modifying operations from other, auxiliary, function definitions. A state-based model, in addition to definitions of values, types and functions, contains the following:

A state definition: a collection of variables which represent the state of the system, each variable having a type. The state represents the persistent data: the information that is stored between occurrences of operations and which is read or modified by operations.

Operations: The operations on the system are those procedures which can be invoked by the system's users (humans or other systems). In this book, they will always be defined implicitly (via pre- and postconditions), although the full VDM-SL language provides facilities for explicit operation definition.

Auxiliary definitions: These are local definitions of types and functions which are used in the definitions of the state and operations. They follow the syntax for type and function definitions used in the functional models introduced so far.

This structure is reflected in those VDM-SL models containing value definitions, type definitions, function definitions, the state definition and operation definitions. These need not appear in any particular order (apart from the restriction on value definitions mentioned in Subsection 5.3.3), but a model may not have more than one state definition.

The explosives storage controller from Chapter 6 is one example of a system which could be described via a state-based model, and this forms the subject of Section 10.3, which introduces state and operation definitions in VDM-SL. The choice of state variables and operations is often an important factor in developing a state-based model and this is examined in Section 10.4, where the model of the trusted gateway from Chapter 7 is discussed.

10.3   A state-based model of the explosives store controller

Chapter 6 described a model of the controller for an explosives store. Recall that the model represented a store as a collection of objects (its contents) with physical bounds in the x and y directions. A type Point modelled points in the store, with each Object being located at a point and having dimensions. Functions were defined to express the condition that objects fit within store bounds and do not overlap one another. These functions were then used to express the invariant on a store. The main functionality involved defining functions which returned the number of objects in the store, suggested positions free for placement of new objects, placed objects in a store and removed objects from a store. Notice the terminology here: a function would *"place"* an object in a store or *"remove"* objects. In both cases, the function returns a new store, but it would appear more natural to view this as an operation which modifies some persistent store.

Examining the functionality in order to determine which data items can be viewed as persistent state variables leads to the state-based model discussed below.

10.3.1   *A state-based data model*

The persistent data in the system is the description of the store and its contents. The state of the controller therefore consists of variables modelling the contents and bounds of the store. In VDM-SL a model's state is defined using the following syntax:

```
state Name of
  component-name : type
  component-name : type
  . . .
  component-name : type
inv optional-invariant
init initial-state-definition
end
```

Each *component-name* is a state variable which can be accessed and modified by the operations. The invariant records restrictions on the permitted combinations of state values while the **init** part describes the initial value of the state variables.

In the explosives store controller the state would be defined as follows:

```
state Store of
        contents : set of Object
        xbound   : nat
        ybound   : nat
inv mk_Store(contents, xbound, ybound) ==
    (forall o in set contents & InBounds(o,xbound,ybound))
    and
    not exists o1, o2 in set contents & o1 <> o2 and Overlap(o1,o2)
init s == s = mk_Store({},50,50)
end
```

The invariant records the restrictions that all the objects in the store are within bounds and that there is no overlapping. Note that the components of the state are referred to via a record pattern in the same way as components of a record type.

A state definition introduces a new type (in this case **Store**) which is treated as a record type whose fields are the state variables.

An initial value for the state is defined, using the **init** clause, which in this book will always have the standard form

```
init variable == variable = mk_StateName(...)
```

where *variable* is a variable of the record type *StateName*. In the state-based model of the explosives store controller, the **init** state is an empty store of dimensions 50 by 50 units.

10.3.2 *Modelling functionality via operations*

The functionality described in the original store controller model was:

1. return the number of objects in a given store;
2. suggest a position where a given object may be accommodated in a given store;
3. update a store to record that a given object has been placed in a given position;

4. update a store to record that all the objects at a given set of
positions have been removed.

These should now be recorded as operations having "side-effects" on the
state. Operations in a VDM-SL model are preceded by the keyword
"operations". Each operation definition has the following components:

The header with operation name, the names and types of input parameters and any result.

The externals clause which lists the state components to be used by the
operation and indicates whether each component may be read (rd) only
or both read and written to (wr).

The pre-condition which is a logical expression using the input variables
and state variables. It records the conditions which are assumed to hold
when the operation is applied. The pre-condition may be omitted, in
which case it is assumed to be true.

The post-condition which is another logical expression relating the state
and result value after the operation, to the state and inputs before the
operation: it describes the essence of the computation.

The syntax for an operation definition is as follows:

```
OpName (param : type, param : type, ...) result : type
ext wr/rd state-variable : type
    wr/rd state-variable : type
    ...
    wr/rd state-variable : type
pre   logical-expression
post  logical-expression
```

An operation definition can be thought of as a definition for a piece of
code which has input and output parameters and a side-effect on the state
components (global variables). The pre-condition records assumptions
that are made about the conditions in which the operation may be used.
The post-condition records the effect of applying the operation.

Returning now to the model of the explosives store controller, consider
the operation to calculate the number of objects in the store, taking each
section of the operation definition in turn:

The header Let the operation name be NumObjects. This operation must
count the number of elements of the contents state components and so
requires no input parameters. However, it does return a result, which
we will call r, giving the completed header:

```
NumObjects() r: nat
```

The externals clause Access is required to only one state component. In
this case, the component will not be modified, only read, so read-only
access (represented by the keyword **rd**) is all that is required:

```
ext rd contents : set of Object
```

The pre-condition This operation will operate on any set of contents. As
usual, we take care to consider the empty case, but here we will simply
return zero, so the pre-condition can be omitted.

The post-condition The returned number **r** is simply the cardinality of
contents, so the post-condition is straightforward:

```
post r = card contents
```

The completed operation definition is therefore:

```
NumObjects() r: nat
ext rd contents : set of Object
post r = card contents
```

The next operation in the explosives store example suggests a vacant
position at which there is enough room to accommodate a new object.
Here the object is supplied as input and a point is returned as a result,
unless no suitable point is available in the store in which case the value
nil is returned. The header is as follows:

```
SuggestPos(o:Object) p:[Point]
```

What access to state components will be required? The operation needs
to read the **contents** to check for possible overlapping, and also needs to
read the bounds to ensure that the returned point is within them. This
operation makes no modifications to the store, so read-only access is again
sufficient:

```
ext  rd contents : set of Object
     rd xbound    : nat
     rd ybound    : nat
```

The operation, once again, can be applied to any input and any state, so
the pre-condition is omitted. The post-condition must say (as does the
implicit function version in Chapter 6) that, if there exists a point where
there is room for the object o, then the result **r** must be such a point.
Otherwise, the result must be **nil**. To determine if there is room at a

point, the auxiliary function `RoomAt` may be used but the signature of
`RoomAt` is modified slightly to take the contents and bounds of the store
as arguments directly. We could continue to define a function over the
type `Store`, but this modification simply makes it easier to see how the
function is used. The modified version of `RoomAt` is:

```
RoomAt: Object * set of Object * nat * nat * Point -> bool
RoomAt(o,contents, xbound, ybound, p) ==
    let new_o = mk_Object(p,o.xlength,o.ylength) in
        InBounds(new_o,xbound,ybound) and
        not exists o1 in set contents & Overlap(o1,new_o)
```

and the completed definition of the `SuggestPos` operation is:

```
SuggestPos(o:Object) p:[Point]
ext   rd contents : set of Object
      rd xbound    : nat
      rd ybound    : nat
post if exists pt:Point & RoomAt(o,contents,xbound,ybound,pt)
     then p <> nil and RoomAt(o,contents,xbound,ybound,p)
     else p = nil
```

The operation `Place`, which places an object at a position in the store,
involves some modification to the state: the store's contents are to be updated with the new item. The operation will take the object and position
as input, and will require read and write access (indicated by the keyword
`wr`) to the `contents` state component. Since it is also necessary to check
that there is room at the proposed point, the bounds of the store will also
be read. This gives the following header and externals clause:

```
Place(o:Object, p:Point)
ext   wr contents : set of Object
      rd xbound    : nat
      rd ybound    : nat
```

The pre-condition should record the assumption that sufficient space exists at the proposed point:

```
pre RoomAt(o,contents,xbound,ybound,p)
```

The post-condition describes the modification to the state resulting from
placing the object at the point. The `contents` state component after
the operation is applied is equal to the `contents` component before the
operation, with the object added. In order to record this formally, we will

require a means of referring to the state before and after the operation. The convention in VDM-SL is that a state component name is decorated with a "~" after the name to indicate the component *before* application. Thus, the modification to `contents` could be described as follows:

```
contents  = contents~ union {new_o}
```

where `new_o` is the object with the new coordinates added as its position. The completed operation is as follows:

```
Place(o:Object, p:Point)
ext  wr contents : set of Object
     rd xbound   : nat
     rd ybound   : nat
pre RoomAt(o,contents,xbound,ybound,p)
post let new_o = mk_Object(p,o.xlength,o.ylength) in
     contents  = contents~ union {new_o}
```

The final operation, `Remove`, given a set of points, removes the objects at those points from the store. Note that this operation does not require access to the bounds of the store, since no objects are being added. The operation is presented in its entirety:

```
Remove(sp:set of Point)
ext  wr contents : set of Object
post let os = {o | o in set contents & o.position in set sp} in
     contents = contents~ \ os
```

10.4   A state-based model of the trusted gateway

Recall that the trusted gateway receives a stream of messages as an input and sends each message to one of two output streams depending on whether or not it finds strings from a special category in the input message. In the functional model developed in Chapter 7, types were defined to model character strings (sequences of characters), messages (strings with a certain maximum size), classifications of messages (either <HI> or <LO>), and the category (a set of strings).

The functionality of the gateway was defined first by a recursive function which directed one message at a time to the correct output port, and also by a function which used sequence comprehension to describe the processing of a sequence of inputs. Here we will consider the following operations:

1. `ProcessMessage`, which describes how a single given message could be processed;
2. `Gateway`, which describes the overall functionality, where messages are handled as an input stream.

First, what will go into the state? The gateway contains one input port and two output ports, along with a category. The operations process the inputs, write messages to the outputs and examine the category, so these all seem to be sensible state components. The resulting type and state definitions are given below:

```
types

    String = seq of char
    inv s == s <> [];

    Message = String
    inv m == len m <= 100;

    Classification = <HI> | <LO>;

    Category = set of String;

state TrustedGateway of
    input : seq of Message
    cat   : Category
    outHi : seq of Message
    outLo : seq of Message
init gate == gate = mk_TrustedGateway([],{},[],[])
end
```

Notice that an initialisation clause has been added to the state definition, indicating that the gateway starts with empty streams of messages at its ports and an empty category. The operations in the model should allow a system to progress from its initial state. In practical terms, this means that there should be at least one operation whose pre-condition is implied by the `init` clause in the state definition, otherwise no progress will be possible. Operations to add and remove messages and category strings are considered in the exercises below.

Consider now an operation which takes a message as an input parameter and adds it to the appropriate output port. The operation header will give the input parameter and the operation returns no result:

```
ProcessMessage(m:Message)
```

The operation will need to be able to read the category in order to determine the classification of the message m, so the externals clause will require read-only access to cat:

```
ProcessMessage(m:Message)
ext rd cat : Category
```

The operation will also be writing values to the output ports. We cannot tell which output port will be modified, because that depends on what particular values are passed in m. The externals clause will therefore give read/write access to both output ports:

```
ProcessMessage(m:Message)
ext rd cat    : Category
    wr outHi : seq of Message
    wr outLo : seq of Message
```

It is often best to begin sketching the post-condition before defining the pre-condition. The form of the post-condition helps to determine what assumptions must be recorded in the pre-condition to ensure that uses (partial) operators are defined and that invariants are respected. The ProcessMessage operation is intended to add the message m to the head end of the appropriate output port. If the classification of m is <HI> then

```
outHi = [m]^outHi~
```

and if the classification of m is <LO> then

```
outLo = [m]^outLo~
```

The auxiliary functions Occurs and Classify as previously defined do not have side-effects and so can continue to be defined as functions. Using Classify, a first draft of the operation ProcessMessage is as follows:

```
ProcessMessage(m:Message)
ext rd cat    : Category
    wr outHi : seq of Message
    wr outLo : seq of Message
post if Classify(m,cat) = <HI>
     then outHi = [m]^outHi~
     else outLo = [m]^outLo~
```

This definition suffers from an interesting but common deficiency. Consider the case where

```
Classify(m,cat) = <HI>
```

The post-condition says that the high-classification port must be updated
with `m` added at the head end. However, we also have write access to
the low-classification output port and the post-condition says nothing
about what should happen to this port in the case where the message
is high-classification. Recall that the operation definition could be seen
as a definition for a piece of code which satisfies the post-condition under the assumptions stated in the pre-condition. Here, the operation
definition could be satisfied by code which writes anything at all to the
low-classification port, as long as the high-classification port is updated
correctly! In more general terms, the following two operation specifications achieve the same thing:

```
OP(in:A) r:R                    OP(in:A) r:R
ext wr s : SomeType             ext rd s : SomeType
pre ...                         pre ...
post ... and s = s~             post ...
```

The question of how state components not explicitly mentioned should
be modified is known from artificial intelligence research and is called the
frame problem. The lesson for the author of a VDM-SL formal model is
simply to ensure that updates to all write-access state components are
correctly described in the post-condition.

   The post-condition of the operation `ProcessMessage` should be revised
to say that, in each case, the output port which is not modified is itself
left unchanged:

```
ProcessMessage(m:Message)
ext rd cat   : Category
    wr outHi : seq of Message
    wr outLo : seq of Message
post if Classify(m,cat) = <HI>
     then outHi = [m]^outHi~ and outLo = outLo~
     else outHi = outHi~ and outLo = [m]^outLo~
```

No pre-condition is required for this operation: the post-condition is sensible for all possible states and input parameters.

   Recall from the functional model of the trusted gateway that it is possible to describe the gateway's behaviour as it processes a whole series
of input messages. The `ProcessMessage` function was incorporated into
a recursive function `Gateway` which handled the sequence of messages at
the input one-by-one. Alternatively, sequence comprehension can also be
used to describe the same behaviour without needing recursion.

Within the limited notation introduced in this book, recursion within operations appears clumsy, so we will generally prefer comprehension in operation definitions. The overall functionality of the gateway can be described by an operation using sequence comprehension as follows:

```
Gateway()
ext  rd input : seq of Message
     rd cat   : Category
     wr outHi : seq of Message
     wr outLo : seq of Message
post outHi = [input(i) | i in set inds input &
                            Classify(input(i),cat) = <HI>]
     and
     outLo = [input(i) | i in set inds input &
                            Classify(input(i),cat) = <LO>]
```

10.5 Validation of state-based models

The validation of state-based models proceeds in a very similar way to that of models written using only functions. However, the introduction of the state and operations brings with it some additional proof obligations.

Consider a state definition as follows:

```
state NewState of
  component-name : type
  component-name : type
  ...
  component-name : type
inv optional-invariant
init ns == ns = mk_NewState(...)
end
```

The initialisation only makes sense provided the initial state satisfies the invariant, so we have an additional obligation to show that

```
inv_NewState(mk_NewState(...))
```

The satisfiability obligation for operations is much the same as for implicitly defined functions, except that we must include the "before" and "after" states as well as the inputs and results. Consider an operation specification OP of the form

```
OP(p1:T1,...,pn:Tn) r:R
ext ...
pre ...
post ...
```

working on a state s of type NewState. The obligation involves showing that

```
forall a1:T1, ..., an:Tn, s~:NewState &
    pre_OP(a1,...,an,s~) =>
        exists r:R, s:NewState & post_OP(a1,...,an,s~,s,r)
```

The same validation techniques are available for operations as for implicit functions, including testing (by evaluating the post-condition) and proof.

Summary

- In many cases it is appropriate to model a system and its functionality as a collection of state variables representing persistent data and operations which take inputs, produce a result and have side effects on the state variables. A *state-based* model in VDM-SL contains a *state definition* which lists the state variables, and a number of *operation definitions*.
- Although a state-based model has extra complexity in the definition of the state and operations, it often reflects more closely the nature of the computing system being modelled. A state-based model is appropriate when a functional model would involve passing large data structures as inputs to functions, especially when the functions return an output which differs from the input in only a small number of components. State-based modelling is appropriate if the purpose of a model is to document the design of a software system which uses global variables.
- The state definition lists the state variables, along with their representing types. The variables may be restricted by an invariant. The initial values of the state variable are determined by an init clause.
- The operation specifications covered in this book have all been implicit, with a header giving the inputs and result, and an *externals* clause defining the access (read-only or read/write) which the operation may have to the state variables. The functionality of the operation is described by means of a post-condition which relates

the result and "after" values of the state variables to the inputs and the "before" values. The post-condition must respect the restrictions in the externals clause. It is important to ensure that the post-condition defines all the "after" values of write-accessible state variables. The operation may have a pre-condition restricting its application.

- Explicit operation definitions are possible in VDM-SL, but are not covered in this book.

Exercise 10.1 We have omitted some important operations from the trusted gateway model. Extend the model with the following, using Toolbox Lite to test your answers:

1. Add a new string to the category. Return a special error value if the string is already present in the category.
2. Remove a given string from the category if it is present. If the given string is not in the category, leave it unchanged.
3. Add a new input message to the tail end of the input stream.

□

11

Large-Scale Modelling

Aims

In this chapter, we aim to provide an awareness of the issues involved in constructing and analysing large-scale models. We will introduce modular structuring facilities in VDM-SL as an illustration of the features required in a structuring mechanism. On completion of this chapter, the reader should be able to exploit modular structuring and the potential for re-use in large models.

11.1   Introduction

In any course on modelling, one is naturally limited in the size of model which can be developed and presented. However, in any realistic application of modelling technology, questions of scale must be addressed. How can one manage the complexity of developing and analysing a model which contains many related parts?

Before answering this question, it is worth remembering that models should be kept as simple as possible while still capturing the aspects of the system which are felt to be relevant to the analysis. Careful use of abstraction means that many systems can be usefully modelled without encountering problems of scale. However, for some applications, particularly where the product is safety-related, a formally-defined language such as VDM-SL must be applied to the production of a substantial model, and so the management of the model's size and complexity becomes a significant issue.

In programming languages, the management of complexity has led to the adoption of modular structuring mechanisms for programs, and this approach has also been applied to VDM-SL. All the models presented so far have been *flat* in the sense that they have consisted of a series of definitions in a single document. In order to understand part of the model, one might possibly have to read the whole document. In contrast, a modular model consists of a number of separate modules, each of which contains a collection of definitions just as in a flat model. Given a good division of a model into separate modules, it should be possible to complete the analysis of the modules relatively independently. Ultimately, the separate modules are brought together into a "top-level" unit. The task of analysing the whole model, whether by visualisation, testing or proof, can then be split into analyses of the component modules.

The remainder of this chapter presents the modular structuring facilities available in VDM-SL. These are illustrated on the tracker model introduced in Chapter 8. The facilities are those supported by the full IFAD VDM-SL Toolbox[1]. The ISO Standard for VDM-SL does not, at the time of writing, mandate any particular modular structuring mechanism. It is expected that a future part of the standard will formalise a module construct along similar lines to those presented here.

11.2   A structure for the tracker model

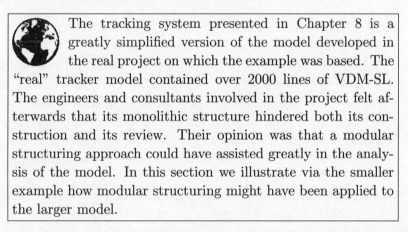 The tracking system presented in Chapter 8 is a greatly simplified version of the model developed in the real project on which the example was based. The "real" tracker model contained over 2000 lines of VDM-SL. The engineers and consultants involved in the project felt afterwards that its monolithic structure hindered both its construction and its review. Their opinion was that a modular structuring approach could have assisted greatly in the analysis of the model. In this section we illustrate via the smaller example how modular structuring might have been applied to the larger model.

First, we consider the overall division of the model into component modules. The model presented in Chapter 8 has three main aspects: containers, phases and the overall tracker. We might consider a structure for the model which puts each of these concepts in a separate module:

- The *Containers* module would hold information relating to the modelling of containers and material they contain.
- The *Phases* module would model the structure of the plant and define properties such as safety of materials stored in phases. In

---

[1] These facilities are not available in Toolbox Lite.

Figure 11.1 *Modular structure for the tracker model*

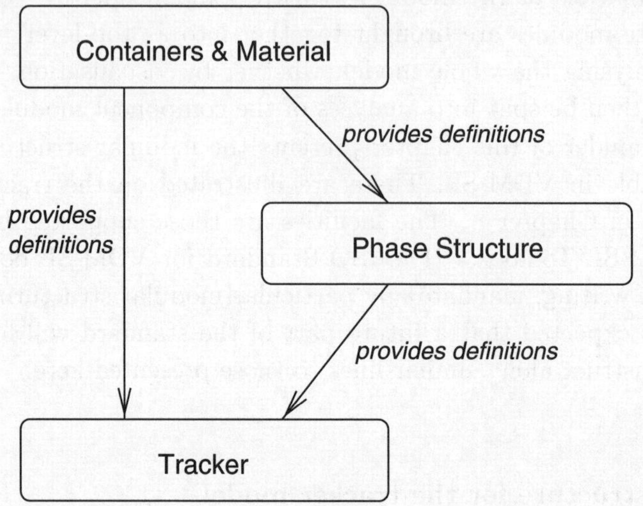

order to do this, it will need to use some of the types defined in the *Containers* module.

- The *Tracker* module brings together the *Containers* and *Phases* modules, providing a definition of the information held by the tracker and the functions which may be applied to the tracker, such as granting permission for containers to move between phases.

Figure 11.1 shows the general structure suggested here. Many alternatives are possible. For example, materials might be defined in a separate module. However, this would lead to a structure where several modules have little content.

There comes a point where the ratio between the size of a module's interface definition and its content is too heavily weighted towards the interface for the module to be useful. The advantages and disadvantages of each possible modular structure should be weighed up before a commitment is made.

The Containers module

This module will hold the definitions of the types and functions relating to containers and materials. The relevant type definitions from the flat model are as follows:

```
ContainerInfo = map ContainerId to Container;

Container :: fiss_mass : real
             material  : Material;

ContainerId = token;

Material = token
```

To place these definitions in a module, we first have to name the module. For brevity, we will call the module CTRS. The basic definitions are enclosed in module ... end keywords:

```
module CTRS
   ⋮
   types

   ContainerInfo = map ContainerId to Container;

   Container :: fiss_mass : real
                material  : Material;

   ContainerId = token;

   Material = token
end CTRS
```

Notice that so far no functions are included in this module. This is because all the functions we require in the model use types like PhaseInfo and Tracker which are defined in other modules. Our intention in producing a modular version is to make it possible to understand the overall model as the sum of its constituent modules, with each individual module being separately defined and analysed. Thus each function must be defined in a context in which its input and result types are available.

Since each module represents a separate part of the overall model, we should provide interfaces between modules. Each module's interface says which constructs (types, functions etc.) it will supply to, and which it will require from, the other modules. This information is given in an *interface section* of the module, separate from the definitions of types and functions. The definitions are separated from the interface by a `definitions` keyword:

```
module CTRS
  ⋮

  definitions

   types

    ContainerInfo = map ContainerId to Container;

    Container :: fiss_mass : real
                 material  : Material;

    ContainerId = token;

    Material = token
  end CTRS
```

This module requires nothing from the other modules, but makes the types it defines available to the others. We say that it *exports* all its defined constructs. This is represented by the keywords `exports all` in the interface section of the module definition:

```
module CTRS

  exports all

  definitions

   types

    ContainerInfo = map ContainerId to Container;

    Container :: fiss_mass : real
                 material  : Material;

    ContainerId = token;

    Material = token

  end CTRS
```

The Phases module

The phases module defines the phases, the `PhaseInfo` type and relevant functions, namely the auxiliary functions: `Consistent`, which checks that all the contents of containers in the phases of the plant are known; `PhasesDistinguished`, which checks that no containers occur in more than one phase; and `MaterialSafe`, which checks that all containers in all phases contain only those kinds of material expected for that phase.

Recall from the flat model that the type definitions relevant to phases were as follows:

```
PhaseInfo = map PhaseId to Phase;

Phase :: contents            : set of ContainerId
         expected_materials: set of Material
         capacity           : nat
inv p == card p.contents <= p.capacity;

PhaseId = token
```

When placed in the phases module, these definitions will require the use of types defined in the containers module CTRS. The interface part of the phases module should record this dependency. We say that the phases module will *import* all the definitions from CTRS. Suppose it is decided that this module should also export all of its defined types and functions. If the phases module is called PHS for brevity, this yields the following skeleton module definition:

```
module PHS
 imports from CTRS all
 exports all

 definitions

  types

   PhaseInfo = map PhaseId to Phase;

   Phase :: contents            : set of ContainerId
            expected_materials: set of Material
            capacity           : nat
   inv p == card p.contents <= p.capacity;

   PhaseId = token

end PHS
```

There remains a problem with this definition. Suppose one were analysing
the type correctness of PHS. The types `ContainerId` and `Material` could
be imports from CTRS, or they could be locally-defined types whose definitions have been omitted. In order to make the origin of each construct
clear, we prefix the use of imported constructs by the name of the module
from which they have been imported, and we separate the prefix from the
construct's name by the backtick character ('). Thus:

```
module PHS
 imports from CTRS all
 exports all

 definitions

  types

   PhaseInfo = map PhaseId to Phase;

   Phase :: contents           : set of CTRS'ContainerId
            expected_materials: set of CTRS'Material
            capacity          : nat
   inv p == card p.contents <= p.capacity;

   PhaseId = token

end PHS
```

The functions defined in this module also make use of the types imported
from CTRS. The full module definition is as follows:

```
module PHS

   imports from CTRS all
   exports all

   definitions

     types

     PhaseInfo = map PhaseId to Phase;

     Phase :: contents           : set of CTRS'ContainerId
              expected_materials: set of CTRS'Material
              capacity          : nat
     inv p == card p.contents <= p.capacity;
```

```
PhaseId = token

functions

    Consistent: CTRS'ContainerInfo * PhaseInfo -> bool
    Consistent(containers, phases) ==
        forall ph in set rng phases &
            ph.contents subset dom containers;

    PhasesDistinguished: PhaseInfo -> bool
    PhasesDistinguished(phases) ==
        not exists p1, p2 in set dom phases &
            p1 <> p2 and
            phases(p1).contents inter phases(p2).contents <> {};

    MaterialSafe: CTRS'ContainerInfo * PhaseInfo -> bool
    MaterialSafe(containers, phases) ==
        forall ph in set rng phases &
            forall cid in set ph.contents &
                cid in set dom containers and
                containers(cid).material in set
                    ph.expected_materials

end PHS
```

Notice that PHS exports all its constructs. However, the modular structuring facility in the IFAD VDM-SL Toolbox is defined so that it does not automatically re-export the constructs it imported from CTRS.

The Tracker module

The final module in this hierarchy is the Tracker module, which we will call TRACKER. It requires the types and functions from PHS, but also the types exported by CTRS, since it uses the ContainerInfo type. The module is presented in full below. Note again that the names of imported constructs are qualified.

```
module TRACKER

    imports from PHS all,
            from CTRS all

    exports all

    definitions
```

```
types

  Tracker :: containers : CTRS'ContainerInfo
             phases     : PHS'PhaseInfo
  inv mk_Tracker(containers,phases) ==
    PHS'Consistent(containers,phases) and
    PHS'PhasesDistinguished(phases) and
    PHS'MaterialSafe(containers,phases);

functions

  -- introduce a new container to the plant (map union)

  Introduce : Tracker * CTRS'ContainerId * real * CTRS'Material
                        -> Tracker
  Introduce(trk, cid, quan, mat) ==
    mk_Tracker(trk.containers munion
                {cid |-> mk_CTRS'Container(quan, mat)},
                trk.phases)
  pre cid not in set dom trk.containers;

  -- permission to move (simple Boolean function)

  Permission: Tracker * CTRS'ContainerId * PHS'PhaseId  ->  bool
  Permission(mk_Tracker(containers, phases), cid, dest) ==
      cid in set dom containers and
      dest in set dom phases and
      card phases(dest).contents < phases(dest).capacity and
      containers(cid).material in set
                phases(dest).expected_materials;

  -- assign a known container to a given phase

  Assign: Tracker * CTRS'ContainerId * PHS'PhaseId -> Tracker
  Assign(mk_Tracker(containers, phases), cid, pid) ==
      let pha = mk_PHS'Phase(phases(pid).contents union cid,
                             phases(pid).expected_materials,
                             phases(pid).capacity)
      in
        mk_Tracker(containers, phases ++ {pid |-> pha})
  pre Permission(mk_Tracker(containers, phases), cid, pid);


  -- remove a container from the contents of a phase

  Remove: Tracker * CTRS'ContainerId * PHS'PhaseId -> Tracker
  Remove(mk_Tracker(containers, phases), cid, source) ==
    let pha = mk_PHS'Phase(phases(source).contents \ {cid},
```

```
                           phases(source).expected_materials,
                           phases(source).capacity)
    in
        mk_Tracker(containers, phases ++ {source |-> pha})
    pre source in set dom phases and
        cid in set phases(source).contents;

    -- delete a container from the plant

    Delete: Tracker * CTRS'ContainerId * PHS'PhaseId  ->  Tracker
    Delete(tkr, cid, source) ==
        mk_Tracker({cid} <-: tkr.containers,
                   Remove(tkr, cid, source).phases)
    pre pre_Remove(tkr,cid,source)
```

end TRACKER

On a much larger scale, a similar modular structuring could have been effectively applied to the "real" tracker model. It is likely that there would have been many more modules. Some modules would also have contained much larger definitions sections than those shown here. When one has a structure in which modules contain a great deal of detail which may change as individual modules are developed, it may be advisable to limit the use which can be made by other modules of the constructs defined in a given module. This is the subject of the following section.

11.3 Information hiding

In the example presented so far, we have exported all the constructs defined in each module. However, it may sometimes be appropriate to define a more restricted interface to a module. For example, if one defines an auxiliary function which is not meant to be exported, but is used in the definition of an exported function, then the auxiliary function should not be used by any other module. This means that the auxiliary function can be replaced by an equivalent new version at a later stage without any other module being affected.

Support is available for this by means of limiting exports. Instead of using all in the exports list, we can list the individual types and functions which we do wish to export. For example, we could have defined the following version of TRACKER which has the same definitions section, but makes only some of the defined functions available to other modules:

```
module TRACKER_LIMITED

imports from PHS all,
        from CTRS all

exports types Tracker;
        functions Permission: Tracker * CTRS'ContainerId *
                                    PHS'PhaseId  ->  bool;
                  Assign: Tracker * CTRS'ContainerId * PHS'PhaseId
                          -> Tracker;
                  Remove: Tracker * CTRS'ContainerId * PHS'PhaseId
                          -> Tracker
        definitions
        ...
module TRACKER_LIMITED
```

This would allow the authors of other modules to use the tracker functions to move existing containers through the plant, but would not allow them to introduce or delete containers, because those functions are missing from the export list.

The authors of a module can impose self-discipline by restricting imports as well. The **imports** list can contain individual types or functions from a module rather than importing **all**. For example, suppose that, instead of restricting exports, the **TRACKER** module exports all its functions. The authors of a module that describes control of container introduction might use the following imports list:

```
imports from CTRS types ContainerId, Material
from TRACKER
    types Tracker
    functions Introduce : Tracker * CTRS'ContainerId *
                            real * CTRS'Material -> Tracker
```

This would allow them only to use the **Introduce** function from **TRACKER**. Notice that all the types in the signature of the imported function must also be available, otherwise it would not be possible to construct values to which the function can be applied. Hence we import types from **CTRS** as well as **TRACKER**.

A further kind of restriction is available on export. The authors of a module may choose to export a type with or without its representation. This is indicated by the use of a keyword **struct**. Suppose **TRACKER** exports the type **Tracker** with **struct**, written as follows:

```
module TRACKER

  imports ...

  exports types struct Tracker,
          functions all

  definitions
  ...
     Tracker :: containers : CTRS'ContainerInfo
                phases     : PHS'PhaseInfo
     inv mk_Tracker(containers,phases) ==
        ...

  ...
  module TRACKER
```

Now any module which imports TRACKER has access to the type Tracker and its definition. The importing module can use the fact that Tracker is a record type with two fields called containers and phases. This could cause difficulties where separate teams of developers are responsible for their own modules. For example, if the authors of the TRACKER module added another field to record the history of container movements, the users of the TRACKER module would have to update all their uses of mk_Tracker expressions to ensure that they now had three arguments. To guard against the consequences of such change, it is often advisable to export types without struct. The use of the all keyword on export implies export of types with their representations.

Finally in this section, a note on renaming. The prefixed names used for imported types and functions can become cumbersome. It is possible to rename constructs on import. For example, we could have avoided the use of prefixed names in the PHS module by renaming them as follows. Renaming is indicated by the use of the renamed keyword:

```
module PHS

  imports from CTRS types ContainerInfo renamed CtrInfo,
                          Container renamed Ctr, ...
  exports all

  definitions
  ...
     Consistent: CtrInfo * PhaseInfo -> bool
     Consistent(containers, phases) ==
        forall ph in set rng phases &
           ph.contents subset dom containers
  ...
```

11.4   Supporting reuse through parameterisation

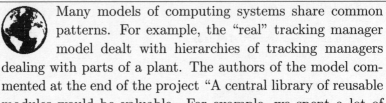
Many models of computing systems share common patterns. For example, the "real" tracking manager model dealt with hierarchies of tracking managers dealing with parts of a plant. The authors of the model commented at the end of the project "A central library of reusable modules would be valuable. For example, we spent a lot of time defining operations over a tree structure in our architecture: this must have been done before."

Modular structuring mechanisms provide for the parameterisation of modules, allowing them to be used many times with different actual parameters on each occasion. For example, a general tree structure could be parameterised over the type of the data stored at the nodes. Such a module would have been useful to the authors of the real tracker model, because the tree structure could have been instantiated with tracking managers, phase identifiers and other types which occurred in tree structures in the model.

For a simple illustration of the use of parameterisation to promote reuse of modules, we use a simple and familiar example about sorting. Suppose we develop a function for sorting sequences of natural numbers. The sorting algorithm used for illustrative purposes here is very simple and not very efficient. A flat model for sorting would take the following form:

. . .

```
DoSort: seq of nat -> seq of nat
DoSort(l) ==
  if l = [] then
    []
  else
    let sorted = DoSort(tl l) in
      InsertSorted (hd l, sorted);

InsertSorted: nat * seq of nat -> seq of nat
InsertSorted(i,l) ==
  if l = []
  then [i]
  elseif i <= hd l
  then [i] ^ l
  else [hd l] ^ InsertSorted(i,tl l)
```

This model deals only with sorting sequences of natural numbers. How could it be generalised so that it can be used elsewhere?

Using a modular structuring mechanism, the model could be placed in a module:

```
module SORT

exports
 functions DoSort: seq of nat -> seq of nat

definitions

 functions

  DoSort: seq of nat -> seq of nat
  DoSort(l) ==
    if l = [] then
      []
    else
      let sorted = DoSort(tl l) in
        InsertSorted (hd l, sorted);

  InsertSorted: nat * seq of nat -> seq of nat
  InsertSorted(i,l) ==
    if l = []
    then [i]
    elseif i <= hd l
    then [i] ^ l
    else [hd l] ^ InsertSorted(i,tl l)

end SORT
```

Only the function `DoSort` is exported. The function `InsertSorted` is a local auxiliary function introduced in order to make the definition of the main function `DoSort` more straightforward.

Although this provides an encapsulation of the model for sorting, the model is of limited value because it still describes only the sorting of sequences of natural numbers. The module could be more widely used if the type **nat** could be replaced by other types. This can be done by parameterising the module over a type. Let the parameter type be called ELEM. The module then becomes:

```
module SORT

parameters
 types ELEM
```

```
exports
functions DoSort: seq of ELEM -> seq of ELEM

definitions

functions

 DoSort: seq of ELEM -> seq of ELEM
 DoSort(l) ==
   if l = [] then
     []
   else
     let sorted = DoSort(tl l) in
       InsertSorted (hd l, sorted);

 InsertSorted: ELEM * seq of ELEM -> seq of ELEM
 InsertSorted(i,l) ==
   if l = []
   then [i]
   elseif i <= hd l
   then [i] ^ l
   else [hd l] ^ InsertSorted(i,tl l)

end SORT
```

When this module is used, the parameter ELEM will be replaced by an actual type, for example **real**, producing a module which describes sorting of sequences of real numbers. The replacement of module parameters by actual values is called *instantiation*.

Notice that a problem remains. Since **nat** has been replaced by a parameter, there is no way of knowing for certain that the "<=" operator used in the definition of InsertSorted will apply to elements of the actual parameter type when the module is instantiated. For example, if SORT is instantiated with **char** as the actual type, the InsertSorted function would not be well-formed. It would appear that the use of "<=" restricts the instantiation to certain types only. Again, the essence of sorting is not dependent on the way in which order is determined among the elements of the sequence or whether the elements are to be sorted in ascending or descending order. It would therefore appear sensible to make the module parametric over an ordering function. This is done in the example below:

```
module SORT

parameters
```

```
types ELEM
functions Ordered: ELEM * ELEM -> bool

exports
functions DoSort: seq of ELEM -> seq of ELEM

definitions

functions

...

InsertSorted: ELEM * seq of ELEM -> seq of ELEM
InsertSorted(i,l) ==
  if l = []
  then [i]
  elseif Ordered(i, hd l)
  then [i] ^ l
  else [hd l] ^ InsertSorted(i,tl l)

end SORT
```

This new version of SORT will be instantiated by the type of the elements
to be sorted and the ordering function to be applied over that type.

Now that a genuinely reusable sorting model has been defined, it is
worth briefly examining how it might be instantiated. Suppose a model
is being developed for some other part of the nuclear plant. In particular,
consider an early phase in the plant, in which sequences of containers arrive ready for allocation of identifiers and sorting on the basis of contents.
In a model of this phase, one may wish to order the containers in order of
decreasing fissile mass, so that the containers with highest fissile mass are
dealt with first. In this case, the element type to be sorted is Container
and the sorting function compares the fiss_mass fields of containers.

Suppose we are defining a module ARRIVAL which models the handling
of containers on arrival in the plant.

```
module ARRIVAL

imports from CTRS all

definitions

types

Arrivals = seq of CTRS'Container
```

```
functions

...

end ARRIVAL
```

To describe the sorting of containers, we will have to instantiate the SORT module and define a function giving the desired ordering on containers. The sorting would be on the basis of fissile mass, and so could be defined by a function HigherMass as follows:

```
HigherMass: CTRS'Container * CTRS'Container -> bool
HigherMass(c1, c2) ==
  c1.fiss_mass >= c2.fiss_mass
```

The instantiation of SORT is given in the interface using an instantiations list:

```
module ARRIVAL

imports from CTRS all

instantiations
 CSORT as SORT(ELEM -> CTRS'Container,
               Ordered -> HigherMass) all

definitions
...
```

This makes available a module called CSORT which is the instantiation of SORT with Container as the actual type and HigherMass as the ordering function. In particular, CSORT now has a sorting function CSORT'DoSort which operates on sequences of containers sorting them so that they are in order of decreasing fissile mass. Now it is possible to define a function which orders the containers in the arrival sequence. This function, called Prioritise, simply calls the sorting function.

```
Prioritise: Arrivals -> Arrivals
Prioritise(arr) ==
  CSORT'DoSort(arr)
```

The completed ARRIVAL module showing the instantiation is used as follows:

```
module ARRIVAL

imports from CTRS all
```

```
instantiations
 CSORT as SORT(ELEM -> CTRS'Container,
               Ordered -> HigherMass) all

definitions

 types

  Arrivals = seq of CTRS'Container

 functions

  HigherMass: CTRS'Container * CTRS'Container -> bool
  HigherMass(c1, c2) ==
    c1.fiss_mass >= c2.fiss_mass;

  Prioritise: Arrivals -> Arrivals
  Prioritise(arr) ==
    CSORT'DoSort(arr)

end ARRIVAL
```

A range of modular structuring facilities has been presented: import and export, providing information hiding; renaming, to make qualified names more acceptable to the reader; and parameterisation, as a way of promoting reuse of modules. These have been illustrated on a simple functional model. The effect of modular structuring on a state-based model is one of a number of more advanced topics which are beyond the scope of this text. Readers seeking further information are directed to a VDM language manual such as that accompanying the full IFAD VDM-SL Toolbox.

11.5   Object-orientated structuring

Modular structuring provides a basic means of organising large-scale models. The approach nevertheless entails some care in deciding what should be included in each module participating in a larger structure. Object-oriented modelling approaches such as Universal Modelling Language (UML) [Booch&97] and Object Modelling Technique (OMT) [Rumbaugh&91] provide support for structuring models of complex systems by basing structures around objects which may have local state and which interact through methods at their interfaces. Classes of objects share common properties and may inherit properties from super-classes.

Although object-oriented methods play a major role in system modelling, they could benefit from exploiting the combination of abstraction and suitability for rigorous analysis which comes from the use of a formally-defined modelling language such as VDM-SL. There has been some considerable work on the extension of VDM-SL to be compatible with object-oriented design, notably the development of VDM++, [UserManPP, LangManPP], an extended VDM-SL which incorporates notions of class and inheritance. Tool systems such as the VDM++ Toolbox can provide for coupling between object-oriented models (e.g. in OMT and UML) and their formal counterparts.

Summary

The construction and analysis of large-scale models necessitate a structuring mechanism. A modular structuring mechanism provides for:

- separation of models into syntactic units;
- information hiding through restrictions on imported and exported constructs and the provision of an option to export types with or without their representations;
- the ability to rename imported modules so as to maintain "readability" of modules;
- parameterisation of modules as a means of promoting reuse of models which describe frequently-recurring patterns. Such parameterised modules are then instantiated.

The extension of modular structuring methods to object-oriented structuring is achieved in VDM++.

12

Using VDM in Practice

Aims

The aim of this chapter is to clarify how the VDM modelling technology introduced in this book can be used in an industrial development context. This chapter will enable the reader to understand where in the traditional life-cycle this technology can be applied beneficially and indicate how take-up can be initiated in an organisation.

12.1 Introduction

The focus of this chapter is the application of the modelling technology presented in this book in a commercial software development context. Modelling in a formal language is not a panacea which solves every problem in system and software development. However, if used thoughtfully it can yield significant process improvements. We will use the term *"VDM technology"* to refer to the combination of the VDM-SL notation and the full IFAD VDM-SL Toolbox[1].

The central motivation for using VDM technology has to be cost-effectiveness and/or quality increase. The cost of developing a formal system model should be recouped in later development stages when the improved understanding of system functionality reduces the reworking required to deal with "surprises" which arise during testing and maintenance.

This chapter begins by discussing the traditional software development life-cycle used in many industrial companies and the most common problems that arise with it. The main part of this chapter explains how VDM technology can be used to address some of these problems. Finally, some hints on how to get started using this technology are presented. This

---

[1] The Toolbox Lite version used with this book is designed as a training tool and as a "taster" for the kind of tool support which can be obtained. Its limitations make it unsuitable for serious commercial application.

advice may be useful in avoiding pitfalls in successfully deploying formal modelling in commercial practice.

12.2   The traditional life-cycle model

Many organisations use a development process which is a variant on the well-known "V" life-cycle model [Sommerville96] shown in Figure 12.1. The name of this model follows from the structure of the figure. It is essentially a derivative of the "waterfall" model, a name which emphasises the flow of design information from one phase to another. The V model stresses the validation and verification products and activities in the various development phases. In different companies the phases and the products resulting from these phases may be given different names, but generally speaking the same kind of life-cycle is used. Other life-cycle models exist but the V model is by far the most widely adopted, although, in practice, it may not be followed exactly. A main reason for the V life-cycle's popularity is the process visibility which comes from the production of clear deliverables by each phase. Such deliverables can be used to assess progress and predict resource levels for future development phases.

The borderlines between the different phases vary from company to company and even from project to project. However, the phases in Figure 12.1 can be explained as:

System Analysis: This phase involves the analysis of requirements for the system under development, carried out in consultation with the customer and the domain experts. The overall system architecture may also be constructed in this phase and the requirements partitioned into those to be implemented in hardware and software respectively. The deliverables produced in this phase are usually a requirements specification as well as an acceptance test plan to be used for the system when it is completed. Typically the requirement specification uses natural language and various informal diagrammatic notations.

Software Design: In this phase, a more detailed design of the software components of the system is produced by software engineers using the requirements specification. The deliverables produced in this phase are usually a software design describing the software architecture in terms of modules and their functionality as well as a test plan for each of the modules. Typically the software design is expressed with

Figure 12.1 *The V life-cycle model*

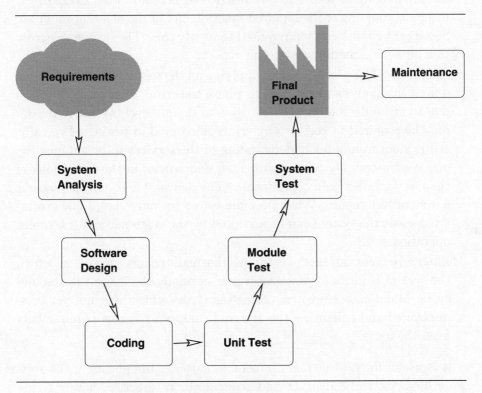

pseudo-code and various diagrammatic notations supported by Computer Aided Software Engineering (CASE) tools.

Coding: In this phase, the software design is realised as code in a programming language. The code is compiled by a compiler and an executable is produced. The deliverables produced in this phase are the actual program code and the corresponding executable.

Unit Test: In this phase each of the functions are tested separately by the developers. The deliverable from this phase is a report of the unit test results. Possibly certain test coverage criteria must be fulfilled in the unit testing and this must be documented in the report. Coding errors discovered at this stage are comparatively straightforward and cheap to correct.

Module Test: This phase involves carrying out the module tests produced in the software design phase. If some inputs yield incorrect results the error must be discovered and corrected at the right level of description.

In this phase the integration of modules produced by different teams usually also takes place. Errors discovered here are often caused by a misunderstanding of the required functionality of the different modules. Significant rework is often required to rectify this. The deliverable from this phase is a module test result report.

System Test: This phase involves applying all the tests produced in the requirement analysis phase. In this phase the errors discovered are often due to misunderstandings at the system design level, so major rework may be required to correct any errors uncovered in testing. Typically, errors stem from a misunderstanding of the services to be supplied by one system component to another, or deficiencies in the definitions of the interfaces between components. The deliverable from this phase is a system test report. When no more errors (or only acceptable errors) are present the system can be accepted by the customer and taken into operation.

Maintenance: For successful systems the maintenance phase, in which the system is put into practical use, is normally the longest in the life-cycle. Maintenance involves correcting errors which have not yet been discovered and enhancing the system in response to new requirements from the users.

It is useful for project management to consider the phases of the software life-cycle to be distinct and sequential. In practice, however, the development process does not follow a linear model. Phases overlap and feed information back, for example when problems with requirements are identified during design or design errors are discovered during coding. To ensure progress, it is often a management necessity to limit iterations through development activities by "freezing" deliverables at baselines for periods of time. Without keeping control over the deliverables produced, it may be very difficult to avoid version problems. The balance between the use of baselines and the freedom to change documents in response to errors has to be struck by project management.

As an alternative to the V life-cycle model, evolutionary development processes involve a strong element of prototyping. A prototype can be used to help clarify the client's requirements. In some development processes, an initial prototype is progressively enhanced, following customer feedback at each stage. This continual client involvement is intended to lead to a product which more precisely matches requirements than a product developed in a waterfall model. Nevertheless, the process suffers from some deficiencies, notably the difficulty of developing well-structured software when development consists of continual improvements to an initial prototype.

12.3 Common development problems

The traditional life-cycle presented above does have a number of problems. Here we focus on the problems that VDM technology can help to alleviate. Thus, we will not go into problems with staffing, scheduling, cost estimation and configuration management.

Premature coding

Coding of software components is often begun before the functional requirements have been fully analysed. The motivation for this is clearly that the running program in the developed system acts as a final arbiter of system acceptance. However, it often happens that deficiencies in understanding the functional requirements of the system return to haunt the development team in later stages of the development. If design errors stemming from an erroneous understanding of the functionality are found late in the development process their correction can be very costly in terms of required rework.

Lack of confidence in descriptions

The system descriptions used in early development phases often use informal ways of representing the model, such as natural language and pseudo-code. Confidence in such descriptions is typically gained through reviews and inspections. The main problem with this approach is that success in discovering errors depends largely up on the skills and intuition of the reviewers to spot problems. Typically this problem is compounded by the variety in backgrounds of customers, domain experts, system and software developers. The members of such a team often use terminologies which are so different that misunderstandings are not uncovered. In addition, it is a very labour-intensive way to gain confidence in the descriptions.

Errors discovered too late

At module integration time it is often discovered that developers have misunderstood each other, so that the functionality relied on by one module may not be correctly provided by another. The consequence of this is that a significant amount of rework must be carried out. Since projects are often very close to the delivery deadline by the time such errors are discovered, the documentation may not be updated to reflect the changes made at this late stage of development.

Late feedback from customer

Customers cannot always provide feedback on the system before the final implementation has been completed. As a result, deficiencies in the expression of requirements or in their interpretation may not become clear until the testing or maintenance phases. A solution chosen by some organisations is to develop prototypes of the system and use these to get earlier feedback from the customer in an evolutionary model.

Overly late delivery

The overall development time from formulation of requirements to the production of the final system is often longer than planned, in no small part due to errors discovered late in the development. It is desirable to get a more predictable route to a product. Often the time to market is an essential parameter determining the success of a product.

Understanding design in the maintenance phase

The engineers maintaining a system may not have taken part in its development. If the documentation is not accurate or up-to-date it is difficult to understand how a reported bug can be corrected without introducing new bugs. The problem is that the code may be complex, and without an understanding of the design principles of the system the level of abstraction is simply so low that bug fixing can become a "trial and error" process. The engineer does not necessarily understand why a correction works but the bug seems to have disappeared. Without an understanding of the system's design principles, there is an increased risk that the bug fix simply introduces other errors.

12.4 Advantages of VDM technology

For most of the needs described above VDM technology can be used to improve the situation. Below we discuss the areas of the life-cycle that show the greatest potential benefit from using modelling technology.

Better clarification of requirements

As this book illustrates, VDM-SL provides a medium for the systematic formulation and analysis of requirements. The development of a model involves capturing a range of requirements and clarifying them through the questions which arise during the formulation of the model.

Abstraction is the key technique used to moderate the complexity of models. Throughout the book we have focussed on the formulation of abstract VDM models for a number of different systems. The abstract model provides an overview of the data structures in the system and an overview of its required functionality. The choice of modelling abstraction should be grounded by a clear understanding of the model's purpose.

Earlier feedback from customer

The ability to execute models allows early demonstration of the intended functionality to a customer (see Section 9.3). A dynamic link facility allows *visualisation* of an executable model. The visualised model can be demonstrated to a customer with no understanding of the VDM modelling notation behind it. A heterogeneous model is presented in which a part of the system is modelled in VDM-SL while another part, for example existing code, is implemented in C++. Typically the part which is implemented is a relatively simple piece of code used to visualise the system in the form of a user interface. With such a demonstration it is possible to get feedback from a customer at the system analysis stage of the development, long before an expensive commitment has been made to a particular design (data structures and algorithms).

In effect, we are advocating that some of the prototyping aspects of the evolutionary development model can be incorporated into more conventional processes. Rather than developing a prototype in an implementation language and subsequently transforming this prototype into a product, we are suggesting the use of a special-purpose modelling language in conjunction with visualisation software which allows the client to interact with the abstract model. The model can then form the basis of subsequent design and validation activities. This allows a strong element of customer involvement, while still permitting the development of a well-structured system.

Raising confidence in descriptions

In order to carry out automatic consistency checking it is necessary to have a precise notation in which to describe the system in the early phases of development. Here the availability of powerful analysis tools is an important aid to raising confidence in such descriptions. As demonstrated in Chapter 9 different levels of checks can increase the confidence in the correctness of a model.

The generation of proof obligations can provide an indication of places where run-time errors could occur. Because of their ability to identify and protect parts of the model which have not been guarded against misapplication of partial operators, proof obligations are an important aid in ensuring the well-definedness of the model produced. In addition, it is possible to provide dynamic checking of restrictions such as invariants and pre-conditions and post-conditions. Formulating such restrictions is an excellent way to document the limitations and assumptions made by the different components of a system.

In Chapter 9 we considered the ability to test VDM models systematically at the early stages of design as another way to increase confidence in the correctness of the model. The ability to show test coverage directly in the VDM model is an important way of documenting the level of trust one can have in a model. The ability to test the model in the system analysis phase may be a productive way to ensure that system tests produced by the development phase have a high level of coverage.

Shorter time to market

The production of a model is usually accompanied by an improvement in the developer's understanding of the functional requirements. Thus, major rework carried out in the later stages of development, such as the integration stage, is less likely to occur. This in turn makes it easier to control the budget because the system will be less prone to the risk of major errors discovered late in development. Thus, VDM technology helps to provide a safer route to the development of the system.

If the requirements for the speed of the final code are not especially high, the time to market can also be shortened by the use of automatic code generation. Embedded software with highly demanding speed requirements would currently have to be coded manually. It is possible that improvements in the code generators will be able to change this situation in the future. However, in cases where optimised code is to be produced it is also essential to have a correct understanding of the required functionality. Otherwise the rework is likely to be particularly costly. By reusing the tests from the model for the implementation, the testing of the implementation will also be faster. The tests on the model can also be used as oracles at the implementation level.

Reducing maintenance costs

In the maintenance phase of a system, requests for incorporation of new features need to be considered. Using VDM in the development of (a part of) a system, this situation would be tackled by first adding the feature to the VDM model. The modifications are then tested at the VDM level before the differences are incorporated in the code. This approach makes it easier to keep the documentation up-to-date with the system. In addition, it will be easier to analyse the impact of the change request on the rest of the system. This can also be advantageous in estimating the efforts required to incorporate the desired change.

The maintenance phase also entails handling bug reports for the delivered system. Using VDM it is natural to try to reproduce the bug at the VDM level first. At that more conceptual level it is usually easier to understand what causes the bug to appear using the debugging facilities. When this cause is understood the VDM models can be corrected. The test environment at the VDM level is then reused in the manner of regression testing. The complexity of the application software can make the impact of corrections difficult to assess and often the correction of one bug introduces others. In this way the regression test environment can be used to identify such erroneous corrections before they are incorporated in the code. Because of better documentation of the design principles for the system, the usual approach is replaced by one in which the cause of the error is more thoroughly analysed.

12.5   Getting started

If the arguments for using VDM technology are so strong, why is it not already being used by everybody? There are both technical and non-technical reasons for this, and in this section we discuss them. In addition we suggest how these problems can be overcome.

The organisation and people involved

Small, medium and large organisations that develop software as part of their work can benefit from applying modelling techniques to essential parts of their software systems. Whatever the size of organisation, a number of people may be involved in deciding whether or not to use these techniques as part of a trial or real product development. Apart from engineers who have a technical view on the benefits of applying formal modelling, managers will have concerns about changes to the development process and the cost-effectiveness of the technology. All these concerns have to be addressed, and experience suggests that the introduction of a new technology of the kind discussed in this book is greatly assisted if it has "champions" within the organisation: people who are confident of the benefits of the techniques, have some experience of their application on the small scale and can develop a rough model.

Champions need to be aware of the costs and benefits of the technology they support. The costs of applying formal modelling techniques include training, initial consultancy and tool support, along with a longer systems analysis phase. However, this has to be measured against the effort which is taken up in the software process due to the problems identified in Section 12.3. When the cost-effectiveness has been justified this must be used to convince individuals at different levels in the company about the feasibility of introducing the technology.

The development process

The most important advice with respect to the development process is to change by evolution rather than revolution. It is important to make progress by a series of small "deltas" to the stages of the development process currently in use. Many industrial organisations already have a very sophisticated and efficient development process which has been the subject of considerable investment (e.g. to achieve ISO9000 qualification). Thus, it is important to investigate how to fit the modelling technology and its products into the existing process and assess the impact of the technology on the level of qualification.

The discussion above suggests that it is not difficult to embed VDM technology in the traditional V life-cycle model. The embedding of the VDM technology can be done at relevant points in any standardised software development process such as ESA PSS-05 or MIL-STD-498. Emerging standards such as MoD 00-55 even mandate the use of this kind of technology in certain critical applications. This trend is likely to continue, at least in the area of critical systems.

Often the result will be to designate VDM or some other modelling technology as a viable technique for some tasks. The way it is used, and the life-cycle products to which it is contributing, depend on the phase of the development where it is used.

For project managers leading a team of developers using VDM it is worth providing some guidance about what can be expected in terms of the time spent in the different phases of development. Our experience has generally been that the first system analysis phase is expanded, with 25% or more additional time using formal modelling, and validation using testing, as described in this book. However, this additional effort is saved in the later development phases. If project managers measure progress using the number of lines as a metric, it is also worth noting that usually it is when the size of a formal model is starting to decrease that a full understanding of the functionality of the system has emerged amongst the development team. Thus, this should not be seen as a bad sign, but as an indication that the formal model soon will be finished, and that in the implementation from that model, a much better mental understanding of the conceptual requirements exists. Thus, the code will be written much more quickly and will be much more structured.

Integration with other tools

An evolutionary approach to the introduction of modelling technology necessitates integration with tools already used by the company, such as CASE tools supporting structured methods. However, at least initially, it is advisable to aim for a relatively simple form for integration.

When more experience about the best way to combine the different tools has been gained, tighter integration can be investigated. It is possible to continue to use graphical notations such as Object Modelling Technique (OMT), Universal Modelling Language (UML) and Structured Analysis (SA), and then use VDM-SL to add rigour to the products produced using the conventional tools – for example by enhancing data dictionary entries with type definitions, and process specifications with function or operation definitions.

VDM technology can also be integrated into version and revision control systems. Most of these systems simply operate at the file level and since the VDM-SL Toolbox also operates on files it is easy to apply the existing technology for this purpose. The same holds for requirements-traceability tools such as RTM® [RTM].

Where can formal modelling be applied?

Even though most of the examples we have presented in this book have been related to early development phases, formal methods can be used beneficially in other arenas. In the more detailed software design phases, VDM models can replace pseudo-code. When VDM is used at this more detailed level it is typically combined with structured methods supporting a graphical overview of the system such as data flow or object-oriented design techniques. Here the formal models are used to formally define the data being passed between processes and to formally define the detailed functionality of the methods or functions inside the different processes. Commercial tool support with tight integration between graphically oriented CASE tools and formal methods tools have started to appear.

Many industrial organisations have huge amounts of legacy code they need to maintain and continue to evolve in different directions. In the area of reverse engineering and in development of new components added to existing systems, VDM can also play an important role. When a part of such a large system either contains too many errors, or the staff who developed it have moved on, leaving very limited documentation, the development of an abstract description can be beneficial for the future maintenance of the system. When a new component is to be developed for an existing large system, it is also possible to model the interface between the existing system and the new component. The dynamic link facility from the IFAD VDM-SL Toolbox can then be used to validate the interaction between the new component under development and the existing code.

Another rather new application domain where we feel that VDM can play a major role, is in the modelling of components whose development will be subcontracted or outsourced to other companies. Here it is important to be able to supply a combination of a precise description of the required functionality and the interface required at the code level. For the functionality description, abstract formal models can be very beneficial in increasing confidence in the system which is delivered by the subcontractor.

Finally, VDM can play a role in the testing phase. Here the benefits will be in being able to automate a larger part of the test case selection process. Testing is a very expensive part of the development of critical systems; it has already been demonstrated how effort can be reduced by automating parts of this phase.

Starting the first project(s)

Before starting a pilot project using modelling techniques it is important to decide which phase of the development life-cycle is to be the subject of the application. The success criteria for the project should be defined so that the expectations are clear to all the involved personnel. This also includes an estimate of the cost-effectiveness of the new technology.

The pilot project should be selected so that, if it is not a success, it will not cause too much damage for the organisation. On the other hand the project should not be so small and trivial that, even if it is a success, there is doubt about the technology when used on a more realistic scale. It is often a good idea to take a complex challenge and be able to show that VDM can bring new and valuable insight, enhancing the solution.

Training

Before a project is started it is vital to obtain training in abstraction using a notation such as VDM-SL and getting hands-on experience in tool support. In essence this is exactly what this book is trying to provide, but if it has been used for self-study it would be advisable to take at least a short course given by an experienced VDM expert. In

addition, one should not forget that, in order to carry out reviews satis-
factorily, it is important that quality assurance personnel involved with
the project are at least trained to read and understand the formal models
being developed.

Following training, we advocate a project-specific workshop, where the
parts of the system to be formally modelled are selected and the general
structure of them are laid out. Generally, only part of a system is to be
modelled, and a significant amount of experience is required to be able to
select those parts of the system which would benefit from application of
this technology. Thus, at such a workshop, it is important that there is an
experienced modeller or consultant present to assist in decision making.
In addition, the experience from the expert can be used to get the best
structure of the system at an early stage.

After the workshop we advocate use of consultancy from an internal or
external source. Such a consultant can be used for reviews of draft models
and above all, for help in choosing appropriate abstract representations.

Information resources

For those wishing to use modelling technology of the kind described in this book, there are a wide range of available sources of information. These include:

- reports on industrial applications of formal techniques;
- guidelines for the application of modelling technology (such as the
  NASA Guide Book);
- bibliographies on a range of formal modelling techniques;
- technical descriptions of models;
- electronic mailing lists;
- industrial seminars and courses;
- conferences on industrial use and research in modelling technology.

Most of these resources are accessible electronically. Rather than risk
giving addresses which are soon out of date, we refer the reader to the
web site accompanying this text, where full details and links to these
resources are available. The URL is

```
http://www.csr.ncl.ac.uk/modelling-book/index.html
```

Summary

The modelling techniques set out in this book aim to address some of the problems which beset development of software in the commercial context. The kind of benefits one can expect from using modelling technology such as VDM can be characterised as follows:

Better clarification of requirements: A high-level abstract VDM model encourages systematic analysis of requirements. The complexity of a full system model or prototype is avoided by using abstractions relevant to the model's purpose.

Earlier feedback from customer: Constructing a high-level model makes it is possible to get feedback from customers and/or domain experts about the initial capture and understanding of the requirements. The feedback can be obtained through a range of validation techniques, including visualisation, testing and proof.

Raising confidence in descriptions: The rigour of the notation makes it possible, when desired, to automatically carry out a number of consistency checks which raise the level of confidence one can have in the description.

Shorter time to market: Having captured the user's requirements early on there is less rework in the late stages of the development and tools can also be used to automate parts of this process.

Reducing maintenance costs: An abstract formal model of the software developed can help in predicting the consequences of changes in requirements during maintenance and evolution.

A
Language Guide

A model written in VDM-SL is a collection of the following:

- data type definitions;
- function definitions;
- operation definitions;
- value (constant) definitions; and
- a state definition.

Each collection of definitions is prefixed by a keyword (e.g. **types**). Individual definitions are separated by semicolons.

This appendix provides an overview of the constructs in the subset of VDM-SL treated in this book and supported by Toolbox Lite. Finally there is a BNF grammar for the subset of VDM-SL covered in this book and supported by Toolbox Lite. For ease of referencing an HTML version of this BNF grammar is provided on the CD-ROM.

A.1 Identifiers

The different kind of definitions which can be made in VDM-SL are named using identifiers. The naming conventions used in this book are:

- Functions, operations and types begin with an upper-case letter for each word or abbreviation of which the name is composed.
- Constant values begin with lower-case characters and use underscore between word or abbreviations of which these are composed.
- Local identifiers are always sequences of lower-case characters and usually rather short names are used.

However, this is only a convention and is not mandatory.

A.2   Type definitions

As in traditional programming languages it is possible to define data types in VDM-SL and give them appropriate names. For example:

```
Amount = nat
```

Hereby we have defined a data type with the name "Amount" and stated that the values which belong to this type are natural numbers (nat is one of the basic types described below). One general point about the type system of VDM-SL which is worth mentioning at this point is that equality and inequality can be used between any value. In programming languages it is often the case that it is required that the operands have the same type. Because of a construct called a union type (described below) this is not the case for VDM-SL.

It is also possible to define record types in VDM-SL. As it can be seen from Subsection A.4.8 this is done using a : : notation rather than the equality sign used in the type definition of Amount above.

Invariants

In VDM-SL it is possible to attach invariants to a type definition.

```
Type-name == type-expression
inv pattern == logical-expression
```

The *pattern* can be a single identifier or a more complex pattern if the invariant is attached to a complex type. In the latter case the pattern must match the structure of all values belonging to the type denoted by the type expression. Invariants can be used both for types defined using the equality sign and the double colon notation (::).

A.3   Basic data types and type constructors

In VDM-SL there is a distinction between types (which can contain infinitely many values) and sets of values (which always are finite). The basic types from VDM-SL are:

- The positive natural numbers starting from 1 written as nat1;
- The natural numbers starting from 0 written as nat;
- The integers written as int;

- The real numbers written as `real`;
- The Booleans written as `bool`;
- The characters written as `char`;
- The token type written as `token`;
- The quote types written as ordinary identifiers surrounded by angle brackets e.g. `<Red>`.

In addition VDM-SL contains type constructors to produce:

- sets constructed by the `set of` _ operator;
- sequences constructed by the `seq of` _ operator;
- mappings constructed by the `map` _ `to` _ operator;
- tuples constructed by the _ `*` _ operator;
- unions constructed by the _ `|` _ operator;
- optional types constructed by the `[` _ `]` operator;
- records which can be constructed using a `::` notation in the type definition as shown in Subsection A.4.8.

A.4   Data type operator overview

This section provides an overview of all the basic operators for each of the basic types and all the types which can be constructed. The basic constructors are also presented here. The basic constructors for the compound types are all explained informally. For each type a table shows each operator in use, its name and its signature.

A.4.1   *The Boolean type*

The operations on the Boolean type are explained in Chapter 4.

Operator	Name	Signature
`not b`	Negation	`bool` $\rightarrow$ `bool`
`a and b`	Conjunction	`bool` $*$ `bool` $\rightarrow$ `bool`
`a or b`	Disjunction	`bool` $*$ `bool` $\rightarrow$ `bool`
`a => b`	Implication	`bool` $*$ `bool` $\rightarrow$ `bool`
`a <=> b`	Biimplication	`bool` $*$ `bool` $\rightarrow$ `bool`
`a = b`	Equality	`bool` $*$ `bool` $\rightarrow$ `bool`
`a <> b`	Inequality	`bool` $*$ `bool` $\rightarrow$ `bool`

See also Subsection A.5.3.

A.4.2 *The numeric types*

The operators on the numeric types are not explained in detail anywhere because they are well-known from most programming languages.

Operator	Name	Signature
-x	Unary minus	real → real
abs x	Absolute value	real → real
x + y	Sum	real ∗ real → real
x - y	Difference	real ∗ real → real
x * y	Product	real ∗ real → real
x / y	Division	real ∗ real → real
x div y	Integer division	int ∗ int → int
x mod y	Modulus	int ∗ int → int
x**y	Power	real ∗ real → real
x < y	Less than	real ∗ real → bool
x > y	Greater than	real ∗ real → bool
x <= y	Less or equal	real ∗ real → bool
x >= y	Greater or equal	real ∗ real → bool
x = y	Equal	real ∗ real → bool
x <> y	Not equal	real ∗ real → bool

A.4.3 *The character, quote and token types*

Characters, quotes and token values can only be compared to each other. The characters from VDM-SL are presented in Table A.1. Quote literals are written by the use of angle brackets around an identifier as described in Subsection 5.3.1. Token values are written with a token constructor mk_token preceeding a value surrounded by parentheses as shown in Subsection 5.3.3.

Operator	Name	Signature
c1 = c2	Equal	char ∗ char → bool
c1 <> c2	Not equal	char ∗ char → bool

The characters which can be used in VDM-SL are:

Table A.1 *Character set*

---

plain letter:

a	b	c	d	e	f	g	h	i	j	k	l	m
n	o	p	q	r	s	t	u	v	w	x	y	z
A	B	C	D	E	F	G	H	I	J	K	L	M
N	O	P	Q	R	S	T	U	V	W	X	Y	Z

delimiter character:

,	:	;	=	(	)	|	–	[	]
{	}	+	/	<	>	<=	>=	<>	.
*	->	+>	==>	||	=>	<=>	|->	<:	:>
<-:	:->	&	==	**	^	++			

digit:

0   1   2   3   4   5   6   7   8   9

other characters:

_   '   '   "   @   ~

newline:

white space:

These have no graphical form, but are a combination of white space and line break. There are two separators: without line break (white space) and with line break (newline).

A.4.4   *Set types*

The use of sets is described in Chapter 6. In this section the set constructors and set operators are described.

Set enumeration: {e1, e2, ..., en} constructs a set of the enumerated elements. The empty set is represented as {}.

Set comprehension: {e | bd1, bd2, ..., bdm & P} constructs a set by evaluating the expression e on all the bindings for which the predicate P evaluates to true. A binding is either a set binding or a type binding[1]. A set binding bdn has the form pat in set s, where pat is a pattern (normally simply an identifier), and s is a set constructed by an expression. A type binding is similar, in the sense that "in set" is replaced by a colon and s is replaced with a type expression.

Set range: The *set range expression* is a special case of a set comprehension. It has the form {e1, ..., e2} where e1 and e2 are numeric expressions. The set range expression represents the set of integers from e1 to e2 inclusive. If e2 is smaller than e1 the set range expression represents the empty set.

Operator	Name	Signature
e in set s1	Membership	$A * \mathtt{setof}\,A \to \mathtt{bool}$
e not in set s1	Not membership	$A * \mathtt{setof}\,A \to \mathtt{bool}$
s1 union s2	Union	$\mathtt{setof}\,A * \mathtt{setof}\,A \to \mathtt{setof}\,A$
s1 inter s2	Intersection	$\mathtt{setof}\,A * \mathtt{setof}\,A \to \mathtt{setof}\,A$
s1 \ s2	Difference	$\mathtt{setof}\,A * \mathtt{setof}\,A \to \mathtt{setof}\,A$
s1 subset s2	Subset	$\mathtt{setof}\,A * \mathtt{setof}\,A \to \mathtt{bool}$
s1 = s2	Equality	$\mathtt{setof}\,A * \mathtt{setof}\,A \to \mathtt{bool}$
s1 <> s2	Inequality	$\mathtt{setof}\,A * \mathtt{setof}\,A \to \mathtt{bool}$
card s1	Cardinality	$\mathtt{setof}\,A \to \mathtt{nat}$
dunion ss	Distributed union	$\mathtt{setofsetof}\,A \to \mathtt{setof}\,A$
dinter ss	Distributed intersection	$\mathtt{setofsetof}\,A \to \mathtt{setof}\,A$

Operator Name	Semantics Description
Membership	tests if e is a member of the set s1.
Not membership	tests if e is not a member of the set s1.

---

[1] Notice that type bindings cannot be executed by the interpreter because they in general are not executable.

Operator Name	Semantics Description
Union	yields the union of the sets s1 and s2, i.e. the set containing all the elements of both s1 and s2.
Intersection	yields the intersection of sets s1 and s2, i.e. the set containing the elements that are in both s1 and s2.
Difference	yields the set containing all the elements from s1 that are not in s2. s2 need not be a subset of s1.
Subset	tests if s1 is a subset of s2, i.e. whether all elements from s1 are also in s2. Notice that any set is a subset of itself.
Cardinality	yields the number of elements in s1.
Distributed union	the resulting set is the union of all the elements (these are sets themselves) of ss, i.e. it contains all the elements of all the elements/sets of ss.
Distributed intersection	the resulting set is the intersection of all the elements (these are sets themselves) of ss, i.e. it contains the elements that are in all the elements/sets of ss. ss must be non-empty.

A.4.5 *Sequence types*

The use of sequences is described in Chapters 7.

Sequence enumeration: `[e1,e2,..., en]` constructs a sequence of the enumerated elements. A text literal is a shorthand for enumerating a sequence of characters (i.e. `"ifad"` = `['i','f','a','d']`). The empty sequence will be represented as `[]`.

Sequence comprehension: `[e | id in set S & P]` constructs a sequence by evaluating the expression `e` on all the bindings for which the predicate `P` evaluates to `true`. The expression `e` can use the identifier `id`. `S` is a set of numbers and `id` will be matched to the numbers in the normal order (the smallest number first).

Subsequence: A *subsequence* of a sequence `l` is a sequence formed from consecutive elements of `l`; from index `n1` up to and including index `n2`.

It has the form: 1(n1, ..., n2) where n1 and n2 are positive integer expressions (less than the length of 1). If the lower bound n1 is smaller than 1 (the first index in a non-empty sequence), the subsequence expression will start from the first element of the sequence. If the upper bound n2 is larger than the length of the sequence (the largest index which can be used for a non-empty sequence), the subsequence expression will end at the last element of the sequence.

Operator	Name	Signature
hd l	Head	$\text{seqof}\,A \to A$
tl l	Tail	$\text{seqof}\,A \to \text{seqof}\,A$
len l	Length	$\text{seqof}\,A \to \text{nat}$
elems l	Elements	$\text{seqof}\,A \to \text{setof}\,A$
inds l	Indices	$\text{seqof}\,A \to \text{setofnat1}$
l1 ^ l2	Concatenation	$(\text{seqof}\,A) * (\text{seqof}\,A) \to \text{seqof}\,A$
conc ll	Distributed concatenation	$\text{seqofseqof}\,A \to \text{seqof}\,A$
l ++ m	Sequence modification	$\text{seqof}\,A * \text{mapnatto}\,A \to \text{seqof}\,A$
l(i)	Sequence index	$\text{seqof}\,A * \text{nat1} \to A$
l1 = l2	Equality	$(\text{seqof}\,A) * (\text{seqof}\,A) \to \text{bool}$
l1 <> l2	Inequality	$(\text{seqof}\,A) * (\text{seqof}\,A) \to \text{bool}$

Operator Name	Semantics Description
Head	yields the first element of 1. 1 must be a non-empty sequence.
Tail	yields the subsequence of 1 where the first element is removed. 1 must be a non-empty sequence.
Length	yields the length of 1.
Elements	yields the set containing all the elements of 1.
Indices	yields the set of indices of 1, i.e. the set $\{1,\ldots,\text{len 1}\}$.
Concatenation	yields the concatenation of l1 and l2, i.e. the sequence consisting of the elements of l1 followed by those of l2, in order.

Operator Name	Semantics Description
Distributed concatenation	yields the sequence where the elements (these are sequences themselves) of `ll` are concatenated: the first and the second, and then the third, etc.
Sequence modification	the elements of `l` whose indices are in the domain of `m` are modified to the range value that the index maps into. `dom m` must be a subset of `inds l`
Sequence index	yields the element of index `i` from `l`. The index `i` must be in the indices of `l`.

A.4.6 *Mapping types*

The use of mappings is described in Chapters 8.

Mapping enumeration: {a1 |-> b1, a2 |-> b2, ..., an |-> bn} constructs a mapping of the enumerated maplets. The empty mapping will be represented as {|->}.

Mapping comprehension: {ed |-> er | bd1, ..., bdn & P} constructs a mapping by evaluating the expressions `ed` and `er` on all the possible bindings for which the predicate `P` evaluates to `true`. `bd1, ..., bdn` are bindings of free identifiers from the expressions `ed` and `er` to sets or types.

Operator	Name	Signature
dom m	Domain	$(\text{map}A\text{to}B) \rightarrow \text{setof}A$
rng m	Range	$(\text{map}A\text{to}B) \rightarrow \text{setof}B$
m1 munion m2	Map union	$(\text{map}A\text{to}B) * (\text{map}A\text{to}B) \rightarrow \text{map}A\text{to}B$
m1 ++ m2	Override	$(\text{map}A\text{to}B) * (\text{map}A\text{to}B) \rightarrow \text{map}A\text{to}B$
merge ms	Distributed merge	$\text{setof}(\text{map}A\text{to}B) \rightarrow \text{map}A\text{to}B$
s <: m	Domain restrict to	$(\text{setof}A) * (\text{map}A\text{to}B) \rightarrow \text{map}A\text{to}B$
s <-: m	Domain restrict by	$(\text{setof}A) * (\text{map}A\text{to}B) \rightarrow \text{map}A\text{to}B$
m :> s	Range restrict to	$(\text{map}A\text{to}B) * (\text{setof}B) \rightarrow \text{map}A\text{to}B$
m :-> s	Range restrict by	$(\text{map}A\text{to}B) * (\text{setof}B) \rightarrow \text{map}A\text{to}B$
m(d)	Mapping apply	$(\text{map}A\text{to}B) * A \rightarrow B$
m1 = m2	Equality	$(\text{map}A\text{to}B) * (\text{map}A\text{to}B) \rightarrow \text{bool}$
m1 <> m2	Inequality	$(\text{map}A\text{to}B) * (\text{map}A\text{to}B) \rightarrow \text{bool}$

Two mappings `m1` and `m2` are compatible if any common element of `dom m1` and `dom m2` is mapped to the same value by both mappings.

Operator Name	Semantics Description
Domain	yields the domain (the set of keys) of m.
Range	yields the range (the set of information values) of m.
Map union	yields a mapping combined by m1 and m2 such that the resulting mapping maps the elements of dom m1 as does m1, and the elements of dom m2 as does m2. The two mappings must be compatible.
Override	overrides and merges m1 with m2, i.e. it is like a map union except that m1 and m2 need not be compatible; any common elements are mapped as by m2 (so m2 overrides m1).
Distributed merge	yields the mapping that is constructed by merging all the mappings in ms. The mappings in ms must be compatible.
Domain restricted to	creates the mapping consisting of the elements in m whose key is in s. The set s need not be a subset of dom m.
Domain restricted by	creates the mapping consisting of the elements in m whose key is not in s. The set s need not be a subset of dom m.
Range restricted to	creates the mapping consisting of the elements in m whose information value is in s. The set s need not be a subset of rng m.
Range restricted by	creates the mapping consisting of the elements in m whose information value is not in s. The set s need not be a subset of rng m.
Mapping apply	yields the information value whose key is d. The value d must be in the domain of m.

A.4.7   *Tuple types*

Values belonging to a tuple type are called tuples; they can only be constructed using a tuple constructor written as mk_(a1,a2,...,an) where the different a's are arbitrary values.

Operator	Name	Signature
t1 = t2	Equality	$T * T \rightarrow \texttt{bool}$
t1 <> t2	Inequality	$T * T \rightarrow \texttt{bool}$

A.4.8   *Record types*

Values belonging to a record type are called records and they can only be constructed using a record constructor which we write as mk_TagId(a1,a2,...,an) where the different a's are arbitrary values and TagId is a tag incorporated into all values from the type with this name such that the origin is known.

Typically record types are used as alternatives in a union type definition (see A.4.9) such as:

```
MasterA = A | B | ...
```

where A and B are defined as record types themselves. In this situation the is_ predicate can be used to distinguish the alternatives.

Operator	Name	Signature
r.i	Field select	$A * Id \rightarrow Ai$
r1 = r2	Equality	$A * A \rightarrow \texttt{bool}$
r1 <> r2	Inequality	$A * A \rightarrow \texttt{bool}$
is_A(r1)	Is	$Id * \texttt{MasterA} \rightarrow \texttt{bool}$

Record types are defined as:

```
Type :: component name : type
        component name : type
        ...
        component name : type
```

For example, for a type defined:

```
Date :: day   : Day
        month : Month
        year  : Year
```

The record constructor for Date is

```
mk_Date(_,_,_)
```

The field selectors are

```
_.day
_.month
_.year
```

A.4.9 *Union and optional types*

Union types are written as:

```
MasterA = A | B | ...
```

The types used with the union type constructor A and B should either be basic types or record types. This makes it easy to detect which (component) type an element of a union type belongs to using either pattern matching or the is-expression.

An optional type is written as:

```
[T]
```

where the brackets indicate a union between the elements from the type T and the special value nil.

Operator	Name	Signature
t1 = t2	Equality	$A * A \rightarrow$ bool
t1 <> t2	Inequality	$A * A \rightarrow$ bool

A.5 Expressions

Where the previous section presented all basic operators, constructors (using enumeration and comprehension) and selectors, this section will provide an overview of the more complex expressions used for structuring large constructs conveniently.

A.5.1 *Let expressions*

A *let expression* has the form:

```
let p1 = e1, ..., pn = en in e
```

where p1, ..., pn are patterns, e1, ..., en are expressions which match the corresponding pattern pi, and e is an expression, of any type, involving the pattern identifiers of p1, ..., pn. The value of the entire let expression is the value of the expression e in the context in which the patterns p1, ..., pn are matched against the corresponding expressions e1, ..., en.

A *let-be-such-that expression* has the form:

```
let b be st e1 in e2
```

where b is a binding of a pattern to a set value (or a type), e1 is a Boolean expression, and e2 is an expression, of any type, involving the pattern identifiers of the pattern in b. The be st e1 part is optional. The value of the let-be expression is the value of the expression e2 in the context in which the pattern from b has been matched against either an element in the set from b or against a value from the type in b^2. If the be st e1 expression is present, only such bindings where e1 evaluates to true in the matching context are used.

A.5.2 Conditional expressions

The *if expression* has the form:

```
if e1
then e2
else e3
```

where e1 is a Boolean expression, while e2 and e3 are expressions of any type. The value of the if expression is the value of e2 evaluated in the given context if e1 evaluates to true in the given context. Otherwise the value of the if expression is the value of e3 evaluated in the given context.

The *cases expression* has the form:

```
cases e :
    p11, p12, ..., p1n -> e1,
    ...                -> ...,
    pm1, pm2, ..., pmk -> em,
    others             -> emplus1
end
```

where e is an expression of any type, all pijs are patterns which are matched one by one against the expression e. The ei's are expressions of any type, and the keyword others and the corresponding expression

---

[2] Remember that only the set bindings can be executed by means of the interpreter from the Toolbox.

`emplus1` are optional. The value of the cases expression is the value of the `ei` expression evaluated in the context in which one of the `pij` patterns has been matched against `e`. The chosen `ei` is the first entry where it has been possible to match the expression `e` against one of the patterns. If none of the patterns match `e` an `others` clause must be present, and then the value of the cases expression is the value of `emplus1` evaluated in the given context.

A.5.3 *Quantified expressions*

There are two forms of quantified expressions: *universal* (written as `forall`) and *existential* (written as `exists`). Each give a Boolean value `true` or `false`, as explained in the following.

The *universal quantification* has the form:

```
forall bd1, bd2, ..., bdn & e
```

where each `bdi` is a binding `pi in set s` (or if it is a type binding `pi:type`), and `e` is a Boolean expression involving the pattern identifiers of the `bdi`'s. The universal quantified expression has the value `true` if `e` is `true` when evaluated in the context of every choice of bindings from `bd1, bd2, ..., bdn` and `false` otherwise.

The *existential quantification* has the form:

```
exists bd1, bd2, ..., bdn & e
```

where the `bdi`'s and the `e` are as for a universal quantification. It has the value `true` if `e` is `true` when evaluated in the context of at least one choice of bindings from `bd1, bd2, ..., bdn`, and `false` otherwise.

A.6   Patterns

A pattern is always used in a context where it is matched to a value of a particular type. Matching consists of checking that the pattern can be matched to the value, and binding any pattern identifiers in the pattern to the corresponding values, i.e. ensuring that the identifiers are bound to those values throughout their scope. In some cases where a pattern can be used, a binding can be used as well (see the next section).

Matching is defined as follows:

1. A *pattern identifier* fits any type and can be matched to any value. If it is an identifier, that identifier is bound to the value; if it is the "don't care" symbol -, no binding occurs.

2. A *match value* can only be matched against the value of itself; no binding occurs. If a match value is not a literal like e.g. 7 or <RED> it must be an expression enclosed in parentheses in order to discriminate it from a pattern identifier.

3. A *set enumeration pattern* is written as {p1,p2,...,pn} and it fits only set values with n elements. The patterns p1,p2,...,pn are matched to distinct elements of a set; all elements must be matched.

4. A *set union pattern* is written as p1 union p2 and it fits only set values. The two patterns, p1 and p2 are matched to a partition of two subsets of a set. In the Toolbox the two subsets will always be chosen so that they are disjoint.

5. A *sequence enumeration pattern* is written as [p1,p2,...,pn] and it fits only sequence values with length n. Each pattern is matched against its corresponding element in the sequence value; the length of the sequence value and the number of patterns must be equal.

6. A *sequence concatenation pattern* is written as p1^p2 and it fits only sequence values. The two patterns are matched against two subsequences which together can be concatenated to form the original sequence value.

7. A *tuple pattern* is written as mk_(p1,p2,...,pn) and it fits only tuples with the same number of elements. Each of the patterns are matched against the corresponding element in the tuple value.

8. A *record pattern* is written as mk_TagId(p1,p2,...,pn) and it fits only record values with the same tag TagId. Each of the patterns are matched against the field of the record value. All the fields of the record must be matched.

A.7　Bindings

A *binding* matches a pattern to a value. In a *set binding* the value is chosen from the set defined by the set expression of the binding. In a *type binding* the value is chosen from the type defined by the type expression. Notice that type bindings *cannot* be executed by the interpreter from the Toolbox. This would require the interpreter to potentially have to search through an infinite number of values such as the natural numbers.

A.8 Explicit function definition

An explicit function definition has the form:

```
f: T1 * T2 * ... * Tn -> R1 * R2 * ... Rm
f(a1,a2,...,an) ==
    expr
pre preexpr(a1,a2,...,an)
```

This definition has four parts:

The signature with the function name, the types of input parameters, and the type of the result (here `f: T1 * T2 * ... * Tn -> R1 * R2 * ... Rm`);

A parameter list, naming the parameters to the function using patterns which usually are simply names (here `(a1,a2,...,an)`);

The body which is an expression stating the value of the result in terms of the values of the inputs (here `expr`);

The pre-condition which is a logical expression stating the assumptions made about the inputs (here `preexpr(a1,a2,...,an)`). If a pre-condition is absent, the default is `true`.

A.9 Implicit functions

An implicit function definition has the form:

```
f(a1:T1,a2:T2,...,an:Tn) res:R
pre preexpr(a1,a2,...,an)
post postexpr(a1,a2,...,an,res)
```

This definition has three parts:

The function heading with the function name, the names and types of input and the result identifier (here `f(a1:T1,a2:T2,...,an:Tn) res:R`);

The pre-condition which is a logical expression stating the assumptions made about the inputs (here `preexpr(a1,a2,...,an)`;. If omitted, the default pre-condition is `true`.

The post-condition which is a logical expression stating the property between the parameters and the result which holds after application of a function (in this case `postexpr(a1,a2,...,an,res)`).

A.10   Operations

An implicit operation definition has the form:

```
op(a1:T1,a2:T2,...,an:Tn) res:R
ext wr s1: ST1
    rd s2: ST2
       ...
    wr sm: STm
pre  p(a1,a2,...,an,s1,s2,...,sm)
post q(a1,a2,...,an,res,s1~,...sm~,s1,s2,...,sm)
```

This definition has the following components:

The header with the operation name, the names and types of input parameters, and any result (in this case op(a1:T1,a2:T2,...,an:Tn) res:R);

The externals clause which lists the state components to be used by the operation and indicates whether each component may be read or written (here ext wr s1: ST1 rd s2: ST2 ... wr sm: STm);

The pre-condition which is a logical expression stating the conditions that are assumed to hold when the operation is applied. The pre-condition may be omitted, in which case it defaults to true (here p(a1,a2,...,an,s1,s2,...,sm)).

The post-condition which is another logical expression relating the state and result value after the operation, with the state and inputs before: it describes the essence of the computation (here q(a1,a2,...,an,res, s1~,...sm~,s1,s2,...,sm)).

Note that the value of the state components in wr mode are distinguished by a "~" symbol to mean the value before the operation was called.

A.11   The state definition

The state definition has the form:

```
state ident of
   id1 : T1
    ...
   idn : Tn
inv  pat1 == inv
init id == id = mk_ident(expression list)
end
```

A state component identifier `idi` is declared of a specific type `typei`. The invariant `inv` is a Boolean expression describing a property which must hold for the state `ident` at all times. The `init` part describes a condition which must hold initially. It should be noticed that in order to use the interpreter from the Toolbox, it is necessary to have an initialisation predicate (if any of the operations using the state are to be executed). The body of this initialisation predicate must be a binary equality expression with the name (which also must be used as the pattern) of the entire state on the left-hand side of the equality and the right-hand side must evaluate to a record value of the correct type as shown above. This enables the interpreter to evaluate the `init` condition.

In the definition of both the invariant and the initial value the state must be manipulated as a whole, and this is done by referring to it as a record *tagged* with the state name. When a field in the state is manipulated in some operation, the field must however be referenced directly by the field name without prefixing it with the state name.

A.12 Syntax overview

Wherever the syntax for parts of the language is presented in the document it will be described in a BNF dialect. The BNF notation which is used employs the following special symbols:

,	the concatenate symbol
=	the define symbol
|	the definition separator symbol (alternatives)
[ ]	enclose optional syntactic items
{ }	enclose syntactic items which may occur zero or more times
' '	single quotes are used to enclose terminal symbols
meta identifier	non-terminal symbols are written in lower-case letters (possibly including spaces)
;	terminator symbol to represent the end of a rule.

A.12.1 *Definitions*

definition block =   type definitions
                  | state definition

| value definitions
| function definitions
| operation definitions   ;

Type definitions

type definitions =   'types', type definition, { ';', type definition } ;

type definition =   identifier, '=', type, [invariant]
              | identifier, '::', field list, [invariant]   ;

type =   bracketed type
      | basic type
      | quote type
      | union type
      | tuple type
      | optional type
      | set type
      | seq type
      | map type
      | type name ;

bracketed type =   '(', type, ')' ;

basic type =   'bool' | 'nat' | 'nat1' | 'int' | 'real' | 'char' | 'token' ;

quote type =   quote literal ;

union type =   type, '|', type, { '|', type } ;

tuple type =   type, '*', type, { '*', type } ;

optional type =   '[', type, ']' ;

set type =   'set of', type ;

seq type =   'seq of', type ;

map type =   'map', type, 'to', type ;

function type =   discretionary type, '->', type ;

discretionary type =   type | '(', ')' ;

type name =   name ;

field list = { field } ;

field = [identifier, ':'], type ;

State definition

state definition = 'state', identifier, 'of', field list,
                       [invariant], [initialisation], 'end' ;

invariant = 'inv', invariant initial function ;

initialisation = 'init', invariant initial function ;

invariant initial function = pattern, '==', expression ;

Value definitions

value definitions = 'values', value definition, { ';', value definition } ;

value definition = name, [':', type], '=', expression ;

Function definitions

function definitions = 'functions', function definition,
                       { ';', function definition } ;

function definition = explicit function definition |
                       implicit function definition ;

explicit function definition = identifier, ':', function type,
                         identifier, parameters,
                         '==', expression,
                         ['pre', expression], ;

implicit function definition = identifier, parameter types ,
                         identifier type pair,
                         ['pre', expression],
                         'post', expression ;

identifier type pair = identifier, ':', type ;

parameter types = '(', [pattern type pair list], ')' ;

pattern type pair list = pattern list, ':', type,
                       { ',', pattern list,':', type } ;

parameters = '(', [pattern list], ')' ;

Operation definitions

operation definitions = **'operations'**, operation definition,
　　　　　　　　　　　　　{ ';', operation definition } ;

operation definition =　identifier, parameter types, [identifier type pair],
　　　　　　　　　　　　[externals],
　　　　　　　　　　　　[**'pre'**, expression],
　　　　　　　　　　　　'post', expression ;

operation type =　discretionary type, '**==>**', discretionary type ;

externals = **'ext'**, var information, { var information } ;

var information =　mode, name list, [':', type] ;

mode = **'rd'** | **'wr'** ;

Expressions

expression list =　expression, { ',', expression } ;

expression =　bracketed expression
　　　　　|　let expression
　　　　　|　let be expression
　　　　　|　if expression
　　　　　|　cases expression
　　　　　|　unary expression
　　　　　|　binary expression
　　　　　|　quantified expression
　　　　　|　set enumeration
　　　　　|　set comprehension
　　　　　|　set range expression
　　　　　|　sequence enumeration
　　　　　|　sequence comprehension
　　　　　|　subsequence
　　　　　|　map enumeration
　　　　　|　map comprehension
　　　　　|　tuple constructor
　　　　　|　record constructor

| apply
| field select
| is expression
| name
| old name
| symbolic literal ;

Bracketed expressions

bracketed expression =   '(', expression, ')' ;

Local binding expressions

let expression =   'let', pattern, '=', expression,
                            { ',', pattern, '=', expression }, 'in', expression ;

let be expression =   'let', bind, ['be', 'st', expression], 'in', expression ;

Conditional expressions

if expression =   'if', expression, 'then', expression, { elseif expression },
                      'else', expression ;

elseif expression =   'elseif', expression, 'then', expression ;

cases expression =   'cases', expression, ':', cases expression alternatives,
                         [',', others expression], 'end' ;

cases expression alternatives =   cases expression alternative,
                                       { ',', cases expression alternative } ;

cases expression alternative =   pattern list, '->', expression ;

others expression = 'others', '->', expression ;

Unary expressions

unary expression =   unary operator, expression ;

unary operator =   '+'
                   | '-'
                   | 'abs'

	'not'
	'card'
	'dunion'
	'dinter'
	'hd'
	'tl'
	'len'
	'elems'
	'inds'
	'conc'
	'dom'
	'rng'
	'merge' ;

Binary expressions

binary expression =   expression, binary operator, expression ;

binary operator =	'+'
|	'−'
|	'*'
|	'/'
|	'div'
|	'mod'
|	'<'
|	'<='
|	'>'
|	'>='
|	'='
|	'<>'
|	'or'
|	'and'
|	'=>'
|	'<=>'
|	'in set'
|	'not in set'
|	'subset'
|	'union'
|	'\'

|	'inter'
|	'^'
|	'++'
|	'munion'
|	'<:'
|	'<-:'
|	':>'
|	':->' ;

Quantified expressions

quantified expression =   all expression
                      | exists expression ;

all expression = 'forall', bind list, '&', expression ;

exists expression = 'exists', bind list, '&', expression ;

Set expressions

set enumeration = '{', [expression list], '}' ;

set comprehension = '{', expression, '|', bind list, ['&', expression], '}' ;

set range expression = '{', expression, ',', '...', ',', expression, '}' ;

Sequence expressions

sequence enumeration = '[', [expression list], ']' ;

sequence comprehension = '[', expression, '|', set bind,
                             ['&', expression], ']' ;

subsequence = expression, '(', expression, ',', '...', ',', expression, ')' ;

Mapping expressions

map enumeration = '{', maplet, { ',', maplet }, '}' | '{', '|->', '}' ;

maplet = expression, '|->', expression ;

map comprehension = '{', maplet, '|', bind list, ['&', expression], '}' ;

Tuple constructor expression

tuple constructor =   'mk_', '(', expression, expression list, ')' ;

Record expressions

record constructor =   'mk_',[3]name, '(', [expression list], ')' ;

Apply expressions

apply =   expression, '(', [expression list], ')' ;

field select =   expression, '.', identifier ;

Is expressions

is expression =   'is_',[4]name, '(', expression, ')'
       | is basic type, '(', expression, ')' ;

is basic type =   'is_', ('bool' | 'nat' | 'nat1' | 'int' | 'rat' | 'real' | 'char'
       | 'token') ;

Names

name =   identifier, [' '' ', identifier] ;

identifier =   (plain letter),
       { (plain letter) | digit | ' '' ' | '_' } ;

name list =   name, { ',', name } ;

old name =   identifier, '~' ;

Literals

symbolic literal =   numeric literal | boolean literal | nil literal
       | character literal | text literal | quote literal ;

numeral =   digit, { digit } ;

---

[3] **Note:** no delimiter is allowed
[4] **Note:** no delimiter is allowed

numeric literal = numeral, ['.', digit, { digit }], [exponent] ;

exponent = ('E' | 'e'), ['+' | '-'], numeral ;

boolean literal = 'true' | 'false' ;

nil literal = 'nil' ;

character literal = ' ' ', character – newline, ' ' ' ;

character = plain letter
   | digit
   | delimiter character
   | other character
   | separator ;

separator = newline | white space ;

text literal = ' " ', { ' " " ' | character – (' " ' | newline) }, ' " ' ;

quote literal = distinguished letter, { '_' | distinguished letter | digit } ;

Patterns

pattern = pattern identifier
   | match value
   | set enum pattern
   | set union pattern
   | seq enum pattern
   | seq conc pattern
   | tuple pattern
   | record pattern ;

pattern identifier = identifier | '-' ;

match value = '(', expression, ')' | symbolic literal ;

set enum pattern = '{', [pattern list], '}' ;

set union pattern = pattern, 'union', pattern ;

seq enum pattern = '[', [pattern list], ']' ;

seq conc pattern = pattern, '^', pattern ;

tuple pattern = 'mk_', '(', pattern, ',', pattern list, ')' ;

record pattern   =   'mk_',[5]name, '(', [pattern list], ')' ;

pattern list   =   pattern, { ',', pattern } ;

Bindings

pattern bind   =   pattern | bind ;

bind   =   set bind | type bind ;

set bind   =   pattern, 'in set', expression ;

type bind   =   pattern, ':', type ;

bind list   =   multiple bind, { ',', multiple bind } ;

multiple bind   =   multiple set bind | multiple type bind ;

multiple set bind   =   pattern list, 'in set', expression ;

multiple type bind   =   pattern list, ':', type ;

---

[5] **Note:**   no delimiter is allowed

B
Solutions to Exercises

Solutions for most of the exercises are given in this appendix. However, for exercises where the solutions are large and probably only can be feasibly handled using the Toolbox the solutions are given on the CD-ROM only.

Chapter 2

2.1 (1) It is correct that the `Data` field is not used in any of the functions defined so far. However, the engineer may envisage that the data will be needed for other functions to be defined later. Thus, for the model presented, the `Data` could be entirely abstracted away. In this case no definition is present at all so one may wonder whether the engineer has carried out a type check of the model.

(2) This is ensured by the pre-condition of `Request`. This states that `forall t1 in set dom ans & t1 < t`, i.e. all requests made since the system was started should be at a time earlier than (i.e. less than) the current time `t`.

(3) `Clear` is to be used for initialisation of the system.

(4) `RaiseAlarm` would have to be changed to reflect such a change.

Chapter 3

3.1   See Toolbox Lite.

3.2   See Toolbox Lite.

3.3 (1) 1

(2) 3

(3) {mk_token("Monday day"),mk_token("Tuesday day")}

(4) {}

(5) {mk_token("Tuesday day")}

3.4
```
ChangeExpert: Plant * Expert * Expert * Period -> Plant
ChangeExpert(mk_Plant(plan,alarms),ex1,ex2,per) ==
```

251

```
        mk_Plant(plan ++ {per |-> plan(per)\{ex1} union {ex2}},alarms)
    pre per in set dom plan and
        ex1 in set plan(per) and
        ex2 not in set plan(per) and
        forall a in set alarms &
            QualificationOK(plan(per)\{ex1} union {ex2},a.quali)
```

Chapter 4

4.1 (1) `true`

(2) `false`

(3) `true`

4.2 (1) `true`

(2) `false`

(3) `false`

4.3
```
((false and false) or true) => false
(false or true) => false
true => false
false
```

4.4 (1) `forall i in set inds temp &`
`temp(i) < 400 and temp(i) > 50`

(2) `forall i in set inds temp\{1} &`
`temp(i - 1) > temp(i) and temp(i - 1) + 10 >= temp(i)`

(3) `exists i,j in set inds temp &`
`i <> i and temp(i) > 400 and temp(j) > 400`

4.5   See Toolbox Lite.

4.6   `functions`

```
Xor: bool * bool -> bool
Xor(a,b) ==
  not (a <=> b);

Nand: bool * bool -> bool
Nand(a,b) ==
  not (a and b)
```

4.7   This is identical to the truth table for `A => B`.

Chapter 5

5.1   `forall con in set conflicts & inv_Conflict(con)`

5.2
```
Controller :: lights    : map Path to Light
              conflicts : set of Conflict
inv mk_Controller(ls,cs) ==
     forall c in set cs &
```

```
               mk_Conflict(c.path2,c.path1) in set cs and
               c.path1 in set dom ls and
               c.path2 in set dom ls and
               (ls(c.path1) = <Red> or ls(c.path2) = <Red>)
```

5.3
```
ToRed: Path * Controller -> Controller
ToRed(p,mk_Controller(lights,conflicts)) ==
  mk_Controller(lights ++ {p |-> <Red>},conflicts)
```
and

```
ToAmber: Path * Controller -> Controller
ToAmber(p,mk_Controller(lights,conflicts)) ==
  mk_Controller(lights ++ {p |-> <Amber>},conflicts)
```

5.4   The consequence is that we get a **Run-Time Error** informing us that the pre-condition is broken. This check is only performed when the pre-condition option is switched on.

5.5   It is not possible to change the light for path **p1** at all with the defined values for `controller`. This means that the light for path **p1** cannot be changed in the current state. For path **p3** it is possible to change it to amber which can be seen from the pre-condition for **ToAmber** yields **true**.

5.6   For example:

```
print ToColour(p3,kernel,8,<Amber>)
print ToColour(p4,$$,10,<Amber>)
print ToColour(p4,$$,15,<Red>)
print ToColour(p3,$$,19,<Red>)
print ToColour(p1,$$,24,<Green>)
print ToColour(p2,$$,28,<Green>)
```

5.7   For example `ToAmber(p1,controller,-9)` will break the **Time** invariant.

Chapter 6

6.1   A singleton set e.g. $\{12\}$ and an empty set $\{\}$.

6.2 (1) $\{1,2,3,4\}$

   (2) $\{2,4,6\}$

   (3) $\{2,3,4,5,6,7,8\}$

6.3 (1) $\{5\}$

   (2) $\{\}$

   (3) $\{10000000000, 285311670611, 8916100448256\}$

6.4 (1) 4

   (2) 0

   (3) 6

6.5 (1) {{1,3},{7,12},{1,5,6}}

   (2) {2,3}

   (3) {2,3,4,5,6,7,8,9,10}

6.6 (1) {89, 33}

   (2) {89, 33}

   (3) {21,23,25,27,29,31,33,35,37,39}

6.7
```
SetDiff: set of nat * set of nat -> set of nat
SetDiff(s1,s2) ==
    {e | e in set s1 & e not in set s2}
```

6.8 (1) `false`

   (2) `true`

   (3) `false`

6.9   See Toolbox Lite.

6.10 (1) {1,3,4,5,11,12}

   (2) {}

   (3) {1,2,3,4,5,6}

   (4) {1,2,{1}}

6.11
```
ListBigItems: Site * nat * nat -> Inventory
ListBigItems(site,xmin,ymin) ==
    {inve | inve in set SiteInventory(site) &
            inve.item.xlength > xmin and
            inve.item.ylength > ymin}
```

6.12 (1) {3,4,5}

   (2) {5}

   (3) {1,2,3,4,5,6}

   (4) {}

6.13   `forall s1,s2 in set s & s1 <> s2 => s1 inter s2 = {}`

6.14   The entire solution is placed on the CD-ROM as `explo3.vdm`.

   (1) `Class = <Expl> | <Fuse>`

   (2)
```
Object :: class    : Class
          position : Point
          xlength  : nat
          ylength  : nat
```

   (3)
```
SafeSpace: Object -> set of Point
SafeSpace(o) ==
  {mk_Point(x,y)
  | x in set {Bottom(o.position.x),...,o.position.x + 10},
```

```
            y in set {Bottom(o.position.y),...,o.position.y + 10}}
(4)  Overlap: Object * Object -> bool
     Overlap(o1,o2) ==
       Points(o1) inter Points(o2) <> {} or
       (o1.class <> o2.class and
        SafeSpace(o1) inter Points(o2) <> {});
```

Chapter 7

7.1 (1) `[5, 3, 3, 9]`

   (2) `[9, 3, 2, 3]`

   (3) `[9]`

   (4) `[]`

7.2
```
FilterBig: seq of int * int -> seq of int
FilterBig(s,n) ==
  [s(i) | i in set inds s & s(i) <= n]
```

7.3 The call stack expands to:
```
SeqSum([2,8,5,6])
SeqSum([8,5,6])
SeqSum([5,6])
SeqSum([6])
SeqSum([])
```

7.4
```
Indices: seq of int -> set of nat1
Indices(l) ==
  {1,...,len l}
```

7.5 (1) `{<Red>}`

   (2) `{2,5,4}`

   (3) `{}`

   (4) `{[5,4,5]}`

7.6 (1) `[<Green>]`

   (2) `[5,4,6]`

   (3) `[8,8,8,2,3,4]`

7.7
```
SumTree: Tree -> nat
SumTree(t) ==
  cases t:
    mk_Node(l,r) -> SumTree(l) + SumTree(r),
    others       -> t
  end
```

7.8 See using Toolbox.

7.9
```
MaxGenTree: GenTree -> nat
MaxGenTree(t) ==
  cases t:
```

```
      mk_Node(l) -> MaxSeq([MaxGenTree(l(i)) | i in set inds l]),
      others    -> t
   end;


MaxSeq: seq of nat -> nat
MaxSeq(s) ==
   cases s:
     [n]     -> n,
     others -> max(hd s, MaxSeq(tl s))
   end
 pre s <> [];


SumGenTree: GenTree -> nat
SumGenTree(t) ==
   cases t:
     mk_Node(l) -> SumSeq([SumGenTree(l(i)) | i in set inds l]),
     others    -> t
   end;


SumSeq: seq of nat -> nat
SumSeq(s) ==
   if s = []
   then 0
   else hd s + SumSeq(tl s)
```

7.10   types

```
   Expr = Value | BinaryExpr | UnaryExpr;

   Value = int;

   BinaryExpr :: left  : Expr
                 op    : BinaryOp
                 right : Expr;

   BinaryOp = <Add> | <Sub> | <Mult> | <Sub>;

   UnaryExpr :: op      : UnaryOp
                operang : Expr;

   UnaryOp = <Minus> | <Plus>
```

functions

```
   Eval: Expr -> int
   Eval(e) ==
     cases e:
       mk_BinaryExpr(l,op,r) -> EvalBinaryOp(op,Eval(l),Eval(r)),
       mk_UnaryOp(op,expr)   -> EvalUnaryOp(op,Eval(expr)),
       others                -> e
```

```
        end
    pre is_BinaryExpr(e) =>
        pre_EvalBinaryOp(e.op,Eval(e.left),Eval(e.right));

    EvalBinaryOp: BinaryOp * int * int -> int
    EvalBinaryOp(op,l,r) ==
        cases op:
            <Add>  -> l + r,
            <Sub>  -> l - r,
            <Mult> -> l * r,
            <Div>  -> l div r
        end
    pre op = <Div> => r <> 0;

    EvalUnaryOp: UnaryOp * int -> int
    EvalUnaryOp(op,r) ==
        cases op:
            <Minus> -> -r,
            <Plus>  -> r
        end
```

7.11
```
    SetSum: set of nat
    SetSum(s) ==
        if s = {}
        then 0
        else let e in set s
                in
                   e + SetSum(s\{e})
```

Chapter 8

8.1 (1) {1 |-> 2,2 |-> 4,3 |-> 6,4 |-> 8}

(2) {2 |-> true,4 |-> true,6 |-> true}

(3) {2 |-> 2,3 |-> 3,4 |-> 4,5 |-> 5,6 |-> 6}

If subtraction is used instead of addition for this exercise a run-time error will occur because the mapping is no longer unique. One should always be careful about this when one is defining mappings using comprehensions.

8.2 (1) {3, 4, 7}

(2) {4, 8}

(3) {}

8.3 (1) {9,10,11,12,13,14,15}

(2) {1,4,27,256,3125}

8.4
```
    Compatible: (map nat to nat) * (map nat to nat) -> bool
    Compatible(m,n) ==
        forall a in set dom m inter dom n & m(a) = n(a)
```

8.5 (1) {1 |-> 3,2 |-> 4,3 |-> 8,4 |-> 8,7 |-> 4}
    (2) {3 |-> 8,4 |-> 8,5 |-> 4,7 |-> 4}
    (3) {8 |-> true, 9 |-> false}

8.6 (1) {1 |-> 3,2 |-> 4,3 |-> 8,4 |-> 8,7 |-> 4}
    (2) {3 |-> 3,4 |-> 8,5 |-> 4,7 |-> 4}
    (3) {8 |-> true, 9 |-> false}

8.7
```
m :-> as = {x |-> m(x) | x in set dom m & m(x) not in set as}
m :>  as = {x |-> m(x) | x in set dom m & m(x) in set as}
```

8.8 By debugging calls of the inv_Tracker function with values violating this.

8.9
```
Find(db:Tracker, cid:ContainerId)
    p: PhaseId | <NotAllocated> | <UnknownContainer>
post if cid not in set dom db.containers
     then <UnknownContainer>
     elseif exists pid in set dom db.phases &
                     cid in set db.phases(pid).contents
     then p in set dom db.phases and cid in set
          trk.phases(p).contents
     else p = <NotAllocated>
```

8.10 This solution is available in the solutions directory as explo3.vdm and explo4.vdm. Note that the invariant for Site no longer is needed:

```
types

Site = map StoreName to Store;

StoreName = token;

Store :: contents : set of Object
         xbound   : nat
         ybound   : nat
inv mk_Store(contents, xbound, ybound) ==
   forall o in set contents & InBounds(o,xbound,ybound)
   and
   not exists o1, o2 in set contents &
              o1 <> o2 and Overlap(o1,o2);

Inventory = set of InventoryItem;

InventoryItem :: store : StoreName
                 item  : Object

functions
```

```
SiteInventory: Site -> Inventory
SiteInventory(site) ==
  dunion {StoreInventory(name,site(name).contents)
          | name in set dom site};

StoreInventory: StoreName * set of Object -> Inventory
StoreInventory(name,objects) ==
  {mk_InventoryItem(name,o) | o in set objects}
```

8.11
```
Over: seq of (map A to B) -> map A to B
Over(map_seq) ==
  if map_seq = []
  then {|->}
  else hd map_seq ++ Over(tl map_seq)
```

8.12
```
Merge: set of (map A to B) -> map A to B
Merge(map_s) ==
  if map_s =
  then |->
  else let m in set map_s
       in
          m munion Merge(map_s\{m})
pre forall m1, m2 in set map_s &
        forall d in set (dom m1 inter dom m2) &
              m1(d) = m2(d)
```

Chapter 9

9.1
```
forall trk: Tracker, cid: ContainerId, ptoid:PhaseId &
      pre_Move(trk,cid,ptoid)
      =>
      ptoid in set dom trk.phases
```

9.2 Assume the following value definitions:

```
values
  cid = mk_token(1);
  pid = mk_token(2);
  mid = mk_token(5);
  cinfo = {cid|->mk_Container(3.5,mid)};
  pinfo1 = {pid|->mk_Phase(cid,mid,1)};
  pinfo2 = {pid|->mk_Phase(cid,mid,6)}

Permission(mk_Tracker(cinfo,{|->}),cid,pid)

Permission(mk_Tracker(cinfo,pinfo1,cid,pid))

Permission(mk_Tracker(cinfo,pinfo2,cid,pid))
```

9.3   This solution is available in the solutions directory as
`testtracker.vdm`.

```
values

glass = mk_token("Glass");

liquid = mk_token("liquid");

metal = mk_token("metal");

plastic = mk_token("plastic");

all_material = {glass,liquid,metal,plastic};

unpacking_initial = mk_Phase({},all_material,5);

sorting_initial = mk_Phase({},all_material,6);

assay_initial = mk_Phase({},all_material,5);

compaction_initial = mk_Phase({},{glass,metal,plastic},3);

storage_initial = mk_Phase({},{glass,metal,plastic},50);

coninfo_initial = {|->};

phases_initial = {mk_token("Unpacking")  |-> unpacking_initial,
                  mk_token("Sorting")    |-> sorting_initial,
                  mk_token("Assay")      |-> assay_initial,
                  mk_token("Compaction")|-> compaction_initial,
                  mk_token("Storage")    |-> storage_initial};

tracker_initial = mk_Tracker(coninfo_initial,phases_initial)}

functions

SetUp: () -> Tracker
SetUp() ==
  tracker_initial
```

Chapter 10

10.1   This solution is available in the solutions directory as
`op-gate-ext.vdm`.

```
operations
```

```
AddString(str: String) err: <Ok> | <AlreadyThere>
ext wr cat: Category
post if str in set cat
     then cat = cat~ and and err = <AlreadyThere>
     else cat~ union {str} = cat and err = <Ok>;

RomoveString(str: String)
ext wr cat: Category
post cat = cat~ \ {str};

AddMessage(m: Message)
ext wr input : seq of Message
post input = input~ ^ [m]
```

BIBLIOGRAPHY

[Ammann95]   Paul Ammann. A Safety Kernel for Traffic Light Control. In *COMPASS'95: Proceedings of the Tenth Annual Conference on Computer Assurance*, pages 71–82, June 1995. Gaithersburg, MD.

[Ammann96]   Paul Ammann. A Safety Kernel for Traffic Light Control. *IEEE Aerospace and Electronic Systems Magazine*, 11(2):13–19, February 1996.

[Bicarregui&94]   Juan Bicarregui, John Fitzgerald, Peter Lindsay, Richard Moore and Brian Ritchie. *Proof in VDM: A Practitioner's Guide. FACIT*, Springer-Verlag, 1994. 245 pages. ISBN 3-540-19813-X.

[Booch&97]   Grady Booch, Ivar Jacobson and Jim Rumbaugh. *The Unified Modelling Language, version 1.1*. Technical Report, Rational Software Corporation, September 1997. Available at: http://www.rational.com/.

[Fitzgerald&95]   John Fitzgerald, Peter Gorm Larsen, Tom Brookes and Mike Green. Developing a Security-critical System using Formal and Conventional Methods. In M. J. Hinchey and J. P. Bowen, eds., *Applications of Formal Methods*, Prentice-Hall, 1995.

[Fitzgerald&98]   J.S. Fitzgerald and C.B. Jones. Proof in the analysis of a model of a tracking system. In J.C. Bicarregui, editor, *Proof in VDM: case studies*, Springer-Verlag, 1998.

[ISOVDM96]   D.J. Andrews (ed.). Information technology — Programming languages, their environments and system software interfaces — Vienna Development Method — Specification Language — Part 1: Base language. ISO, Geneva, http://www.iso.ch, December 1996. ISO/IEC 13817-1.

[LangManPP]   The VDM Tool Group. *The IFAD VDM^{++} Language.* Technical Report, IFAD, September 1997. IFAD-VDM-44, Available from IFAD, Forskerparken 10, 5230 Odense M, Denmark.

[Larsen&96]   Peter Gorm Larsen, John Fitzgerald and Tom Brookes. Applying Formal Specification in Industry. *IEEE Software,* 13(3):48–56, May 1996.

[Mukherjee&93]   Paul Mukherjee and Victoria Stavridou. The Formal Specification of Safety Requirements for Storing Explosives. *Formal Aspects of Computing,* 5(4):299–336, 1993.

[Naur&69]   P. Naur and B. Randell, (eds.). Software Engineering: Report on a Conference sponsored by the NATO Science Committee. 231 pages. Garmisch, Germany, 7th to 11th October 1968, Brussels, Scientific Affairs Division, NATO, January 1969.

[RTM]   Marconi Systems Technology. Requirements & Traceability Management. 1997. Manual 300/HD/01553/002.

[Rumbaugh&91]   James Rumbaugh, Michael Blaha, William Premerlani, Frederick Eddy and William Lorensen. *Object-Oriented Modeling and Design.* Prentice-Hall International, 1991. ISBN 0-13-630054-5.

[Rushby86]   John Rushby. Kernels for safety? In Tom Anderson, ed., *Safe and Secure Computer Systems,* pages 210–220, Blackwell Scientific Publications, October 1986.

[Sommerville96]   I. Sommerville. *Software Engineering.* Addison-Wesley, 5th edition, 1996. ISBN 0-201-42765-6.

[UserManPP]   The VDM Tool Group. *The IFAD VDM^{++} Toolbox User Manual.* Technical Report, IFAD, September 1997. IFAD-VDM-43, Available from IFAD, Forskerparken 10, 5230 Odense M, Denmark.

SUBJECT INDEX

$$, **90**, 109

abs, **227**, 246
abstraction, **2**, 3, 9, 12, 17–19, 26, 214, 215
and, **57**, 67, 69, 84, 89, 150, 226, 246

biimplication, **59**, 68, 226, 246
bool, **52**, 54, 100, 150, 226
boolean data type, **52**, 54, 100, 150, 226
break point, **46**, 120

card, 26, **103**, 144, 246
CASE tools, 211, **220**
cases expression, **88**, 236, 237, 245
char, 18, 21, **78**, 226, 229, 230
conc, **129**, 231, 232, 246
configure, **38**, 41
conjunction, **57**, 67, 69, 84, 89, 150, 226, 246
continue, **46**
cost-effectiveness, 209, **218**
critical systems, **1**, 66, 73, 92, 172, 219, 221

data type, *see* type
debug, **46**, 120
DefaultMod, **39**
dinter, **113**, 229, 230, 246
disjunction, **55**, 67, 69, 226, 246
distributed operators, **110**, 129, 156
div, **227**, 246, 256
dom, 20, **145**, 232, 233, 246
domain checking, **161**
dunion, **112**, 229, 230, 246
dynamic link, 167, **167**, 169, 170, 175, 215

elems, **128**, 231, 246
encapsulation, **203**
equality, 52, **91**, 226, 227, 229, 231, 232, 234, 235, 246
ESA PSS-05, **219**
execution, **44**
exists, **62**, 63, 105, 146, 237, 247
ext, **180**, 181, 186, 188, 240, 244
externals, **180**, 181, 186, 188, 240, 244

false, **52**, 55, 56, 58–60, 66–68
flat model, **191**
forall, **62**, 63, 82, 111, 147, 161, 164, 165, 237, 247
frame problem, **186**
function
    definition, 7, 11, 54, **82**, 243
        explicit, 12, 25, 54, **82**, 164, 239, 243
        implicit, 9, 12, 25, 27, 104, **104**, 165, 239, 243
    parameter, **83**, 239, 243
    recursive, **120**, 132, 135, 136, 183, 186, 187
    signature, **83**, 239, 242
function trace, **46**, 120

hd, **120**, 231, 246
help, **37**

if expression, **104**, 106, 120, 123, 124, 155, 236, 245
implication, **58**, 67, 89, 161, 165, 226, 246
in set, **108**, 229, 246
inds, **119**, 125, 231, 246
inequality, **91**, 226, 227, 229, 231, 232, 234, 235, 246

264

information hiding, **207**, 208
init, **44**
int, **76**, 92, 95, 225
integers, **76**, 95, 225
inter, **101**, 229, 230, 247
interpreter, **44**, 120
invariant, 6, 11, 23, 28, 31, **80**, 81, 82,
    90, 100, 111, 122, 144, 145, 163,
    165, 216, 225, 243
is expression, **234**, 248
ISO9000, **218**

len, 52, **122**, 231, 246
let be expression, **136**, 236, 245
let expression, **105**, 107, 109, 152, 235,
    245
life-cycle, 210, **210**
logic, **50**
looseness, 27, 28, **105**, 136
LPF, **66**

maintenance, **212**, 214, 217
map to, 7, 20, **139**, 143, 226, 242
mapping
  application, **146**, 150, 232, 233
  comprehension, **140**, 232, 247
  distributed merge, **156**, 232, 233, 246
  domain, **137**, 145, 232, 233, 246
  domain restriction, **153**, 232, 233, 247
  domain subtraction, **153**, 232, 233,
    247
  empty, **139**, 232
  enumeration, **139**, 232, 247
  maplet, **137**, 139, 232, 247
  override, 84, 85, 88, **151**, 232, 233,
    247
  range, **137**, 145, 232, 233, 246
  range restriction, **153**, 154, 232, 233,
    247
  range subtraction, **153**, 232, 233, 247
  type, 7, 20, **139**, 143, 226, 242
  union, **148**, 149, 161, 232, 233, 247
match value, **238**, 249
merge, **156**, 232, 233, 246
MIL-STD-498, **219**
mod, **227**, 246
MoD 00-55, **219**
module
  export, **194**, 197, **200**, 207, 208

import, **195**, 196, 197, **200**, 201, 207,
    208
instantiation, 204, 205, **206**, 208
interface, **192**, 193
parameters, 202, **202**, 203, 204, 207,
    208
reuse, **202**, 208
test, **211**
munion, **148**, 149, 161, 232, 233, 247

nat, 23, **76**, 92, 99, 143, 225
nat1, **76**, 92, 225
natural numbers, 23, **76**, 99, 143, 225
negation, **55**, 226, 246
nil, 72, **91**, 104
not, **55**, 226, 246
not in set, 9, **149**, 154, 162, 197, 229,
    246, 251, 254, 258

object-orientation, 208, **208**
OMT, **207**, 208, 220
operation
  definition, 176, 177, 180, **180**, 188,
    240, 244
  parameter, 180, **180**, 184, 240
operator
  partial, **73**, 161
  total, **73**
optional type, 72, 91, **91**, 104, 226, 235,
    242
options
  dynamic type, **47**
  invariant, **47**
  pre-condition, **47**
or, **55**, 67, 69, 226, 246

pattern, 105, 136, 237, **237**, 249
  don't care, **111**, 238, 249
  for records, 27, **81**, 83, 87, 100, 111,
    152, 238, 249
  for sequences, **238**, 249
  for sets, **238**, 249
  for tuples, **238**, 249
  identifier, **105**, 238, 249
post-condition, 9, 28, 31, **104**, 166, 180,
    185, 186, 216, 239, 240
pre-condition, 8, 12, 28, 29, 31, **83**, 84,
    89, 104, 107, 149, 151, 161, 162,
    165, 166, 180, 216, 239, 240

predicate, **52**, 95
print, **45**, 46
proof, **172**
  obligation, 29, 160, 175
  rule, **174**
proposition, **52**

quantification
  existential, **62**, 63, 105, 146, 237, 247
  expression, 24, 62, **62**, 237, 247
  universal, **62**, 63, 82, 111, 147, 161,
      164, 165, 237, 247
quote, 17, **76**, 92, 123, 226
quote type, **76**, 242

rd, **180**, 181–183, 185–187, 240
real, **76**, 92, 143, 226
record
  constructor, 79, **79**, 83, 127, 234
  field, 79, **79**, 81, 86, 87, 92, 243
  pattern, 27, **81**, 83, 87, 100, 111, 152,
      238, 249
  selector, **79**, 81, 152, 234, 248
  type, 18, 21, 73, **79**, 99, 142, 143, 226
renaming, **201**, 207, 208
requirements
  analysis, xi, 3, **15**
  specification, 10, **13**
rigour, **2**, 220
rng, 20, **145**, 232, 233, 246
run-time error, **47**, 68, 96, 253

satisfiability, 166, **166**, 175
seq of, 18, 78, **117**, 122, 226, 242
sequence
  comprehension, **118**, 127, 230, 247
  concatenation, **126**, 231, 247
    distributed, **129**, 231, 232, 246
  elements, **128**, 231, 246
  empty, **118**, 230
  enumeration, **118**, 230, 247
  head, **120**, 231, 246
  index, **119**, 231, 232
  indices, **119**, 125, 231, 246
  length, 52, **122**, 231, 246
  modification, **130**, 231, 232
  subsequence, **118**, 231, 247
  tail, **120**, 231, 246
  type, 18, 78, **117**, 122, 226, 242

set
  binding, **63**, 96, 118, 140, 229, 230,
      238, 250
  cardinality, **103**, 144, 229, 230, 246
  comprehension, 26, **96**, 102, 108, 112,
      229, 247
  difference, **107**, 229, 230, 247
  empty, **94**, 229
  enumeration, **95**, 229, 247
  intersection, **101**, 229, 230, 247
    distributed, **113**, 229, 230, 246
  membership, **108**, 229, 246
  range, 62, **95**, 125, 229, 247
  subset, **109**, 146, 229, 230, 246
  type, 18, **95**, 226, 242
  union, **106**, 123, 229, 230, 246
    distributed, **112**, 229, 230, 246
set of, 18, **95**, 143, 226, 242
signature, 22, **83**, 101, 123
silence, **28**
software design, **210**
state
  definition, 10, **178**, 187, 188, 240, 243
  initialisation, **178**, 187, 188, 241, 243
  invariant, **178**, 187, 241, 243
struct, **200**
structured analysis, **220**
subsequence, **118**, 231, 247
subset, **109**, 146, 229, 230, 246
syntax checking, **39**

test
  coverage, **171**, 175
  phase, **214**
time to market, **214**, 216
tl, **120**, 231, 246
token, 18, 19, 21, **77**, 78, 92, 111, 143,
    226
Toolbox Lite, xii, 4, **36**
tools menu, **47**
true, 29, **52**, 55, 56, 58–60, 66–68, 100,
    105, 150
truth table, **55**, 69
tuple
  constructor, **233**, 248
  type, **233**, 242
tuple type, **226**

type
  basic, 52, 76, **76**, 77, 242
  binding, 46, **63**, 96, 97, 140, 229, 238,
    250
  definition, 5, 16, **76**, 225, 242
  invariant, 6, 11, 23, 28, 31, **80**, 81, 82,
    90, 100, 111, 122, 144, 145, 163,
    165, 216, 225, 243
  membership, **91**, 164
type checking, **40**

UML, **207**, 208, 220
undefinedness, **66**, 68, 120, 149
union, **106**, 123, 229, 230, 246

union type, 17, **72**, 76, 226, 235, 242
unit test, **211**

validation, 4, **167**, **170**, 219
  by proof, 158, **172**, 173, 175
  by testing, 158, **170**, 175
  conjecture, **172**, 175
value definition, 44, **78**, 86, 243
VDM, xi, **4**
VDM++, 208, **208**
VDM-SL, xi, 4, **4**, 11
vdmlite, **37**
verification, xi, **172**

what, not how, **4**, 7, 27
wr, **180**, 182, 183, 185–187, 240

DEFINITIONS INDEX

AircraftPosition, 6
Alarm, 18, 21
AmberChange, 86
AnyHighClass, 128

Bottom, 115

Category, 123, 184
Censor, 130, 131
ChgLight, 85
ChgTime, 88
Classification, 122, 123, 184
Classify, 124
Conflict, 79, 80
Container, 143
ContainerId, 143
ContainerInfo, 143
ContOverLimit, 57

Delete, 153, 154, 161

Expert, 18, 21, 24
ExpertId, 19, 21
ExpertIsOnDuty, 26, 27
ExpertToPage, 28

FilterBig, 119
Find, 155, 166
FlattenMessages, 129
FlatternMessages, 129

Gateway, 123, 124, 187
Gateway2, 128

InBounds, 101
Indices, 125
Introduce, 150, 162
Inventory, 111

InventoryItem, 111

Kernel, 79–81, 86

Latitude, 6
Light, 76, 91
LightFail, 91
ListBigItems, 113

Material, 143
MaterialSafe, 147
Merge, 156
Message, 122, 184
MinimumGreen, 86
Move, 152, 163

NewAircraft, 8, 9
NumberOfExperts, 25, 26
NumObjects, 103, 181

Object, 99
Occurs, 125
Over, 156
Overlap, 102
OverLimit, 56, 62

Path, 77
Period, 19, 21
Permission, 150, 162, 171
Phase, 143, 144
PhaseId, 143
PhaseInfo, 143
PhasesDistinguished, 147
Place, 107, 182, 183
Plant, 21, 28
Point, 99
Points, 102
Ports, 123

ProcessMessage, 124, 125, 127, 185, 186

Qualification, 17, 21
QualificationOK, 29

RadarInfo, 7
RaiseAlarm, 59
RedClearance, 86
Remove, 108, 109, 150, 151, 165, 183
Rising, 54
RoomAt, 105, 182

Safe, 58
SafeSpace, 114
Schedule, 20, 21, 25
SelectForLanding, 9

SeqSum, 120
Site, 111
SiteInventory, 112
Store, 99, 100, 110, 179
StoreInventory, 112
StoreName, 111
String, 78, 122, 184
SuggestPos, 104, 106, 181, 182

TempRead, 52
Time, 77, 82
ToAmber, 85, 88
ToColour, 88, 89
ToGreen, 83, 84, 87
ToRed, 85, 87
Tracker, 142, 144, 145
TrustedGateway, 184